CULTURAL POLITICS

Border traffic

CULTURAL POLITICS

Border traffic

Strategies of contemporary women writers

Maggie Humm

MANCHESTER UNIVERSITY PRESS
MANCHESTER and NEW YORK

distributed in the USA and Canada by ST. MARTIN'S PRESS, New York

Published by Manchester University Press
Oxford Road, Manchester M13 9PL, UK
and Room 400, 175 Fifth Avenue,
New York, NY 10010, USA

Distributed exclusively in the USA and Canada
by St. Martin's Press, Inc.,
175 Fifth Avenue, New York, NY 10010, USA

A catalogue record for this book is available from the British Library

Library of Congress cataloging in publication data
Humm, Maggie
    Border traffic: strategies of contemporary women writers / Maggie Humm.
        p.   cm. – (Cultural politics)
    Includes bibliographical references and index.
    ISBN 0-7190-2703-9. – ISBN 0-7190-2704-7 (pbk.)
    1. English literature–Women authors–History and criticism.
    2. American literature–Women authors–History and criticism.
    3. American literature–20th century–History and criticism.
    4. English literature–20th century–History and criticism.
    5. Feminism and literature–History–20th century. 5. Women and
    literature–History–20th century. 7. Authorship–Sex differences.
    I. Title. II. Series.
    PR116.H8   1991
    820.9'9287'0904—dc20   91-10252

ISBN 0 7190 2703 9 hardback
     0 7190 2704 7 paperback

Typeset in Joanna
by Koinonia Limited, Manchester
Printed in Great Britain
by Bell & Bain Ltd, Glasgow

Contents

For Dan:

> the air   through which child and mother
> are running   the boy singing
> the woman   eyes sharpened in the light
> heart stumbling   making for the open

Adrienne Rich, 'Mother-Right'

Preface

The literary canon in the West is a means by which 'women' and 'men' are imaginatively constructed, it is a site of construction, and an area of policing. In order to read literature, criticism demands a removal of our intuitions, our mother-knowledges, of what we are, before it allows us to 'understand' literary forms. Criticism devalues racial and sexual differences unless it can critically embrace such experience as 'minority literature'. It paws and shreds the cognitions of difference into pieces of essentialism all the better to eat them up. As Catharine MacKinnon so pertinently suggests: 'Difference is the velvet glove on the iron fist of domination' (MacKinnon, 1989, p. 219).

Literature, in feminist light, is not made up of universal values. It is an organised, aesthetic representation of what society wants politically, which inevitably focuses on borders, as limits to the power of Others. Feminist criticism locates the relation of women's literary experience to her life experience in a place of struggle: on the border between literary constructions and the turn towards transformation.

As I explored these issues I came to realise that in many books written by women authors just as in lives lived by many women readers, the border figures as a dynamic force. In the 1990s feminist writers of detective fiction are plotting revisionary ways of deploying domesticity just as women Co-operators, in the 1910s, read transgressively together in their homes in order to 'open the doors and the windows so that we may see the City Beautiful' (Llewellyn Davies, 1977, p. 101).

Border traffic offers a fresh synthesis of the ways in which women writers from different races, cultures and nationalities often choose similar, alternative routes across the border of their literary place. I am using the term 'border' to identify texts which manipulate specific strategies, for example a use of 'women's time' and women's friendship, to subvert the conservative ideologies of literary forms.

This book is intended as the first of a two volume study of 'border' writing. In this volume *Border traffic* I offer an overview of border issues in some Anglo-American and Caribbean writing and in my next book I intend to trace responses in the writing of Third World women to the political and cultural barriers of racism and sexism. For example

Buchi Emecheta and Bessie Head's personal 'exiles' in Britain and Botswana structure the form as well as the content of their writing. The second volume will set this theme of women's difference within the wider context of colonial and post-colonial oppression. Taken together both volumes will, I hope, help to illuminate the radical transformation of contemporary writing by border women. Issues of cultural displacement in Nayantara Sehgal's This time of morning (1965), and the transformation of images of Central American women and the breaking of 'feminine' taboos in the writing of Rosario Castellanos mean that, as Mineke Schipper argues, women 'who do not keep to their "own territory" find themselves in difficulty' (Schipper, 1985, p. 14).

Since the subversion of the literary canon is more than a simple matter of extending a list of literary texts both volumes aim to adopt new reading practices, for example juxtaposing the bilingualism of La Malincha and Zora Neale Hurston, to highlight revisionary 'writing'. It is these manoeuvres, as much as the reading of a feminist tradition, which are the focus of my work.

Border traffic is also a personal journey. Like many women of my generation, the British 1944 Education Act, which laid a duty on government for the first time to provide tertiary education, enabled us much later, often unwittingly, to cross the borders of region, of class and of politics. So that the subject matter of Border traffic is as emotionally charged for me as a critic as it is for its women authors as writers.

This book owes most of all to my son Dan Humm whose support and love kept me writing during a period of great pain for us both. I am indebted to Harold and Maggie Jaffe who deepened my understanding of Central America and of criticism; to colleagues in the British Women's Studies organisation and in Network who offered helpful comments and suggestions at HETE and the many conferences where sections of this book were tried out as papers. Numerous individuals, for example Helen Taylor, Jackie Jones, have provided helpful suggestions and support probably without realising how important these were to me. I owe a great deal to my Women's Studies colleagues at PEL and to my Women's Studies students for their energetic discussions and continuing encouragement. I also wish to thank Chitra Aloysius for sharing her life history with me. Of course my poor writing could never have been turned into a manuscript and hence Border traffic without the expert skill and care of Joyce Lock.

Acknowledgements

The author and publishers wish to make the following acknowledgements:

Every effort has been made to trace copyright holders, but if any has been inadvertently overlooked the publishers will be pleased to make the necessary arrangement at the first opportunity.

Lines from 'This is a photograph of me', from Circle game by Margaret Atwood, Copyright © 1966 Margaret Atwood and the House of Anansi Press, Toronto.

Lines from 'I Was That Woman' from I was that woman by Debjani Chatterjee, Copyright © 1989 by Debjani Chatterjee, Copyright © 1989 Hippopotamus Press.

Lines from Notebook and The dolphin from Robert Lowell's poems Copyright © 1974 by Faber and Faber Ltd.

Lines from 'Leaflets', 'Pierrot Le Fou' from Poems: selected and new 1950-1974 by Adrienne Rich, Copyright © 1974 by Adrienne Rich, Copyright © 1975 by W. W. Norton Company, Inc.

Lines from 'Twenty-one Love Poems' and 'Mother-Right' from The Fact of a doorframe: poems selected and new 1950-1984 by Adrienne Rich, Copyright © 1984 by Adrienne Rich, Copyright © 1984 by W. W. Norton & Company, Inc.

'No Customs' is a longer and substantially revised version of 'Landscape for a literary feminism: British women writers 1900 to the present' reprinted from H. Forsas-Scott (ed.), Textual liberation: European feminist writing in the twentieth century, Routledge, 1991.

'Simultaneous translators' is a longer and substantially revised version of 'Translation as survival: Zora Neale Hurston and La Malincha' reprinted 17:2 from Fiction international, 1987.

'Legal aliens' is a longer and substantially revised version of 'Feminist thrillers' reprinted from C. Bloom (ed.), Twentieth century suspense: the thriller comes of age, Macmillan, 1990.

Mapping the territory: Bakhtin, Douglas, Bernstein, Cixous

This book is about women's writing which crosses borders, writing which has no single 'ism' to orchestrate identity. These borders are, in most cases, metaphoric since it is impossible to argue a convincing case that there is anything inherently feminine in any one literary form. This book wears a theory as a lens against astigmatism: the proposition that women writers who cross the different borders of genres, of history, of sexual preference, of bodies or of politics write 'differently' in similar ways.

Border traffic is also a book about critical journeys – about the way feminist criticism can map ethnic, cultural as well as sexual differences with the tangents of border theory. One of the most striking developments in feminist criticism from the mid-1970s on has been its assault on the traditional borders of disciplines and on the fixed limits of the literary canon.[1]

The introduction of postmodernist theory into the field of literary criticism has created a new impulse in feminist criticism: a recognition that while in contemporary capitalism, both women and men who move between cultures and languages develop special responses to questions of identity and representation, that it is women with our long-term history of crossing between received languages and undervalued ways of speaking who can be said to have a poetics of displacement.[2] For women, the condition of patriarchy presupposes the reality of borders, even if, for some women, these are often internalised borders experienced as exclusion.

The contemporary phenomenon of border journeys, in which women writers adjust their writing to their experiential and historical sense of gender exclusion rather than to the demands of the academy is one illustration of the traffic across disciplines and writing codes now transforming literary studies. In contemporary writing by women the border functions both as a strategy and as a shape. The title of my book is intended to highlight the active role played by this complex criss-crossing of the margins of identity and writing possibilities. The focus is on an analysis of several particular writers who interweave these dynamics in striking and perhaps exemplary ways. In writing about hysteria, in contestation with the genres of traditional literature, in moments of 'coming out', in anorexia, in a revulsion from racial stereotypes, some women's texts may be viewed as scripts of boundary crossing.

Of course each crossing is differently experienced, depending on race, sexual preference and historical moment. But although the specific historical and national meanings are different, similar literary mechanisms, I suspect, are at work in all these writers. In these women writers the literary journey is a form of sexual politics. Sylvia Townsend Warner's outward attention to extra literary fairy tales and to characters such as witch women who rarely featured in 1930s novels; Margaret Atwood's use of anorexia and Shamanism to dramatically transform literary representations of femininity; Adrienne Rich's coherent movement into a new lesbian voice — are all border crossings. It is as though these particular writers are speaking to us in a form of feminist theory where their writing signifies what they perhaps could not state or embody in their contemporary societies.

Many literary critics react strongly against theory because, for them, literature is largely the place where women are *aesthetically* represented. But literature is often the place from which women, particularly lesbians and Creole women, voice their political ideas. Literature has an intimate relationship with theory. Literary images, like social selves, have to be pushed over the cultural limits of, for example, the 'Creole Jamaican woman'. Cultural hybridity is a form of border traffic. How something is spoken about reveals a great deal about the operation of power relations. Language (and its most generative space, literature) is targeted by many feminists as a major factor in the reproduction of patriarchy. As Sheila Rowbotham points out: where else can an alternative consciousness of ourselves come from? (see Rowbotham, 1973).

Of course the quest for theory often becomes a quest for single truths. Yet meaning has always 'been a function of the languages you have at your disposal' as Terry Eagleton suggests (Eagleton, 1983, p. 107). The whole point of recent feminist theory is not to construct a theory of knowledge but to put forward a series of methods for examining the production of knowledges. Theory can also separate into opposites features which have a more complex and shifting relationship. Literary texts, in particular, aim to tamper with fixed judgements so that readers can embrace different possibilities in life. The nature of literature, its ability to sustain different meanings both formal and ideological, is what moves us, and often with passion, to struggle in the real world. But feminist theory like feminist fiction is a series of useful stories, open to multiple readings and experiences. Indeed many French feminists, in particular Hélène Cixous and Monique Wittig, do not claim a truth status for theory but create theory in the form of fiction and write fiction as if it were theory.

The treatment by writers of the feminist themes I describe reveals certain typical features. Writers deliberately choose to describe those kinds of women and those forms of female resistance which the representational practices of traditional literature tend to marginalise or ignore. Witch women, Creole women, lesbian women are examples. Important themes include time journeys back into intense memories of mothering and woman-identified relationships. A steady motif in all these writings is that of the literary journey as an embodied feminist protest, which can be an issue of translation within a culture as well as between several cultures. This book proposes to contest the boundaries established by the literary tradition and its iterations of 'writing women' washed clean from the murky differences of race and sexual preference.

What first appears to be an uncertain voice or an inexorable movement among genres, become components of a survival routine. If it is methodologically unsound to look for intrinsic gender difference in writing, we can search for gender differences in the systems of relations in which women's writing situates itself and which it refracts. Of course, to simply read women's writing in terms of its fidelity to fixed ideas about female experience denies differences in literary meanings. Yet we are always confused at the boundary of gender representation, as Marge Piercy wittily illustrated in *Woman on the edge of time* with her bearded breast-feeding man. The logic which runs through *Border traffic* is associative, rather like beads on a necklace. Rather than aiming to construct a single overarching, feminist literary theory, this book offers to link literature and feminism by examining some literary themes relevant to feminist concerns – body imagery, relationships with fathers, mothers and women lovers – as boundary movements. For, as Virginia Woolf argued in *Three guineas*, women are exiled beyond the border of symbolic language which organises social institutions and laws. Women must make border crossings in order to use language at all even if we cannot fully control its laws and its structure.

The chapters in Border traffic offer a cross-section of different ways of rethinking literary theory in the light of border issues. The first chapter explores and constructs a border thematics as a subtext of twentieth century British feminist writing. Chapter two raises the question of paternal boundaries and maternal forces in Jean Rhys and infiltrates the terrain of literature with the guerrilla tactics of history to foreground the limitations of traditional literary criticism. In a 'dialogue' between Zora Neale Hurston and La Malincha, chapter three tries to show how critical writing must itself change in order to re-present the struggles of Black writers against the blind spots of literary studies. The essay about Margaret Atwood draws on theories of border crossing in feminist psychoanalysis and in Shamanism to hypothesise a fresh écriture féminine. Considering border representation from the different perspective of Bloomian psychoanalysis, chapter five examines metaphors of boundary and transformation in Adrienne Rich's 'Twenty-one love poems' and argues that her 'separatism' stems, in part, from her 'completion' of her male precursors. The final chapter follows feminist criticism's current interest in popular culture and in the genre of detective fiction as a site of transgression and resistance.

This book is about the significance of cultural borders which codify women's experience in the West and it studies the ways in which women's writing destabilises literary hierarchies. Contemporary women writers build something metaphysical out of marginality. Borders are where the difference between 'What is a woman?' and 'what is not a woman?' is put to the test. In solving the enigma of the woman writer who vaults over the boundaries of her literary landscape, criticism quickly contains literary athleticism inside a fence crosshatched from periods and genres and glued together with consistency. It is the job of conventional criticism to mark the borders of a text, map its internal consistencies, and its relationship with other texts in the enunciative enclosure of a critical genre. The term genre is applied to texts which all share similar conventions, characters and formulae. Feminist genre writers, for example of detective novels, break with these strategies because they understand that genres carry ideological, not just literary, messages. The view that a woman writer might refuse consistency or violently disrupt genre boundaries is set aside or often transmuted into the fashionable vogue for 'intertextualité'.

Many contemporary thinkers from Roland Barthes onwards have written at length about intertextuality. The impact on linguistic phenomena of larger discourses, form the focus of their research.[3] Julia Kristeva, in particular, following Lacan, notes how metaphors of meaning in texts may have leapt over the dividing line between desire and representation but will always contain traces of the unconscious. Kristeva defines intertextuality as the incorporation of other sign systems by literature (or by any other cultural systems). She believes that all texts are mosaics of references to other texts, images and conventions. Her argument, in Desire in language, is that intertextualité is the place of plurality and subversion. Kristeva's interest, for example in her account of Céline, is in the marginal language which represents sexual identity. Yet in that book, and in her subsequent Histoires d'amour, Kristeva evokes an image of identity which does not promote intertextualité. For example Kristeva argues that language is born out of a chasm between the maternal body and the child and subjectivity. This would emphatically deny the 'different' interrelations of lesbian mothers and daughters.

The relationship between marginality, sexual identity and language described by many border women demands a more open, tolerant understanding of intertextuality than this. But we also need to be cautious of the glib way in which current criticism delights to argue that in broad terms all literature is intertextual anyway. This emphatically emphasises the integrity of literature. Criticism does not hear the desperation which lies inside its truism. Many of the texts considered in this book are involved in complex intertextual practices, ranging from overt borrowings to direct comparisons such as Jean Rhys's Wide sargasso sea. All struggle openly with the rules of genres and with literary traditions and therefore are continually implicating other texts. Also, and more crucially they address a women's world beyond their writing.

The striking feature of border texts is the fact that they are extremely varied. Generalising about women's writing which crosses racial and national boundaries is difficult, to say the least of it. The representation of Zora Neale Hurston's Black women, for example, has been described as grounded in the Harlem Renaissance; in this form it becomes accessible (aesthetically, at least) to period definitions and literary history. By contrast, however, that representation functioned as an exotic appendage to the illustrious all-male list which the period established. In this speculation Hurston's work was also judged to be sensual and unsophisticated, and it was used to authorise (by its exclusion) the masculine cultural canon (see Walker, 1984, p. 84). So that while detailed attention to literary history does bring out Hurston's thematic relationship with a now well defined literary subculture, it occludes the very literary structures with which she opposed that world and therefore occludes the formal structures which run across marginal texts and which all border writing has in common. I call these structures I focus on, 'border traffic' because each writing mode has the potential to overflow the artificiality of genres or periods that govern the literary canon. While it is arguable, a supporter of postmodernism might claim, that all writing is inevitably in tension between aesthetics and the borders of meaning systems because writing, and postmodernist writing in particular, is marked by its own limits and possibilities, I suggest that those structures that are often constituted as 'problems' by the literary canon are particularly important because they reveal the borders of literary meaning specifically in relation to gender. It matters then to stand at literary crossroads, to be self conscious about translation, eclecticism and slippiness in order to challenge critical boundaries from a feminist perspective.

What importance does 'border' have as a meaningful category in women's writing and in the shaping of feminist criticism? The border is not only a question of place which assumes some one dimensional literary plane without hierarchy or class but of difference, since in looking at literary borders we find asymmetry, absence and marginalisation. Hence the border cannot replicate women's writing place as the undifferentiated Other to that occupied by men. There is no point of 'authentic' arrival.The chapter Jean Rhys in particular disavows this 'essentialism' by placing Rhys into a longer history of ethnic and gender identity. Borders are not simply discontinuities, temporary barriers to women's drive for knowledge. Border women are not decentred fragmented individuals but writers who have begun to cohere a core identity by entering the transitional space between self and other. The border is the trope of difference and potential conflict, between races, between cultures and between sexual preferences. As Teresa de Lauretis suggests, 'radical difference cannot perhaps be represented except as an experience of borders' (de Lauretis, 1984, p. 99).

In Alice doesn't and Technologies of gender, De Lauretis's primary concern is with cinema. While cinema and other forms of contemporary culture offer examples of boundary crossing, this book is about the status of the border in literature and specifically in the writing of twentieth century British feminists, Jean Rhys, Zora Neale Hurston, Margaret Atwood, Adrienne Rich, and feminist detective fiction. The guiding concern of these writers is to problematise narrative forms and to question the limits of representation and of consciousness. Based on this writing the term border crossing might describe the 'different' styles of Asian and Black women as well as white women's battles against master narratives. This book rests on the proposition that there is a specifically gendered approach to boundary crossing that for women is best characterised by its rhetorical ambidexterity. This is the ability to be able to handle, while simultaneously refusing to touch, all of the master language which is a technique for concretising 'difference'. Minority, as defined in literary criticism, goes in tandem with liberalism which ignores the literary specificity of border women. Women of colour in particular are often best placed to breach the limits of traditional identities. The question then for a feminist criticism is to discover the features and the effects of ambidexterity.

If we examine the literary history of the twentieth century we can confidently claim that gender difference shapes literary solidarity. For example although the texture of the literary surface of modernism is characterised, for both men and women modernists, by ellipses, ambiguity, phenomenality, and Cubism by a fragmentation of all borders, the entrances to the stage of modernism resemble the entrances to old British primary schools with their separate doors marked 'boys' and 'girls'. More than most modernists, André Gide claimed that his texts were designed to break the limits of literature so that the 'body' of writing would melt away 'deliciously' like sugar. But this pursuit of exteriority and the attempt of male modernists to penetrate the deep structures of modernity and the mystique of capital does not eclipse gender.[4] It is a striking fact, as Griselda Pollock points out in Vision and difference, that the male modernist artists became leaders of the avant-garde by painting pictures about brothels, bars and the commercial exchange of women (see Pollock, 1988). Male literary modernists – Joyce, Eliot, Pound – were colonising and domesticating the urban space while the feminist modernists Virginia Woolf and Gertrude Stein, as we shall see, in their exploration of sexed boundaries and expanded sexual figures can be credited with a triumphant fanfare against the Jericho of gender assignation. Woolf's Orlando stalks through the boundary of historical chronology and gender boundaries and in Three lives, Stein parodies the boundary of realism and hetero-sexuality with her ironic marriage plot. That there can be some concept of border identity, that there are particular literary categories of border women can firmly be demonstrated.

Nevertheless, although we all believe at some level that literature is well versed in the discursive nature of misogyny there is an awkward problem with the conviction of a women's language even one charged with historically fluctuating feminist identities. As Donna Haraway, in her pathbreaking essay 'A manifesto for cyborgs' points out, we are all now in the late twentieth century, women *and* men, theorised and fabricated hybrids of machine and organism. 'The boundary is permeable between tool and myth, instrument and concept, historical systems of social relations and historical anatomies of possible bodies, including objects of knowledge.' (Haraway, 1989, p. 188)[5] Where capitalism relied, Haraway suggests, on an inside/outside antithesis in relation to its borders rendering the dominant international labour force male and the unskilled reserve outsiders Black, and/or women, new biotechnologies resist boundaries with their common computer languages. To fight our way across the historical limitations of 'the woman writer' it is necessary too, to avoid collapsing into a confusion of categories where we can be rescued only by an equivalent technology of an essentialist female language – a feminist cyborg mirroring a greater cybernetic masculine machine.

One means of avoidance is to look at 'other' women writers not simply, or not only, as doubles, parodies or hybrid objects but in the vicissitudes of their contradictions. Artists in the West have always looked East at 'alternative' practices in order to appropriate Third World signifiers into Western representation. From eulogies to Che Guevara or Tahiti, the sudden interest in Muslim women, or concern about *proxenia* or 'arranged' marriages, Western academic affection for the marginal, the non-canonic, the autobiographical is not, or rarely, defined in terms of 'continuous confrontation' but in terms of a new Western generosity to 'forgotten' peoples. For example Rey Chow in 'Rereading Mandarin ducks and butterflies' attacks the appropriation of Chinese literature into Western brands of postmodernism precisely for this reason. As she points out, contemporary Chinese literature is shaped by a reaction to Western imperialism which at first created traditional didactic narratives but that this, in turn, generated a revolutionary literature needing its own Other and 'inferior' writing – women's love stories or Butterfly fiction – to mark revolutionary literature's break with the past. Such a complicated history cannot be reduced to exotic 'difference' (see Chow, 1986). So rather than claiming an absolute difference for the Third World, lesbian or genre breaking woman then, feminist criticism can acknowledge the crucial role of women writers in elaborating border strategies and their invocation of new metaphors along the edges of power and of language. We can only take small steps over this hard ground rather than the giant step of criticism's mankind. Because, as Gayatri Spivak pertinently suggests in answer to the question 'what can criticism do?', feminism can 'name frontier concepts and thus grant itself a little more room to write itself intelligibly, or try frontier styles' (Spivak, 1987, p. 13).[6]

Before my narrative can fall into place, I know perfectly well, humbly following Spivak, that the strategy of these chapters must be polyphonic to match their content. But the strategy is clear. It is to assert the underlying unities of border women. The desire to clarify eclectism is at the core of these chapters. All are about writers who live on borders and who envisage a different cultural horizon for writing and for women. This work of redefinition involves these women in a common effort. Writers like Hurston, Rhys, Rich, Lessing and others do not privilege one 'pure' style but make many moves out of the checkmate of representation.

Each of these writers, by virtue of one border crossing alone, issues a profound challenge to the literary canon, and to the very process of criticism as an exercise in gender proprieties. At the same time, each creates an image of woman derived from a feminist compulsion, which poses an equally weighted challenge to the limits of social narratives. Each writer's story, each writer's crossing, cannot easily be amassed into a single perspective. This is a literature of transgression. Such writing is alert to differences reflected in its enunciation, in its shaping of relationships, in its adherence to women's autobiography. The point of these stories is to emphasise that women's writing is flexible and lively, pregnant from living in dangerous intimacy with tradition.

Look for example at how Adrienne Rich in a work celebrating lesbian sexuality – 'The twenty-one love poems' – actively appropriates the voices of the male poets Robert Lowell and Paul Goodman. When the famous domestic specificity of two women sharing a New York apartment is investigated, the struggle between the limits of literary aesthetics and lesbian desire is scripted as the border confrontation of a masculine sexuality with the profoundly relational vision of lesbian women. In feminist detective writing, excitement coils in the same traits: in the displacement of individualistic, often violent, self seeking in favour of women's friendship. The issue is not simply one of women's plurality posed against a Holmesian singularity but the denial of a specific master genre. To swerve from the formulae of classic detective fiction is to break through the boundaries of characterisation, of content and of endings. The issue of consistency in the work of Zora Neale Hurston parallels that of her sister texts. It is played out by female narrators whose translation tactics are so multivocal and dramatic that they threaten any static versions of Black subjectivity. In *Mules and men*, Black dialect is no exotic and framed miniature of Black culture but subverts the conservative deployment of a fixed racial identity. 'Call and response' highlights the plurality of characters, readers and narrators. Hurston's writing turns the image of a woman split between cultures into a satisfactory ideal.

The writing of Elizabeth Robins, Virginia Woolf, Sylvia Townsend Warner, Rose Macaulay and Doris Lessing also serves this central shaping and contingent function: to take the specific female experience of being non-hegemonic into feminist meaning. The arrangement of women under the banner 'feminist' is enmeshed in boundary crossings. The pole of historically current literary systems of meaning needs its power redirecting, and writers try to prevent the social poles of marriage or mothering from completing an old circuit.

Feminism of late is more ambitious: 'What we women will do and are now doing, is to effect radical change in the electrical charge of words. We are inverting their poles, making them positive or negative depending on our own needs and not following the rules of inherited, phallocentric language' (Valenzuela, 1983, p. 96). Latin American *testimonios* bridge the boundary between autobiography and political representation in the way that Latin American women writers help women to appear in newly broken forms. Luisa Valenzuela significantly shifts and expands women's discursive boundaries with the same critical view of physical categories, the same interest in inversion and transgression which occurs in Adrienne Rich, Margaret Atwood and other writers in this book.

How then can this radical 'charge' of border crossing be demonstrated? In Margaret Atwood's *Surfacing* the protagonist is caught on the border between childhood memory and current events, just as she is caught on the linguistic border of French-speaking Montreal. At the end of the novel the narrator makes an imaginative leap across the boundary of culture into a new body epistemology of Shamanism. In everyday life a 'distorted' woman's body is most frequently construed as the outward and visible sign of a woman out of control. The *edible woman* and *A Handmaid's tale* are powerful statements about the making and patrolling of those body boundaries in patriarchal culture. Both Marian and Offred invoke female power and female powerlessness through metaphors of eating and reproduction. Atwood knowingly puts different registers of discourses: magazines, the literary, and speculative fiction to the service of the anorexic and social protester so that the boundary of 'appropriate' body representation can be stepped over.

Jean Rhys's *Wide sargasso sea* is exactly illustrative of the proposition of this book: that powerful women are those who can speak across linguistic and racial boundaries. Jean Rhys questions the discursive limits of colonialism, and the fixing of racial difference in family history. A family tree has always been one of the simplest of the classificatory schemes based on subsumption and hierarchy. Rhys releases her childhood and her memories of Black women from that bounded past by challenging the arbitrariness and tenaciousness of literary chronology. In Rhys's books marginal women learn to break the specularity of colonial control as they come to inhabit a more fluid psychic identity. Rhys vaults the limits of ethnic representation by contrasting differing temporalities of Black women and Creole women: the historicised images of women from the 1840s (the setting of the *wide sargasso sea*), and those drawn from her childhood and from the nursing homes and hospitals where Rhys stayed in the 1960s (the time of the writing of the *wide sargasso sea*).

In the plots involving Atwood's protagonists, Rhys's Antoinette, Hurston's Janie and feminist detectives and feminist activists, the clear moment of boundary crossing is the moment of rhetorical ambidexterity. Hence, while not all these writers would describe themselves as feminist, for example Jean Rhys would actively resist that term, I can claim that their preoccupation with the differing temporalities of women and of women's different languages may be regarded as feminist. These writers are 'feminist' because they scrutinise the ideological character of femininity in its narrative conventions and substitute the possibility of unstable women for universalism. A writer who organises conceptual manoeuvres to subvert her semantic boundary, arms feminism.

In contemporary feminist theory the boundary of public and private has ceased to be discrete: woman's identity is now recognised as having a relative and shifting positionality. In *Gynesis*, Alice Jardine reflects upon the paradox this sets up for feminists struggling for status in contexts where 'woman' has a fixed and stereotypical place. The paradox, Jardine argues, is between our desire to create an alternative social subject 'woman', and our understanding that 'woman' quickly becomes an essentialist construct. How does feminist criticism escape the impasse? Most obviously perhaps by attention to the changing historical characterisations of literary women, for example as Elaine Showalter does in *New feminist criticism* or by the use of mythology, for example Mary Daly's *Gyn/ecology*. Beyond this there is the development of a woman's language, measured by the extent to which lesbian images and gendered metaphors have been distinguished and crafted, for example in Catherine Clément and Hélène Cixous's *The newly born woman*.

New histories and new languages and a grouping of women as newly conceived literary subjects delegitimate the old tired rules of literary womanhood; yet a positive picture of femininity, one fixed by its own literary grain is still hard to print. The question is how do we speak about feminist literature? Feminism will need to pitch its tent on the axis of paradox so that a concern to question universal stereotypes does not have to result in a slide into a crude form of literary history and an endless plotting of kinds of production and consumption.

'Border traffic', in the terms that will be proposed in this book, takes place on that axis and describes how fluctuating women can write themselves out of the prisons of genres and of periods. Yet there is one obstinate difficulty inherent in using the term border traffic only for women's writing. After all, bilinguality as much as bipartisanship could be said to be the condition of every writing subject. It is not just women writers who turn language through linguistic hoops. For example Freud might be called the first and major translator of women's psyches. Freud used the term 'ubersetzung', or translation, to describe transposing all the hard work of the unconscious. Freud's introjection of 'alien' words and figurative speech has become the subject of much discussion. Currently physics is awash with speculations about the dimensions of borders. For example, Stephen Hawking's *The large scale structure of space-time* outlines a 'no boundary' hypothesis that time and space together form a continuous surface infinite in size. In some ways a translator's tools resemble the unified field concepts of contemporary physics which are used to describe the interaction of systems and phenomena.

Nor is it at all clear what a feminist criticism of boundary crossing should look like when there is no question of holding to essentialism. And it is true that border crossing is about the *lack* of literary place, about the *lack* of typologies, about the *lack* of a substantial narrative realm. What I shall be calling border crossing here then, designates a particular attitude, a certain inclination, in women writers, towards translation, synchronic time, and new significations. The usefulness of 'border traffic' here is that it acts as a pointer to feminist writing. In *Reading women*, Mary Jacobus describes how continental travel (or border crossing) played a significant role in nineteenth century women's writing, for example in the work of George Eliot and Charlotte Perkins Gilman. It was as if the social and sexual freedoms of travel allowed these women to write in a more undomesticated and deviant way.

Border crossing then might be established as crossing a *situación límite*. Existentialism attributes the term *situación límite* merely to a point of ultimate desperation where nothing is forbidden only because nothing matters any more. When women confront their *situación límite* everything matters. I understood, or thought I understood, that the postmodern way of looking at these *situación límites* might engage this desperation productively. Postmodernism, in the work of Jean-François Lyotard and Jean Baudrillard, is based on the proposition that language is eclectic and synchronic, a construct of popular and historical forms with no universal authority. In general, both writers agree, knowledge, at least as it is constructed by the academy, is not neutral or objective. In 'Answering the question: what is postmodernism?' Lyotard offers feminism a useful tool in his attempt to deconstruct totalitarian aesthetics.

Postmodernism works to open up the ontological boundaries between genres and between histories. Postmodernists claim, in particular, that 'fictions' are useful concepts, not just constructs, of knowledge. To be double coded is to be postmodern. Alice Jardine, drawing on postmodernism in *Gynesis*, argues that the 'spaces' in master narratives over which these narratives have lost control *are* women, that is to say these are spaces with feminine connotations. It was tempting not to be swayed by John Fekete's description of the postmodern, in *Life after postmodernism*, as a feminised domestic interior 'whose plan we do not have and which we have never quite finished' (Fekete, 1988, p. xi). Perhaps feminist criticism has a place in the open plan accommodation offered by the postmodern critic. It seemed that much could be understood about borders when I got to this point. The characteristic of postmodernism most specific to feminism is that it works within the very system it attempts to subvert. Postmodern fiction is most likely to revise the boundaries of narration by foregrounding the illusions of history. In postmodern fiction, for example in Gayle Jones's *Corregidora*, the narrator both describes and simultaneously contests her own historical boundaries. Ursa Corregidora has to define her sexuality and personal relationships in a battle with her memories of Corregidora the nineteenth century slave owner who fathered both her mother and grandmother. Both postmodernism and feminism, then, stand at the legislative boundary between what can be represented and what cannot. A critique of representation involves both in a break across the boundaries of history, theory, literature and art.

Art critics see an indefatigable hunger in postmodernism for works that are neither fish nor fowl, that straddle the borderline between the literary and the visual, for example, Barbara Kruger's graffiti. Hal Foster constructs his postmodernism on the boundary between viewer and artist when he claims that postmodern art changes the viewer for all time from a passive contemplator to an active reader (see Foster, 1985). The architect Charles Jencks brings forward the same 'area' of feeling by calling postmodern architecture a metaphysics of the body played out in overlapping planes and exaggerated perspectives (See Jencks, 1977).

Yet the point of postmodernism is to present itself momentarily as complete so that it can be read. Postmodernism, sadly, is no exception to the traditional rules of criticism. Postmodernism answers to post-Fordism: it markets past architecture and dead artists. But language is not a static entity that can be divided into building lots and summarily sold. Language attends to power. It will alter its form depending on who is speaking and from what position it is spoken. When the narratives of the already marginal are allowed to disrupt these literary theories of the *nouveau margineaux* then what makes postmodernism ultimately unsatisfactory is not so much its aesthetic compatibility with capitalism but rather its capitalised pronoun: the masculine gender of its speaking 'I'. Postmodernism's call for experimentation, for Lyotard's 'language games', is cut off from actual *agency*, from actual social reforms and social institutions. Postmodernism ignores the crucial instabilities of ethnicity and homosexuality as historically constituted and in living speakers. Woman's body is absent in postmodernism which has no serious consideration of women's 'subjective' and social experiences of mothering; nor of the emancipatory needs of different ethnic groups; nor of the inequalities of difference and the need of women,Black and white, for agency and historical truth. As Nancy Hartsock argues, 'postmodernist theories...deny marginalised people the right to participate in defining the terms of interaction with people in the mainstream' (Hartsock, 1987, p. 191). It is this absence which makes it difficult to align the proclamations of postmodernism fully with feminism. In these circumstances it is not surprising that the form that difference often takes in postmodern art is parody. In 'Postmodernism and consumer society' Frederic Jameson mourns: 'Each group comes to speak an "idiolect", a curious private language of its own which is spoken at the moment when pastiche appears and parody has become impossible. Pastiche is blank parody that has lost its sense of humour...this is a condition of marginality' (Jameson, 1988, p. 16). Jameson's 'blank page' makes abstract reading. In women's studies classrooms in the 1990s our incredulity towards master narratives is not accompanied by 'pastiche' but often by anger and sometimes humour as we share public accounts of our own marginality. One of feminism's most provocative challenges to existing theory is its insistence that we contemplate our agencies:

> At Gosforth Grammar School in the 1950s I, and all locally born girls, were required to take elocution lessons. Their aim: to rid us of our regional difference. At the University of East Anglia in the 1960s women learnt to lose another 'difference' — the expression of individual and collective femininity — in order to read the (masculine) academic narrative. For a woman who lives in a city in which Geordie is not the standard dialect, for a woman whose peers are middle class but was born working class, for a woman who works in a male dominated institution and has to speak its metalanguage, for a woman who fears her 'bilingualism' will one day be discovered, what recourse is left to her but to turn to border crossing?

Until we can legitimise bilinguilism, with careful study of the developments and effects of these 'sexed' languages, our first and most characteristic interrogation will have to be epistemological: How are we to know? Then we can ask the crucial and material question: Under what conditions can women's experience 'figure'? This is the situational vulnerability of border crossing.[7] So that, as Cixous argues, although all writers write in a foreign language there is always a double tongue which is part of the condition 'woman'.[8]

We open our mouths with double tongues. One tongue uses words like 'astigmatism'
metaphorically, hoping to exercise a livelier criticism. This tongue likes talking about
'the gaze' to Polytechnic students taking Feminist Theory WS201. The other tongue
speaks painfully if at all about her recent and severe astigmatism and her goggle eyed
appearance. Yet feminism, I know, is eloquent only at the border of criticism and
autobiography.

The idea that double tongues could be duplicitly truthful took me
some way for I saw that feminist criticism could similarly zigzag
through the disparate accounts of border crossing. There is a more
extensive theory of border crossing than is generally recognised. The
strength of the tactic is obscured by its fragmented location in many
disciplines. Disciplinary languages drape identical subjects with
voluminous vocabularies of methodological difference. The striking
coincidence of anthropological, or educational, propositions about
boundaries is downplayed in favour of separate disciplinary scenarios
of kinship or class.

No general account of border crossing has been written. Yet the
theme has a persistent draw. We could take up this conviction about
the bilingual force of women's writing and lead it towards dialectics,
anthropology, the sociology of education or French feminism all of
which are shot through with boundary tremors. By necessity this has
to be a very telescoped account of a few thinkers who, I feel have been
especially good at unpacking linguistic systems. Mikhail Bakhtin, Mary
Douglas, Basil Bernstein and Hélène Cixous negotiate most directly
with the repressive borders of language. These writers all recognise
aloud that boundaries are the place of a systematic fighting out of
language difference. In their writing the possibility of an embodied
border thematics has a precisely liminal vocabulary.

Mikhail Bakhtin is generally regarded as the first, and possibly
greatest, theoretician of literature in the twentieth century. In *Marxism*
and the philosophy of language and in *Discourse in the novel* Bakhtin has given
us metaphors of the boundary which are freighted with attraction for
feminist criticism. All language, according to Bakhtin, lives on the
boundary between its own context and another alien context.[9]
Bakhtin's term for his theory of language is a border concept –
translinguistics – and his concepts cross the boundaries of many
disciplines including philosophy, literature and psychology. Bakhtin's
broad view of the novel refers to language in general. The novel crosses
the boundaries of dialect groups and 'high' and 'low' cultures so that

its language is not made up of abstract words but is structured by 'dialogical' intercourse. This is Bakhtin's central metaphor. In his study of Dostoevsky he categorises the various forms of 'dialogism' in language and suggests that 'dialogism' marks the moment when an individual realises that the Other's language is beyond his control. While Bakhtin wrote in the main about male authors and not about gender difference the attraction of Bakhtin's work, from a feminist point of view is, I think, that it acts as a pointer to the value of bilinguilism. This bilinguilism has a political foundation. It is that the organisation of language is enmeshed with the histories of power. To Bakhtin, language is always changing and it is powerfully regenerative because it is always in dialogue with the foreign, the other. In *Marxism and the philosophy of language* he says: 'Indo-European studies have fashioned categories of understanding for the history of language of a kind that preclude proper evaluation of the role of the alien word. Meanwhile that role to all appearances is enormous' (Bakhtin, 1973, pp. 75-76).

Note how Bakhtin applauds the 'alien'. Ethnicity, deviance, the alien other, are at the heart of all language and its regenerative stroke. Bakhtin recognises here that in linguistic etymologies the conservative view prevails. Boundaries in literary studies are imperialistic. Underlying their taxonomies is a relentless and consistent drive to bastardise language difference. It followed, for Bakhtin, that dialogism could not simply be the 'taking into account' of these alien groups, in other words liberalism, but a struggle which actively contests the political conservatism of culture. Parallel to Bakhtin's concept of dialogism, and of equal importance to it, is his concept of 'extopy'. Extopy is active understanding when knowledge takes the form of a dialogue where a 'thou' is equal to 'I' yet appreciated as different from 'it.'

In women's studies we learn to speak in 'extopy'. That is to say, students clarify their research by changing their analyses in recognition of the perspectives of other students in the group not, as in the conventional classroom, by anticipating my likely teaching needs. Students interpellate other students as academic work. For example students write alternative solutions to their research in the style of each other.

In *Discourse in the novel*, Bakhtin describes literature as representing a struggle between languages which subverts a social, (or patriarchal), belief in universal truth. Characters in novels embody the social differences of languages (which are inevitably shaped by the sexual differences which shape society). The relevance of Bakhtin for feminism lies in his recognition of the unequal distribution of power in language and the need for oppositional tactics. The optimistic note, for women who cross languages, is Bakhtin's imaginative prophecy that dialogic forms flourish in moments of transition – in those times between a dead conservatism and a new social structure. Bakhtin's dialogic project can be incorporated into feminist criticism as well as into feminist education. The fundamental theme to recognise here is 'polyphony' which is the plurality of voices existing in any dialogic or literary place. It is fair to speculate that Virginia Woolf's inventive and famous mimicry of historical women in The journal of mistress Joan Martyn is a polyphonic history far more 'real' than much empirical data collected by historians since, like Bakhtin, Woolf makes evident the historical conflicts in language (Woolf, 1979).

The anthropologist Mary Douglas has similar and equally ambitious aims. Her book Purity and danger resembles Marxism and the philosophy of language in its fundamental premises. Douglas argues that all cultures depend on boundaries between animal and human, spirit and matter; and that every great revolution of thought touches on the nature of these boundaries. Time and social organisations are all 'sets of manipulable boundaries' (Douglas, 1975, p. 238). Boundaries are intimately connected both with power and with language because linguistic rituals are how a group maintains its form over time against the foreigner.[10] Douglas shares with Bakhtin a belief that boundary crossing contains a utopian element. When Douglas examines the border in relation to the alien she is struck by the variety of expressions created by the margins of social life. The precise attributes of Douglas's border strategies are ambiguous but are prototypically feminist. They include a movement into intense comradeship where distinctions of rank disappear, when moments, as Virginia Woolf would say, seem 'out of time'. This is how, Douglas claims, 'the fringes of society express their marginality': paradoxically by emphasising their eccentricity as witches or hysterics (Douglas, 1966, p. 114). Much of current anthropology is in debt to literary theory, for example literary terms such as 'image', 'discourse', 'metaphor', shape the way that anthropologists like Mary Douglas make sense of cultural phenomena. The forcefulness of differentiation is dramatised in the double languages that eccentrics speak. Yet the influence of boundaries, Douglas concludes, is always 'thoroughly conservative' (Douglas, 1975, p. 238).

Douglas's analysis of boundary is a much more fully articulated conception of what it means, culturally and historically, to change geographic and metaphorical places. For example the sexual politics of Zora Neale Hurston's verandah encounters becomes clearer if we read her against Douglas's repertoire of interpretative devices. Hurston's characters enact a pedagogics of liminality on the verandah when their 'cussing' and 'conjuring' games work to change gender status. As Douglas argues, danger (and the possibility of border crossing) lies in such transition places which blur the boundary between self and community. Where Bakhtin attends to the internal syntactics of border crossing, Mary Douglas draws bright discursive images of the social location of borders. An interest in the discursive aspects of culture draws attention to a poetics of different voices and positioned speech.

In *Class, codes and control*, Basil Bernstein applies Mary Douglas's analysis to the relation, in British society, between language boundaries and knowledge boundaries. Bernstein's theory of boundaries derives from his investigations into the processes of power in British schools. Changes in education, Bernstein realised, must involve fundamental changes in the nature and strength of educational boundaries. When firm boundaries demarcate curriculum contents and pedagogy then knowledge flows, Bernstein argues, which has a *closed* relation of favoured concepts – for example, 'the educated man'. Loose boundaries lead to integrated curriculae. Loose boundaries are not libertarian *per se*, because loosening is permitted, at least in British education, only in low status areas like infant schools.[11] Like Bakhtin and Douglas, Bernstein argues that strong boundaries lead to a sense of the 'otherness' of educational knowledge and he concludes that the subject is the linchpin of group identity. Any change in the classification and framing of knowledge implies a change in the structure and distribution of power and in its principles of control (Bernstein, 1971, p. 63).

Bernstein's theories became the manifesto of a new sociology of education in Britain and America in the 1970s. Bernstein draws on similar cultural and anthropological connotations of boundary to those in the work of Bakhtin and Douglas but bases his understanding of boundaries firmly on a psychosocial model. What distinguishes Bernstein's work from that of his predecessors Bakhtin and Douglas, is his emphasis on the division of labour and on the family as sources of boundary making. Bernstein's psychosocial model highlights for feminism the significance of internalised boundaries. In schools, boundaries become part of teachers in the mental structures and coding procedures teachers adopt to make sense of events and experience. So, for example, cognitive mappings are qualitatively different for different classes and social groups. Bernstein calls the two major codes 'restricted' (working class) and 'elaborated' (middle class). Marginal groups who use restricted codes create a structure of meanings which, from outside, appear to be 'strung together like beads on a frame, rather than one following a logical sequence' (Bernstein, 1971, p. 67). This definition of marginal social groups resembles the literary techniques of border women. The definition recalls Jean Rhys's unease, in *Good morning midnight*, with the 'sufficiency' of contemporary accounts of femininity in the Paris milieu which was then her home. When Rhys speaks about the different temporalities of women, she speaks in 'restricted beads' of ellipses which hint at imaginative experiences outside the cultural codes which Rhys contested.

Border people are likely to have a heightened perception of symbolic boundaries, the experience of being simultaneously 'insider' and 'outsider'. Bernstein holds out the promise that a movement to loosen boundaries symbolises a 'crisis in society's basic classification and a crisis in its structures of power and control' (Bernstein, 1971, p. 67). Yet, whereas, for Bakhtin and Douglas, the delineation of boundaries is never innocent but its consensual hegemony *can* be broken, for Bernstein nothing finally destroys the *cordon sanitaire* of patriarchal capitalism. Boundaries always displace and make alien certain subjects and transform subjectivity into set discursive routines. Bernstein's sense of the relationship between subjectivity, and social control leans forward to the more radical writings of Hélène Cixous. Where Bernstein's is very much a structuralist model of borders whose significance lies in systems of classification, Cixous, alternatively, takes the meaning of borders to come as an emergent outcome of sexuality.[12]

Cixous gives the theme of boundary particular prominence in the book she co-authored with Catherine Clément, *La Jeune Née, The newly born woman*. Here Cixous is concerned with the ritualistic ways in which women's experience of the world and of their bodies is categorised as alien, witchlike or hysterical by society in order that society can maintain the boundaries of patriarchal power. Cixous's central thesis, arrived at over a period of years, is that boundaries between different experiences of women, for example the boundary between women's writing and women's reading created by literary criticism, obscures sexual identity. Cixous's writing and her teaching (known as 'Etudes

Féminines') is articulated in a style which itself deliberately conflates the fictional and the theoretical. She aims in her work to cross the boundary of `book' and `body' so that her texts can be models of a new, unobjectified women's writing and hence begin to bring about change in the symbolic order. Like Bakhtin, Douglas and Bernstein, what Cixous finds when she examines literary boundaries is hierarchy. Cixous argues that forms of writing serve to legitimate relations of power. For example Cixous defines characterisation in novels as army conscription. Conscription, whether of characters or of army cadets, Cixous argues, is a technique of patriarchal power: `Woman does not perform on herself this regionalisation that profits the couple, that only inscribes itself within frontiers' (Clément and Cixous, 1986, p. 87). Women are at the borders of writing when a woman writes her body. This is because in `writing the body', women will have to make a complex negotiation between sexuality, representation and materialism. The genitality of the exchange will widen the cracks in the overall system. Cixous's decisive shift in focus to a corporeal discourse is a liberating challenge to the boundary of subjectivity and realism. In `conversations' Cixous describes how our gender shapes our perceptions and our knowledge. Portrait of Dora specifically explores this construction of a fresh identity. By stating that the meaning of `literature' is carried in its body (which might be read as the `natural') Cixous refuses the boundary and hierarchy of culture and nature. The body is given its full sign in Cixous's neologisms and syntactical turmoil. Her writing is often associational, built up of permutations of letters, puns, slips of the tongue and other forms of subjectivity. A consequence of this far reaching feminist enquiry into the very `nature' of writing is Cixous's frequent challenge to the logocentrism and phallocentrism of traditional literature. Not surprisingly, Cixous's language, for example in `The laugh of the Medusa' is avowedly metaphoric and quite explicitly autobiographical. Cixous uses cyclical rhythms and feminine imagery to break out of traditional literary forms which bind women's narrative representation.

The alien word plays the same critical role in Cixous's writing as it does in the work of Bakhtin. Cixous deliberately uses untranslated foreign words and in her plays and operas makes constant allusions to other dramas to constitute literature as the place where the issue of boundaries can be explicitly posed. Cixous's plays and criticism, with their multivocal echoes, represent that process of difference. Hence Cixous's main focus of attention, in her Centre d'Etudes Féminines, is on a cross-cultural analysis of the writers Kafka, Clarice Lispector, Tsaevana and other international figures. Passing across the borders of languages is a way of making the arbitrariness of national cultures very visible, just as escaping traditional literary language was a way for expatriate women writers like Gertrude Stein, to escape representations of conventional femininity. Unlike Freudian therapy which uses translation, as Mary Jacobus points out, to *domesticate* women, Cixous's method has the *inner* logic of a psychoanalytic cure which progresses from a sexual innerness to elaborate the construction of a confident femininity.[13]

The realm, par excellence, of the alien is the hysteric. Cixous, specifically in *The newly born woman*, traverses the boundary of hysteria recognising that hysteria and autobiography are related in any woman's search for a social breathing space: 'An entire fantastic world...opens up beyond the limit *as soon as the line is crossed* [my italics]' (Clément and Cixous, 1986, p. 33). Of course, psychoanalysis was first named the 'talking cure' by a woman hysteric Anna O. Breuer and Freud gave to Anna's signs and body language the symptomology of hysteria. It was Anna's entry into English and her refusal of her German mother tongue which led to her estrangement and initial silence. Cixous replaces symptomology with polylingualism since she believes that hysteria is a *positive* symbolisation which enables a writing self to emerge in relation to the Other entombed within us, since hysterics carry the memories of others. The disassociations common to hysterics, when represented in literature for example Marian's drifting perceptions in *The edible woman*, can be seen to be a concretisation of Atwood's dissatisfaction with the cultural boundaries of femininity. Hysteria is a source of communicable positive images because hysterics mimic subversively the master discourse.

Following Cixous we might all be promiscuous with our bodies of knowledge. A 'school' of border crossings will, ultimately, be able to identify these bodies. It is not my concern to demarcate a whole criticism of border crossing nor could I possibly assess the multifarious accounts of every single discipline in such a hammeringly tendentious sweep. I have given a far too brief survey of boundary concepts. This chapter has been an exercise in immersion: in trying to understand the contributions of existing theory. It has constituted an outline, summary and discussion of the work of four key thinkers. Each is a point of reference and a point of departure for feminist criticism. Bakhtin, Douglas, Bernstein and Cixous have been particularly instrumental in developing theories of borders in this century. They provide a number of crucial insights. The following chapters can put these various theories to work against literary texts allowing boundary concepts to introduce new categories of difference into critical theory. Border women are the reserve army of literary labour but they also occupy a liminal, radical place where new literary technologies could be exploited. To put it simply, border theory might provide a dynamic response to the urgent threat of closure in postmodernism's bracketed inattention to gender, race and sexual difference. Border theory can be read as a motivating strategy exploiting a wide range of linguistic tools from the point of view of gender. What I want to do, now, is to place the accounts of Bakhtin and many other critics, for example Nancy Chodorow, against writing by contemporary women in order to make a fresh articulation between psychosocial studies, history and feminist criticism.

> I pose these issues very much here in Britain in the 1990s.
> Chitra Aloysius is now an MA student with me at the Polytechnic of East London. 'My father was an author who also translated many English books into Sinhalese. His translations of The hound of the Baskervilles and Jane Eyre were named the best translations of the year in 1957. As a child who had never experienced winter or snow, I was fascinated by my father's descriptions of icy cold winters at Lowood and the warmth of the nursery fire at Gateshead. I nurtured a secret ambition that one day I would experience the feelings that were conveyed through dad's translations. This indeed came true when I came to England in my early twenties. My father had so absorbed the character of Jane Eyre that he could think and feel as she did. Although he never left the sub-tropical climate of Sri-Lanka he was able to convey in the translation the experience of snow and cold. I realised that my father was an exceptional writer.
>
> | Snow | හිම | -ice cube |
> | Winter | හිම තා කුවේ | -cold season.' |

Cultural critics point to the absurd landscapes depicted as 'natural' by colonial educators. In the *Womb of space* Wilson Harris describes the imaginative subversion fostered in schoolchildren in the West Indies made to write about English snow they had never seen. 'How profoundly has such nature poetry been a form of half-mystical, half-physical humour in refugee peoples around the globe?' (Harris, 1983, p. 134).

Chitra knows the threads that bind together women's experience, borders and the alien word. Chitra also knows the manipulation of difference by the rigid borders of British racism. Immigration controls prevented Chitra from coming to Britain as a graduate in literature and she was permitted entry only as 'unskilled labour for an ancillary job' in the British National Health Service (see Mama, 1984).[14] It took Chitra twenty years to cross another border into British higher education.

For some British women the specific racial and sexual politics of border crossing have never been out of focus.

No customs barriers: feminist literature in Britain 1900 to the present

One of the most striking features of British feminist writing in the twentieth century is the attention to women's everyday experience as a newly conceived literary topic. The precise specifying of 'ordinary' women involves feminist writers in autobiography rather than formal aesthetics, in dialogues rather than framed events. It was the struggle for suffrage reform added to ideas about pacifist feminism at the turn of the century which created new public images of women, entailing a new feminist iconography and, in the process, destabilising conventional notions of femininity. Such a movement demanded a writing which could refuse the boundaries of literary genres and try other literary representations.

These tactics are not always all together claimed by any single writer, nor, of course, are such tactics uniquely feminist. But just as feminist theory opens the ideological fences containing women's subjectivity, it is in the crossing of literary borders that twentieth century literary feminism finds its strength. It is feminist literature in Britain which, until the media explosion of the 1970s, provides the most speculative images of women. Literature is feminism's most visionary terrain. In the outline of feminism from Olive Schreiner, the icon most imaged by subsequent writers, through to Angela Carter's uncompromising allegories, literary texts written by feminists are strategic versions of sexual politics.

Women's writing often rejects and takes apart the 'master' stories of culture. As Rachel Blau DuPlessis has said so clearly, twentieth century women's writing, feminist or feminine, is about 'the delegitimation of cultural conventions about male and female' (DuPlessis, 1985, p. ix). And, as I argue in chapter six, it does not follow that women's fiction need be feminist. Even though there are characteristic tropes of women's writing, feminism does not necessarily shape and inform women's imagery. But now, as a result of contemporary feminist theory, we have arrived at a new understanding of why particular women writers can be called feminist. Women writers are feminist when they ask 'different' questions about female socialisation; or because they begin to take hold of their autobiographies in women's terms; or because they subvert literary boundaries to represent women in positive ways; or, and crucially, because they present topics such as lesbian feminism and attack social and economic discriminations against women. Hence, while contemporary women writers such as Murial Spark and Iris Murdoch frequently make ironic comments about gender, they do not specifically show how gender ideologies and socioeconomic relations might change when women's issues are the focus of literary texts.

This chapter is not about all of the literature written in Britain by feminists in this century. My interest is less in identifying the consciously propagandist text than in trying to read British literature, written by feminist women, as if it were a collective voice speaking a common and transgressive language. First wave feminism was vexed by a traditional politics which ignored women's agency. In the process of attacking the lack of political representation, British feminist writers came to challenge the literary misrepresentation of women and of men.

If there is to be a history of alterations in the literary status of feminism it will need to understand how writers have interpreted their own literary situations. Sheila Rowbotham describes this as a perpetual border crossing:

But always we were split in two, straddling silence, not sure where we would begin to find ourselves or one another. From this division, our material dislocation, came the experience of one part of ourselves as strong, foreign and cut off from the other which we encountered as tongue-tied paralysis about our own identity. We were never all together in one place, we were always in transit into alien territory. (Rowbotham, 1973, p. 31)

To 'understand' the self which Rowbotham describes, is to see how the text which we call a writer's 'work' interacts with the other texts which we call her 'moment'. The study of the historical development of these interactions will help to print a set of positive literary feminisms.

The main shifts in British literary feminism over ninety years are not so much in themes – which show a continuous and obdurate attention to the problems of the family, to work, the public space and to masculine aggression – but in experiences. As a result of second wave feminism, women writers in the 1970s were able to describe more openly a lived experience of transgression. In trying to understand the impact of feminism in this century in relation to boundaries, I am trying, among other things, to understand how literary form relates to ideology and how border crossings in literature might embody feminism.

In 1900 Olive Schreiner first confronted what she called 'sex parasitism' in heterosexual relations at the same time she confronted the bounds of realism and romance in the novel. In the 1910s, after suffrage women broke into the public space, Elizabeth Robins's The convert ends the public silencing of women's experience of sexual violence. The world after the first war enabled Rebecca West and Virginia Woolf to cross boundaries of heterosexuality and class to signify the connections between masculinity and war and to resignify sisterhood. The 1930s was the first full decade of women's suffrage from which so much had been expected. British writers of the period, like Winifred Holtby and Vera Brittain, enlarged the meagre legal definitions of equality by creating narratives critical of private inequalities. The feminist agendas of Storm Jameson and Sylvia Townsend Warner lie at the intersection of modernism and left-wing naturalism. For these writers to dissent from sociocultural constructions of women meant excluding themselves from politically 'acceptable', as well as from historically current, literary systems of meaning. Similarly Rose Macaulay in The world my wilderness, steps aside from conservative post-war Britain to portray London as a bombed wasteland of bourgeois patriarchy. In the 1960s and 1970s Margaret Drabble, Nell Dunn and Fay Weldon could make one more transgressive swerve from post-war family values by criticising, in their fiction, the psychosocial construction of 'motherhood'. Carolyn Steedman, and other feminist autobiographers deny history its linear boundary by mixing the multiple plots of psychoanalysis and sociology to tell their stories. Other writers, like Doris Lessing, were inviting women over the boundary of realism, into psychoanalytic and speculative fictions. The decades since 1970 have witnessed the growth of feminism in the arts and media encouraging the novelist Angela Carter to celebrate female affiliation and the playwright Caryl Churchill to transform the vocabulary of theatre. Finally, in writing in tandem about sexism and racism, Asian and Afro-Caribbean poets like Debjani Chatterjee and Grace Nichols and novelists like Barbara Burford are projecting visions of feminist women for the 1990s and beyond.

Fashions in feminist thought may shift profoundly from one decade to another and clearly women's expectations are shaped by changing economic pressures. But there are continuities. For example the major theoretical question asked by Olive Schreiner – What is the new woman? – is the underlying question of current radical feminism. All twentieth century feminist literature, in Britain at any rate, even the most realistic, typically involves some violation of ontological boundaries. Feminism encourages writers to unpick the seams of misrepresentation with new literary strategies across a broad writing spectrum. For too long feminist history has ignored literary radicalism[1] The breaking of literary boundaries helps to establish the contiguity of the 'work' of literature with the workings of politics. The purpose of my feminist literary history then is not only to fill in some gaps in feminist knowledge, but to challenge the framework of that knowledge. I want to offer this as a tentative model which could engage with the stylistic and generic transformation of the British literary canon by feminist women. The model will support my belief that there are indeed firm grounds for reading narrative dissent as a feminist practice of 'border traffic'.

Most of the major themes of twentieth century feminism are systematically argued in Olive Schreiner's *Woman and labour* (1911). It is an important book in several ways. Not only is it, together with Schreiner's novels, the text most often cited by subsequent feminists, for example Vera Brittain called *Woman and labour* the 'Bible' of feminism just as Doris Lessing, much later, claimed Schreiner's *The story of an African farm* to be the first 'real' novel with Africa as a setting. But Schreiner anticipates the agenda of contemporary feminism by arguing that feminism is as much part of consciousness raising as of equal rights. Olive Schreiner (1855-1920), was an active feminist and socialist who, together with Sylvia Pankhurst, campaigned for the first Women's International Peace Conference at the Hague in 1915. Schreiner's impact on British feminism had begun even before the turn of the century. Her ideas were shaped by her association with a variety of political groups and individuals in London in the 1880s, including Eleanor Marx and Havelock Ellis. In Schreiner's *The story of an African farm* (1883), the heroine Lyndall leaves home to seek a similar new intellectual and social life for herself. Lyndall's allegorical response to conventional womanhood is a powerful critique of realism, for example in the way 'Times and seasons' mixes the languages of nurture and spiritualism: 'This thing we call existence, is it not a something

which has its roots far down below in the dark, and its branches
stretching out into the immensity above ... a living thing, a One'.
(Schreiner, 1883, p. 153).

When Olive Schreiner wrote *Woman and labour* the connection being
made, for example in the writing of the Pankhursts, was between
feminism and equal rights.[2] In *Woman and labour* Schreiner outlines that
much more radical theme of women's essential *differences* from men and
consequent superiority: 'The knowledge of woman, simply as woman,
is superior to that of man; she knows the history of human flesh'
(Schreiner, 1911, p. 173). The book constantly juxtaposes individual
change with social change. Technology has contracted 'the sphere of
woman's domestic labours' and hence unequal pay for woman is a
'wilful and unqualified "wrong" in the whole relation of woman to
society today' (Schreiner, 1911, p. 24). Women's increasing and equal
participation in the work force will change, not only economic
institutions, but also sexuality and femininity. Women's subordination
(or what Schreiner calls 'parasitism') is a general condition in
consciousness and in society. The specific question Schreiner asked –
how is sexual difference constructed? – is the major question of second
wave feminism as much as her depiction of women's unequal rights
informed first wave feminism. Schreiner's commitment to black South
Africans presages Winifred Holtby's concern with the enormities of
Black oppression, just as her argument that *all* women (prostitutes *and*
mothers) suffer the institutionalised objectification of powerful men
is the essence of Caryl Churchill's *Cloud nine*.

Pointing out that gender difference is not biologically given, and
cannot fix 'mental aptitude', Schreiner tackles the issue of essentialism
by promoting a women-centred morality based on women's experience
of, or psychic aptitude for, nurturing. The association of feminism
with maternity anticipates the novels of Margaret Drabble, just as
Schreiner's maternal pacifism flowers in the mobilisation of maternal
iconography by Greenham women. Schreiner draws our attention to
the fact that sexual discrimination is not just an issue of economics but
encoded in the boundaries of culture and of psyche. Schreiner has a
vision of transcendant matriarchy far beyond the liberal battle for equal
rights. For example, this radical focus on nurture and pacifism involves
Schreiner in an acute struggle with literary form. The most significant
sections of *From man to man* (1926) – Rebekah's pregnancy and her
passionate diaries – rupture the bounds of realism and share with the
'Times and Seasons' passage of *The story of an African farm* and sections

of *Woman and labour* a powerful hallucinatory quality. The interpolated languages, the apparent formlessness is the story of *African Farm*, Lyndall and Rebekah are new radical voices speaking openly the language of twentieth century literary feminism.

Of course any critical account of the impact of politics on literature is in danger of the problem of anachronism. In other words, there is always a danger of attributing to past writing a wider, deeper feminist consciousness than actually existed at the time. But between 1900 and the 1920s the suffrage campaign united British women writers and activists more wholeheartedly than any other issue before or since. More important, it created a profound change in women's social images. Inevitably, literature would reflect these changes in women's representation. In 1908 Elizabeth Robins and Cicely Hamilton founded the Women Writers Suffrage League. Edwardian theatre was a special focus for feminism perhaps because, due to their repertory touring, middle class actresses saw the inequalities of class and of the family throughout Britain. The popularity of Henrik Ibsen's plays contributed to their belief that theatre should challenge social attitudes. Karl Marx's daughter Eleanor had first arranged a private reading of *A doll's house* in 1886, and the 'New Woman' became a dominant character in many plays from the 1890s. This climate encouraged Elizabeth Robins to develop an original form of political theatre using agit-prop and by 1912 there were four actresses running London theatres. With the success of independent management, Cicely Hamilton's *How the vote was won* (1909) was performed in commercial theatres as well as at suffrage meetings. While Hamilton's play relied on traditional forms and limited its argument to visualising how the vote would end discrimination against women, Elizabeth Robins (1862-1952) in *The convert* (1907) was to give that more problematic account of sexual politics. Robins's first play *Alan's wife* (1893) had challenged the boundaries of conventional sexuality and motherhood and her second play *Votes for women* manipulates the genre boundaries of sentimental comedy. Retitled the *Convert* when published as a novel, the text focuses on a crucial feminist theme – the issue of sexual violence. The militant heroine Vida Levering 'converts' to suffrage and blackmails her former seducer, the MP Geoffrey Stonor, into supporting a Suffrage Bill. Robins makes a direct correlation between personal and public sexual politics.

It is true that no other work in this period provides as thorough and harrowing a discussion of the sexual politics of feminism, but it is equally true that the period 1900 to 1914 witnessed a massive change in attitudes to masculinity and sexuality.[3] In *The great scourge and how to end it* (1913) Christabel Pankhurst detailed the effects of venereal disease and Cecily Hamilton's *Marriage as a trade* (1909) protests against sexual inequities.[4] Robins's fictional account of the commonplaces of male abuse was potentially more revolutionary. Robins vividly portrays 'the sheer physical loathing' of men to feminist women (Robins, 1901, p. 145). The suffragettes carry dog whips for protection, an inventive practice much like the dog mace defences of second wave feminists. Vida transforms her personal experience of rape and abortion into a public denunciation of the sexual exploitation of women. Male opposition is forcefully depicted. '"Sexless creatures!" … "touched, you know", as he tapped his forehead … "like a Red Indian", and the policeman carried her out scratching and spitting' (Robins, 1901, p. 58). By depicting suffrage as a sexualised battle between the savage and the 'sane' across the boundary of the 'civilised', Robins poses dramatically the question of women's representation. Watching the suffrage meeting, Vida, for the first time, experiences the joy of crossing class boundaries in the large crowd. Robins points to how women might counter misrepresentation by occupying the public space. Feminism introduces Vida to a new and exhilarating urban freedom. 'All the way, from the Battersea Fire Station to Sloane Square, did Ernestine and I walk, talking reform last night', just as their public meetings and demonstrations did open up London to activist women (Robins, 1901, p. 177).

Indeed, the city of London is a significant 'character' in many women's novels of this period. Placing her private bliss in a collective space, Miriam in Dorothy Richardson's *Pilgrimage* similarly evades class boundaries. When Vida shares Ernestine's suffragette speeches, the erotics of public feminism become a substitute for heterosexuality where marriage transforms women into 'slab-like figures' mirroring an all time low in the popularity of marriage in this decade (see Jeffreys, 1982, p. 641). Robins understood that feminism would need to go beyond political campaigns into a whole new evaluation of male and of female psychology. The same critical view of family relationships, the same interest in women's acquisition of gender identity, occurs in May Sinclair's arresting account of mother/daughter bonding in the opening sequences of *Mary Olivier* – 'Mamma's breast: a smooth, cool, round thing that hung to your hands and slipped from them when they tried to hold it' (Sinclair, 1919, p. 4).

There is no doubt that women writers like Robins and Sinclair were passionately aware that women's sexual and social subordination could not be eradicated by equal rights alone. Vida's 'conversion' itself is not simply to a political belief but 'to a view of life' (Robins, 1901, p. 143). The novel shares with Woolf's *Orlando* a utopian vision of 'a world got topsy turvey where all the girls are boys and all the boys are girls' (Robins, 1901, p. 171). Where Radclyffe Hall's *Well of Loneliness* (1928), although a serious and sympathetic study of lesbianism, defines gender as a limited compendium of traits, Robins projects a non-sexist society less in awe of sexed categories: 'Interest in our fellow-women seems queer and unnatural to you because you don't realise Mrs Brown has always been interested in Mrs Jones' (Robins, 1901, p. 195). To describe 'a place where this new campaign must be fought by women alone' is to break the boundary of Edwardian realism (Robins, 1901, p. 290).[5]

Questions of new gender relations were part of a series of structural crises in this period coinciding with campaigns by women to transform male sexual behaviour just before and after the First World War. A state ideology of motherhood was juxtaposed to new ideas about sexual difference which shifted from negative to more positive representations of womanhood.[6] More than any other writers of their time Virginia Woolf and Rebecca West figured this crisis in beliefs about masculine potency and a clearly articulated feminist pacifism. Woolf's *Mrs Dalloway* (1925) and West's *The return of the soldier* (1918) are the two works which explicitly explore violence and sexuality in relation to the psychoanalytic process, but throughout the 1920s and 1930s Woolf and West together with other feminist writers, like Dora Russell and Vera Brittain, were capturing and resignifying masculinity and femininity in psychoanalytic terms. Reading these feminist writers not only prevents us from identifying feminist ideas solely in terms of feminist politics but also fixes our attention on women's literature which is pervaded by new images of women's feelings.

It was in 1908 that Virginia Woolf declared she would reform the novel, but the imperative voice was Woolf's *Three guineas* (1938), that most sustained account of masculinity and fascism and woman's 'difference'. Virginia Woolf (1882-1941) was intermittently a novelist but continually a critic. She wrote over 500 essays which offer substantially the same sympathy to the rights of women as do the ideas in her fiction about marriage and education, female friendship and the representation of women. In all her essays Woolf adopts a narrative stance of open sisterhood by sharing a conversational intimacy with her woman reader. For example, the distance from the assumed male addressee in *Three guineas* contrasts sharply with the first person plural, 'we', which Woolf shares with women in that text. Woolf poses the Outsiders Society, where women work together for equality and peace, against fascistic patriarchy: 'As a woman I have no country. As a woman I want no country. As a woman my country is the whole world' (Woolf, 1938, p. 109). But even in the earlier *A room of one's own* (1929) Woolf was advocating a socialist feminist theory of culture, and Woolf's most condensed and effective metaphor of sexual politics is in *A room of one's own* where she describes women as men's looking glasses 'reflecting the figure of man at twice its natural size' (Woolf, 1929, p. 31). It was Rebecca West who read the book as 'an uncompromising piece of feminist propaganda ... the ablest yet written'.

Rebecca West (1892-1983) began writing at a time of violent political reaction to feminism. At nineteen she wrote for the feminist journal *The freewoman* and went on to produce novels, travel writing, biography as well as political criticism. Like Woolf, West writes in a personal voice judging throughout her work what is significant about male power and what women might do to counter its violence. In *Mrs Dalloway* and *Return of the soldier* Woolf and West celebrate the repressed and submerged semiotic, or the pre-symbolic world of mothers and children, which enables women characters to reassess the social processes of gendering in a negative masculine world. By depicting the claustrophobia of sexual relationships in many of their major novels, Woolf and West highlight the tight bounds of heterosexuality. In order to portray the social implications of masculine aggression both Woolf and West are formally experimental, trying to subvert the patriarchal literary canon as well as neutralise patriarchal social codes. Their novels set 'woman' against a backdrop of public and private relationships. *Orlando's* parodic journey through British history is an emblem of Woolf's critical response to the borders of sex-role stereotypes. *Orlando's* (1928) fantasy plot evades the polarisation of gender and of class. Woolf crosses the boundary of realism by setting Orlando's mixture of 'Kentish earth with Normandy fluid' and his/her affinity with the minority and marginalised groups of gypsies and prostitutes into a narrative landscape of contrasting climates. All Woolf's women characters continually struggle to achieve personhood against the social institutions of family and class. Where Rachel in the early *The voyage out* is her father's daughter, Rose Pargiter joins the suffragette campaigns in The years, Rhoda in The waves refuses narrative causality, and To the lighthouse opposes the heterosexual story with a mother/daughter dyad. Like Woolf's writing, Lily's painting in the novel is made up of absences where the patriarchal Mr Ramsey's dictionary is a militaristic failure – a charge of the Light Brigade.

Many of these themes first surface in Mrs Dalloway. The novel opens with the chimes of Big Ben, Woolf's symbol of masculine authority posed against the different female identities and different possibilities open to Clarissa Dalloway and to her daughter Elizabeth. Clarissa's life is set in a middle class London poised historically in the years immediately following the First World War, where Elizabeth dreams of becoming a professional woman. Clarissa moves between the 'colonial' state of marriage and her subtle and symbolic desire for women's friendship. Mrs Dalloway is a palimpsest of Virginia's affair with Vita Sackville West. Yet masculinity is as much an artefact in Mrs Dalloway as femininity. Woolf makes a structural link between Clarissa and Septimus, the brain damaged 'returned' soldier. The novel exposes their shared misdefinition by imperial power and the sexual frigidity which that power inculcates. Both characters are similarly pervaded by images of rape and compulsion in personal relationships. Septimus and Clarissa fear new experiences and the emotions which these will bring. Yet Septimus, unlike Clarissa, cannot define himself. Shell shock has caused his passive response to aggressive patriarchy. Woolf vividly depicts a society damaged by its suppression of emotions and the resulting alienation of women. But equally vividly she depicts the possibility of change metaphorically with the shifting clouds over London. In order to emphasise the impact of ideas on narrative, Woolf abandoned the conventional organisation of chapters in Mrs Dalloway claiming in June 1923 that 'in this book I have almost too many ideas' (Woolf, 1984, p. 248). The First World War is a vast historical background to another patriarchal institution – psychotherapy.[7] When Sir William Bradshaw consigns Septimus to a sanatorium rather than attending to his symptoms, Woolf is imaging some kind of discontinuity in society. 'Insanity' represents a failure to connect and Clarissa is only 'sane' because she can respond passionately to other women.

Similarly Rebecca West, in The return of the soldier, undercuts the imperialist underpinnings of Edwardian patriarchy by revealing its betrayal of masculinity and resulting male impotence. Choosing the same metaphor – a hero suffering from shell shock – West, too, depicts masculinity as amnesia. The return of the soldier was West's first novel but it draws on Schreiner's ideas of 'parasitic women' which West had explored in her journalism. The novel is Jenny's narrative about her cousin Chris Baldry. West uses the device of amnesia too as a metaphor of the parasitism of women in bourgeois marriages. Chris Baldry remembers neither his estates nor his wife but only his earlier and intense love for working class Margaret. The novel ends when the narrator Jenny, together with Chris's wife and Margaret, collaborate to restore Chris to memory (and hence to patriarchy). Margaret restores Chris to the memory of his son's death, but (and here West is subtle) Margaret points to the death of patriarchy because the end of Chris's paternity is the death of his circulation of representation. In *Return of the soldier* West rescues Chris by using women's intuition where Woolf, more brutally if more radically, sacrifices Septimus. But in *Black lamb and grey falcon* (1941) West wittily identifies patriarchy as 'lunacy', a state in which men see as (if by moonlight) only outlines and never essential nature. The book deliberately crosses the boundaries of literary genres – mixing journalism, fiction and poetry with history.

It is patriarchy, West argues in *Harriet Hume* (1929), which has built London into separate spheres. Art and leisure are the spheres assigned to women and the legal and political institutions of Parliament and the City are reserved for men. It is patriarchy which cannot connect. Public men, West claims, embrace empty causes because they cannot bear things close to them – home, family or self identity. Both *Mrs Dalloway* and *Return of the soldier* go well beyond the conventional depictions of sexuality and pacificism by deeply implicating their readers in the meanings of history and psyche and women's countervailing friendships.[8]

By the 1930s with the achievement of suffrage, the feminist agenda was to be, not Woolf's Outsiders' Society, but one of 'welfare feminism'.[9] The writings of Vera Brittain (1893-1970) and Winifred Holtby (1898-1935) are part of this agenda. Throughout their journalism, autobiographies and fiction both writers were carefully questioning the implications for women of living in a society where women had a legitimate claim to equal treatment but were facing contradictions about motherhood and the sexual division of labour which legislative change could not touch. Winifred Holtby wrote in 'A generation of women's progress' in 1935 that women's 'influence on public affairs is only one indication of the transformed position of women in the world at large ... the profoundest change of all, perhaps, is that which has affected individual minds and social habits' (Brittain and Holtby, 1985, p. 95). So both writers addressed the needs of working mothers and the sexual division of labour, as well as the institutionalisation of motherhood. The discontinuity between social categories of women, the heterosexual couplet and feminist articulations is the border in Holtby and Brittain's writings. Holtby challenged the boundaries of romance in favour of a more communal vision and Brittain subverted the limited representation of heterosexual relations then available to her. The novels of both writers effectively broke the boundary of the realist tradition raising urgent questions about 'private' representations and 'public' roles. Vera Brittain claimed that Olive Schreiner had 'supplied the theory' that could link these public and private experiences of women and Winifred Holtby points to Schreiner's originating argument that if half of humanity 'whether of "inferior" sex or "inferior" race is deprived of the opportunity for development, it endangers the whole progress of civilization' (Brittain and Holtby, 1985, p. 147).

The subordination of women was a continual problem occupying a shifting terrain, and marriage and motherhood made equal opportunity for many women 'an unsubstantial myth' (Brittain and Holtby, 1985, p. 145). The Six Point Group, the focus of much of Brittain's activity, campaigned continually for a 'fair field and no favour' for women entering the public sphere because vertical segregation was increasing steadily between 1911 and 1939.[10] After the First World War the ideology of separate spheres was substantially reinforced by the imposition of a 'marriage bar' on women pursuing professional careers. For educated, political women like Holtby or Brittain the choice they might have to make between marriage and work was obviously an agonising one. Vera Brittain argued that an ideal marriage could be one of 'free, generous and intelligent comradeship' in an 'elastic arrangement of semi-detachment' (Brittain and Holtby, 1985, p. 132). An arrangement very like her own domestic ménage with her husband George Catlin and Winifred Holtby. As Holtby pointed out, 'whenever society has tried to curtail the opportunities, interests and powers of women, it has done so in the sacred names of marriage and maternity' (Brittain and Holtby, 1985, p. 132).

Brittain's fiction makes the same critical response to the 'institution' of marriage. *Honourable estate* (1936) illustrates the old and the new types of marriage. By disrupting the traditional genre of the 'marriage' novel Brittain could openly critique the narrative politics of marriage. Thomas Rutherstone is the outmoded patriarchal husband whose son, Denis, creates a more equal partnership with Ruth who remains an independent career woman throughout her marriage. The novel dramatises the unmet needs of married women as the suppressed subtext of legislative 'equality'. Similarly Winifred Holtby's The crowded street (1924) is a chilling picture of the boundaries of conventional family life. In South riding (1936) Holtby creates a more panoramic picture of local country and family life in order to give space to women's public as well as private conflicts. Holtby's 'voice' is Sarah Burton, the headmistress whose social optimism and urge 'to take the future into our hands' is balanced by the death of Carne her lover, and the ensuing gap between feminist needs and personal tragedy. None of Brittain's or Holtby's fictions suggest that good feminist aspirations can neatly resolve personal and social tensions. Sarah has no victory but reaches a quiet epiphany that children might be 'armaments' for defence in a world of poverty and ugliness.

The contradictions of 1930s feminism are illustrated by Brittain and Holtby's constant oscillation between genres. Where early twentieth century feminists like the Pankhursts could adopt a rhetoric of nationalism Holtby and Brittain chose a more informal style. In 'The whole duty of woman' Brittain describes one evening 'sitting beside my fire rereading the Life of Charlotte Brontë when the post brought to me a request for a speech', on sex differences in education (Brittain and Holtby, 1985, p. 120). Like Woolf in A Room of one's own, Brittain adopts a free-ranging self-reflexivity appropriate to a political world where feminism can no longer focus on single issues like the vote. In her autobiography Brittain hoped to capture that representative experience of feminist women for whom 'love and marriage must be subordinate to work', because war had made them a generation who knew 'stark agonies' (Brittain, 1933, p. 652). Brittain hoped that the impact of the First World War and suffrage might erode class differences and give feminist women a common identity and she tries to contain the tensions of 1930s feminism within a purposeful story. But in the foreword Brittain describes her 'original' idea of writing a long novel which 'turned out a hopeless failure'. Nor could 'reproducing parts of her diaries' absorb Brittain's purpose. Only autobiography, she realises, set against 'the larger background' might challenge distinctions between fiction and history and between public and private. Brittain's 'Forward' self-consciously points to the inherent provisionality of any writing convention, as Brittain implicitly contests the boundaries of genres aware that 'history' is a personal as well as a cultural construct. Although Vera Brittain was not the first writer to speak for a generation she was the first woman to speak *as a woman* about the war. Speaking for a generation forced Brittain to speak in a new form – the generational autobiography.

Brittain's *Testament of youth* (1933), like Ray Strachey's political biography *The cause* (1928), has an active narrative which stretches a plot of psychological 'truth'. In common with many feminist autobiographies, it links the formation of the writer's feminism to her early experiences of discrimination. For example Vera Brittain recalls being 'severely reprimanded' for enjoying conversations with boys which 'aroused in me a rebellious resentment that I have never forgotten' (Brittain, 1933, p. 28). The rebelliousness crystallised when her brother was so easily given the university education that Brittain desperately wanted for herself. Brittain hid from her family, but not from her autobiography, an equally early experience of sexual molestation from 'the pawing and alcoholic' man who shared her railway carriage home from school. The experience finds its politicised plot in Brittain's Six Point Group pamphlet on indecent assault and the age of consent.

Feminist autobiographies often rewrite the family scenario by signalling to the muted but more heightened experience of female affiliations. Brittain admires her aunts because 'they made their way in the world long before independence was expected of middle class women' *and* because they were also 'good-looking and agreeable' (Brittain, 1933, p. 20). Yet there are gaps and tensions which are the inevitable result of Brittain's attempt to create a public face for feminism through the detail of her private life. The sudden rushes into religious imagery are not emotional sublimation but express Brittain's deep desire to make a feminist and therefore 'serious' history, from her life.

It is this public face of feminism which gave writers as apparently disparate in technique as Storm Jameson (1891-1985) and Sylvia Townsend Warner (1893-1978) the strength to evoke a more pluralistic and potent feminist culture. The boundary between public politics and private belief eroded considerably during the 1930s and 1940s, chiefly as a result of women entering the public domain. More single women were employed and legal rights were established in divorce, property and child custody (see Lewis, 1984). Activist women had great faith in the integrity of women's sisterhood. In 1933 Storm Jameson founded 'Writers Against Fascism and for Collective Security' to support the Spanish Republic, which included women contributing to the New left review like Naomi Mitchison, Rose Macaulay, Rebecca West and Sylvia Townsend Warner.

The left-wing feminist agenda, then, lies at the intersection of modernism and socialism. Sometimes, as in Storm Jameson's None turn back (1936), that writing uses a national event like the General Strike of 1926 to make a sharp critique of sexual politics. Alternatively, writers like Sylvia Townsend Warner undermined the left-wing love of realism and its concomitant misogyny by creating fantastic 'historicized' women loving their 'queer' existence. Townsend Warner refuses the boundary of a literary canon with her attention to extraliterary fairy tales and her choice of such unusual characters as witch women, and Black musicians. Much of this writing revolves around a persistent dialectic: the contradiction between women's friendship and the structure of the family and economic relations in patriarchy. More often than not these authors structure their works around a common and central motif: the heroine's growing awareness that to gain her 'true' identity she must break the barriers of family and class. In particular Townsend Warner's writing is characterised by themes of exile, translation and border crossings. Both None turn back and Summer will show (1936) are socialist in their belief that identity is transformed by radical political experience. But the form of this transformation is specific to feminism since, as both Jameson and Townsend Warner reveal, women cross class boundaries primarily by sharing their love of children and each other, not only through political comradeship. Both novels share a particular argument about the relation of women and politics while drawing on very different techniques – of naturalism (Jameson) and of parody and fabulation (Townsend Warner) – in order to portray women struggling with patriarchal forces beyond their immediate control. Both novels depict contemporary society, or a historicised version of that society, as one blind to the strengths of independent women, and to the politics of the outcast. Each heroine's growing conscious awareness of social forces and her transgressive evasion of their constraints places each woman on a border.

For a woman, and in Townsend Warner's case a lesbian communist woman, the 1930s left-wing agenda was profoundly masculinist in both its homophobic view of sexuality and in its literary focus. For example the exclusive 'male club' quality which dominated the group of left-wing intellectuals from Oxbridge[11] forced Warner to displace her lesbianism into the fantastic as she 'made strange' the forms of her novels. If Jameson's dramatic reconstruction of the General Strike lacks the psychological and narrative complexity of Townsend Warner's epic novel of the Paris Commune of 1848, what they share is an understanding that heroines can liberate themselves from the gendered constrictions of class and the economy only with a swerve away from male and family values. Storm Jameson and Townsend Warner combine detailing of the boundaries of class and patriarchy with a portrait of the female artist or writer as a free spirit. This is not an unresolvable conflict in their novels but it does remain a writing tension highlighting the events of transgression.

Storm Jameson's writing reflects her increasing concern with the world of public politics and with the choices women can make that might affect that world. Between 1919 and 1979 she published a total of forty five novels. Her most sympathetic characters are consistently of the left and just as consistently struggle with the social reality of women's oppression. The design of None turn back shares the major motifs of other radical writing in the 1930s. It is both a strike novel, and a novel about the decay of class. Yet by placing the heroine Hervey's thoughts about womb surgery at the beginning of the book, Jameson privileges women's reproductive interests over political production.

The book is replete with episodes where men are depicted as emotional and financial failures like Hervey's husband Nicholas, or as fascists like Julian Swan, the cripple who 'had trained himself to be outside human feelings, she thought'. An assertive masculinity educates Hervey (and the reader) about the hegemony of capitalist patriarchy. The mine owner William Gary, symbolically castrated by a shell in 1918, together with the Jewish financier Cohen and the fascist Swan, represent patriarchy at its most aggressive supported by Swan's prototype Black Shirts, 'young men who will obey anyone who bullies them in the right way' (Jameson, 1936, p. 191). The left opposition is equally patriarchal. The Strike Committee is immersed in a masculine culture which uses a vocabulary of aggressive militarism – of strike 'battalions' and 'discipline'. Hervey's language, in contrast, encapsulates a semiotic lyricism. Jameson allows Hervey a quite extended subjectivity denied to any of the male characters. Significantly this 'semiotic' voice strengthens when Hervey returns to the Hampshire village where she lived when her son Richard was two. Jameson superimposes on the political time of the novel a more diffuse 'women's time', a semiotic space where 'neither past nor future but the whole of her life was present with her' (Jameson, 1936, p. 143). *None turn back* expresses women's yearning for the solidity of 'women' by fashioning episodes that displace the strike events in favour of stories about understanding between women. While taking tea in a working class woman's home Hervey finds a child's toy pig with small teeth marks which resemble 'the same marks on the back of my watch' (Jameson, 1936, p. 172). The sociability of the two women's memories of their maternities, together with the novel's concerted use of the pre-oedipal materials of female identity, contributes to Hervey's understanding of that emotionally denser class crossing that women can make. Hervey's ability to stand outside the bounds of trade socialism stems not from the political events of the novel but from her openness to women's memories and to the semiotic. Hervey remembers again and again the 'sense of responsibility and guilt' she felt as a child herself with her own mother. The title 'A famous victory' for the final chapter is a victory for maternal identity not for the strikers.

In Sylvia Townsend Warner's novels women characters also seek a wilderness of their own away from the patriarchal city and economy. One of Townsend Warner's main themes is the subjection of women in marriage and the forces ranged against independent women by institutions like the Church, marriage or the city. Lolly Willowes retreats to the country to remember the 'body' of her mother. Lolly's knowledge about nature and about witchcraft presages contemporary eco- and radical feminism. But where, in *Lolly Willowes* (1926), women are marginal to the social order and can only *verbally* exorcise 'society, the Law, the Church, the History of Europe', in *Summer will show* the heroine Sophia makes a far more obdurate analysis of marriage and its economic controls.

Set in 1848, the novel traces Sophia's struggle for a new identity which takes her away from the functions of motherhood and educator after the death of her children from smallpox, to Paris where she gains a political consciousness. Townsend Warner's sexual politics are very clear. In England Sophia is trapped by gender, by class and by history when she is deprived of her family estate by the injustice that married women's property was owned by the husband. In Paris, Sophia meets and loves Minna, her husband's ex-mistress, and joins the communards and a *flâneur* existence. The outcast, literally 'mauvais sujets' of Paris, embody a political and aesthetic statement about the liberating possibilities for free women who possess an historical purpose. As in *None turn back*, men are colonisers of psyche and purse. At first Sophia is ironic: 'in some ways men were essential. One must have a coachman or a gardener' (Townsend Warner, 1936, p. 76). Distance and independence bring a concomitant new delight in her own and in other women's eroticism: 'Since she had freed herself of Frederick nakedness was again a pleasure' (Townsend Warner, 1936, p. 176). Speaking in public gives women further power. Minna's gift for story telling shows how women's oppression involves a mutilation of consciousness which can be cured by speaking out. These myriad possibilities assume a different shape when Sophia sleeps with Minna 'in a desperate calculated caress' (Townsend Warner, 1936, p. 250). The script of lesbian desire is their metaphoric free space; 'As one wanders through a new house, where everything is still uncertain or unknown' (Townsend Warner, 1936, p. 236). In a Royal Society of Arts Lecture 'Women as writers' Townsend Warner described the 'ease in low company' which she felt was the mark of women's writing. Warner's lecture shares with Woolf's A room of one's own and Three guineas a similar interest in the 'others' or 'outsiders' of society and the knowledge that woman's alien perspective allows her to 'reject social realism' (Warner, 1959, p. 354). Sophia has ruptured all bourgeois conventions – 'when I looked at the things I had stolen, it re-established me' – to gain identity (Townsend Warner, 1936, p. 229).

There can be, Townsend Warner knew, no romantic telos to a lesbian drama. Yet if Minna has to die melodramatically on the barricades the sheer length and lyricism of her relationship with Sophia supplants the heterosexual economy of patriarchy. Sophia's dream of a new age matches Warner's belief in a possible society free from the conventional boundaries of gender, class and race. Both None turn back and Summer will show make daring, insouciant breaks with the narrative conventions of 1930s left-wing writing as Jameson and Townsend Warner evade the social scripts of 'reasonable' feminism. Yet, scarcely ten years after, some women's writing, (for example the novels of Elizabeth Bowen) was promoting a retreat to the supposed humane values of rural life.[12] While it is true that no single text in the 1940s provides us with the thoroughgoing feminism of Robins, Woolf or Townsend Warner, Rose Macaulay's (1881-1958) The world my wilderness (1950) does forcibly attack the institutions of the family, patriarchy and the bourgeois city. And her earlier social satires Crewe train (1926) and They were defeated (1932) make critical responses to conventional femininity, for example by adopting gender-free names for the adolescent girls Julian and Denham. The world my wilderness is an unmitigating description of the squalor of post-war Britain. Macaulay directly associates the bombed wasteland of London with the 'wasteland' of the patriarchal family epitomised by the young heroine Barbary's name and by her illegitimacy.

Set in 1946, the novel describes the enforced journey of Rose Barbary from her divorced mother's French home to her father's London mansion and to his Scottish vacation retreat. The powerful theme is the contrast between the sensual, semiotic and anarchic world of Barbary's mother Helen and the brutality of her rich aristocratic father, Sir Gulliver, who is dedicated to blood sports and, by implication, 'bloody' wars. Illegitimate Barbary is, metaphorically, outside 'civilized' patriarchy. Macaulay dramatises the 'illegitimate' but necessary struggle of young girls with social authority with Barbary's flight from her father and return to the illicit 'Maquis' morality of her mother.

The novel glows with the sensual warmth of the maternal French Collioure and its 'slumberous sweet garden air' (Macaulay, 1950, p. 10). Helen is a forerunner of the sexually liberated woman of the 1960s: 'She took sex casually in her stride ... with a masculine freedom and sensuousness' (Macaulay, 1950, p. 36). The eroticism of Helen's 'butterfly' kisses as she tucks up her children each night echoes throughout the book. It is the butterfly, but more beautiful, world of maternal anarchy which empowers Barbary to flit across countries and classes to become a genuine female flâneur. In a period when, as Elizabeth Wilson describes, conservative definitions of women's roles took over the progressive ground, it is part of Macaulay's project to create a female subject, Barbary, capable of appropriating knowledge. Barbary is an autonomous voice whose survival tactics among the bombed craters of the city create an agenda of independent womanhood. The world my wilderness shares with its moment that complex act of post-war reconciliation between classes but, and significantly, Barbary's 'reconciliation' is only with her 'spiv' and outsider friends Mavis and Jock and to the mother/daughter dyad. Sir Gulliver knows that Barbary's autonomous 'animal' ethics are 'something rather new ... come on since the war I think' (Macaulay, 1950, p. 134).

Macaulay plays with a humanist notion of universality by ironising an omniscient narrator: 'They sat, though they did not know it, and nor had Messrs Johnson and Brown, and nor did anyone in that year of 1946, in the garden of a great house' (Macaulay, 1950, p. 71). Here, as in her other interpolations, Macaulay deliberately transgresses the boundary of humanism and its secure confidence in its subjects, by using the omniscient narrator ironically to historicise the subject woman (Barbary). Macaulay specifically breaks too, with the bounds of popular religion in the 1940s, through an explicit discounting of two widely read religious texts. In *Passion and society* the Jesuit D. de Rougemont had called for a 'reconciliation' between erotic passion and bourgeois marriage and Father M. C. D'Arcy used de Rougemont's argument as the basis of *The mind and the heart of love* (1945) to claim that only in a Christian marriage did the 'feminine' principle become 'human'. Macaulay's key character, the Jesuit Abbé, is a parodic version of the pro-family argument: 'To sin in our Father's house, that, though sacrilege, has its own blessedness. To stray in the wilderness outside, that is to be lost indeed' (Macaulay, 1950, p. 144).

In other ways, *The world my wilderness* is a feminist bridge between Woolf's attack on psychotherapy in *Mrs Dalloway* and Doris Lessing's repudiation of the behavioural psychiatry of the 1960s. The definition of 'femininity' as a state of nervous instability and the conditioning of women to accept this, is an important part of the patriarchal project. Both Sir Gulliver and Sir Angus, 'the expert on nervous diseases', attempt to secure Barbary inside a language of militarised medicine: 'All he could do for them was to steady them to a point where among other women and girls, they would pass muster' (Macaulay, 1950, p. 96).

If *The world my wilderness* at its best represents resistance, there is a way in which subsequent feminist writing does make one major and transgressive dissent from post-war conservatism. Margaret Drabble and Nell Dunn in the 1960s and Fay Weldon in the 1970s all focus on a phenomenon particularly resonant for women: motherhood. All three writers explicitly locate motherhood 'outside' the bounds of conventional marriage. This relocation of motherhood severs the link between fecundity and subordination. Drabble (1939-), Dunn (1936-) and Weldon (1932-), in their different ways, all argue that women's experience of reproduction is deformed by the institution of marriage but not by motherhood. *The millstone* (1965), *Poor cow* (1967) and *Female friends* (1975) are parallel texts about the relationship of women to children, to class and to other women. All three novels are explicitly about the problems and processes involved in the act of narration and the narrators are themselves 'writers' with a close relationship to each author. All three novels employ various kinds of metafiction or intertextual devices within realistic narratives, for example Drabble refers to nineteenth century women and Dunn uses women's magazines. Drabble, Dunn and Weldon use such devices to problematise the 'feminine' predicaments of their women characters which centre on romantic love and childbirth. Each novel examines in depth the positive and negative facets of mothering for women who are exclusively rearing young children. Each novel pinpoints, with startling accuracy, the key motifs of much contemporary feminist theory. Such questions concerning motherhood have necessarily been crucial to feminist debates about women's liberation. For example in the first major text of British second wave feminism, 'Women: The Longest Revolution' (1966), Juliet Mitchell focused on the family and its four interlocked functions: production, reproduction, sexuality and socialisation.

Drabble continually wrestles with the representation of mothering. To the waterfall renders the physical experiences of giving birth and their interaction with Jane's sense of identity, with such graphic detail that the novel breaks the limits of realism. Heralding radical feminism the graduate researcher Rosamond in Drabble's earlier text, The millstone, chooses to be impregnated but not to marry. A single parent, she names her baby Octavia after the nineteenth century feminist Octavia Hill. Rosamond finds that pregnancy carries her across class barriers into women's shared experience of National Health Service misogyny. Her new immersion in domestic life is a mixture of the personal and the emblematic. In Drabble's work decisive moments of self-understanding are usually expressed in incidents with small children. Drabble illustrates Rosamond's conflict between her intellectual aspiration and her need for maternity with the episode of Octavia's illness for which Rosamond is unprepared by education but can empirically resolve. The conflict has implications for the boundaries of sentence (in Drabble's love of past passive and circumlocution), and structure (a mixture of meticulous social detail and intertextual literary reference). Drabble's women gain a self awareness by battling against the restrictive barriers which limit what women can claim from life. Yet radically, it is motherhood which offers Rosamond a means to evade the stalemate of a heterosexual ending, as she switches 'off' her lover George, a BBC Third programme announcer.

The social reality of single motherhood was, of course, very different. In 1966 the British Social Security Act deprived single mothers of child benefit simply on suspicion of cohabitation. Yet the sociologists Michael Young and Peter Willmott in Family and kinship in east London (1957) and the cultural critic Richard Hoggart in Uses of literacy (1958) had sentimentalised a mythical family culture headed by the working class 'mum'. By making her single mother Joy survive social victimisation Nell Dunn, like Margaret Drabble, could question the misrepresentations in Young and Willmott's and in Hoggart's mistaken histories of working class life. Joy's explicit sexual vocabulary calls attention to the evasions and silences of that masculine sociological terrain. Joy, together with her women friends and relatives, animatedly describes how the Pill makes tits larger and how potash aborts. Neither does Dunn neglect the violence of heterosexuality. Descriptions of wife battering in Poor cow lead directly to feminist theories about sexual molestation in the 1970s and 1980s. In her introduction to Poor cow, on its re-issue in 1988, Margaret Drabble praises Dunn's ability to write across the class barrier. The compensatory mechanism at work in Poor cow, just as in The millstone, is the semiotic. Joy's son Jonny shares her bed 'his wet mouth against my neck' (Dunn, 1967, p. 17). The recognition of reciprocity is represented as a lucid sensuality: 'She buried her head in his stomach till he doubled up in an ecstasy of giggles' (Dunn, 1967, p. 69). The eroticism of motherhood is acutely observed. Dunn makes an equally vivid and plausible break with the boundary of romance: '"I'm so raped up in YOUR love, I never wont to be unraped"' (Dunn, 1967, p. 50). Dunn delegitimates the genre of romance with Joy's misspellings and a mixed narrative made up of Joy's letters to her male lover in prison and her thoughts together with dramatised dialogues.

At first Fay Weldon's Female friends seems to share Drabble and Dunn's rebuttal of the social script of motherhood, 'always having to cope with left-over food, left-over children and left-over washing' (Weldon, 1975, p. 53). But Female friends, together with Little sisters (1978) and Puffball (1980), reveals Weldon's ambivalence about mothering. The male characters Patrick and Oliver have a comic status in Female friends where men function at a displaced distance in The millstone or Poor cow. Yet if the mothers Marjorie, Chloe and Grace appear somewhat as semiological 'types', Weldon creates ambivalence through parody and defamiliarization. Edwin is ludicrously patriarchal in his control of the household economy and the household vegetable patch. Similarly, the returning soldier Dick has none of Chris Baldry's intelligence or Septimus's intuition but suffices as an absurd moment in Marjorie's life. The new divorce legislation of 1969 and the ensuing high rates of divorce are the social background to Weldon's glaring portrayal of the economic inequalities upon which marriage is based, just as Germaine Greer's The female eunuch (1970) and Hannah Gavron's The captive wife (1966) plotted the ideological deployments being carried out in the name of heterosexuality. What Weldon illustrates so well are the contradictions in, and conflict over, discourses of sexuality and she goes on to systematically explode the genre of romance. Weldon's narrative voice, with its mannered and intrusive commentary, wonders bitterly about the sex-class 'women'.

'Well morality is for the rich, and always was. We women, we beggars, we scrubbers and dusters, we do the best we can for us and ours. We are divided amongst ourselves. We have to be for survival's sake' (Weldon, 1975, p. 194). The domestic events which Weldon frequently describes are those of incest, the physical and mental humiliation of wives and single women by men and women's despairing inability to be totally free of marriage. Weldon makes a skilful use of diegesis condensing metatexts of letters and dramatic playlets to give her women control over narration if they cannot yet control their finances. Weldon's highly stylised satire refuses the scripts of conventional femininity. Chloe, Grace and Marjorie share a comic urbanity set against the crippling solipsism of patriarchy, and much of the narration of Down among the women crosses between pairs of women speakers shedding syntactically the designations of heterosexuality. Even if an agenda of transformed motherhood could not be negotiated socially, The millstone, Poor cow and Female friends are a vivid backdrop to feminist theatre's more radical exploration of women's sexuality.

The 1970s was an unusually propitious decade for adapting theatre to feminist needs. A growth in British higher education combined with the abolition of theatre censorship changed the audiences for, and therefore the sexual material of, British theatre. When autonomy becomes an issue for women, women's social struggles and boundary breaks become the content of drama. Doubts about the boundaries of what is 'masculine' and what is 'feminine' inevitably entail issues of appearance.[13] Feminism had its greatest visible impact in the theatre, flooding alternative theatre with the material of sexual politics and transforming the representation of women on the stage. If actresses are emblems of what each era wants its women to be, actresses also 'can remain outside the space defined as "male"' (Blair, 1981, p. 208). For example Caryl Churchill's Vinegar Tom (1976) shows how rebellious, or unmarried, women of all social classes were targets for religious and sexual exploitation. The equation of witchery with social nonconformity is a familiar one in many plays, for example Arthur Miller's The crucible. Yet Vinegar Tom's celebration of the spirituality of witchcraft and hysteria rather than a depiction of its melodrama opposes theatrical convention with the language of the marginalised.

A critical response to theatre structure always involves a critical response to the boundaries of theatre language. The language of feminism differs from other kinds of political rhetoric. It overtly questions the social misrepresentation of 'women' and hence continually questions the gender designations of culture. Female subject matter, much of it taboo, could now be represented, for example in Louise Page's play about breast cancer, Tissue (1982). Feminist theatre explored lesbian life choices (Care and control (1977) and named women among the humanity of history (Light shining in Buckinghamshire). Pam Gems (1925-), urgently specifies women for feminism, either transposing a 'victim' like Edith Piaf to heroic myth or showing how an already mythologised woman, Queen Christina, shared the social reality of other women's oppressions. Queen Christina (1977) is an ambitious play based on feminist themes. Prepared for the throne as a man, Christina joins Orlando and earlier feminist characters testing and crossing the boundary of gender. In Dusa, Fish, Stas and Vi (1977), Gems intersects feminism and left-wing politics. Fish's lover, a Marxist, deserts her for a stereotypical feminine woman which causes Fish to realise that male politics are always patriarchal. Caryl Churchill's (1940-) Objections to sex and violence (1975) similarly focuses on the relationship between political values and women's psychological victimisation. In Traps (1977) Churchill extends her feminist critique to the question of a feminist language. The character Del stays her victimhood by imaginatively manipulating the domestic imagery of ironing and by recourse to her diary.

Light shining in Buckinghamshire (1976) is a more ambitious deconstruction of history. Set in the seventeenth century the play privileges the views of itinerants and outcasts and contests the sermons and the politics of the powerful. Ordinary people are barred from publicly expressing their needs, 'so we can't write now. We can't speak', which epitomises the public power brought to bear on women. The self denial which women characters impose on themselves, 'but women can't preach. We bear children in pain, that's why', is a dramatic statement of the link between language, gender and power (Churchill, 1978a, p. 11). The 'gaze' of patriarchy is momentarily subverted when two peasant women steal mirrors and find that 'they must know what they look like all the time. And now we do' (Churchill, 1978a, p. 11). *Cloud nine* (1979) links colonial patriarchy with the colonisation of women. Beginning his life in Victorian Africa, Clive leads a family of three generations in which the values of patriarchy and imperialism create the repressions of family life. By having women play men and men women, Churchill parodies gender constructions. In *Serious money* (1987) the hegemony of patriarchy is even more obtrusive. A financial cartel, supported by foreign money, controls England and is completed and absorbed by its self-invented violent language of the 'Big Bang'. The differing styles of the play which include free verse, nursery rhymes and monologues suggest that bourgeois definitions of economic 'reality' are as consciously illusory as the lack of stage reality.

Autobiography for other second wave feminists like Carolyn Steedman, Elizabeth Wilson and Sheila Rowbotham, was able to challenge the boundary between private and public realities. The writing of autobiography plays a particularly important part in the development of feminist thinking in Britain in the 1980s. Jean McCrindle and Sheila Rowbotham collected the hidden histories of working class women in *Dutiful daughters* (1979). The novelists Angela Carter, Doris Lessing, Michèle Roberts and poets Elaine Feinstein and others contributed to *Fathers* (1983), a collage of memoir and polemic. In *Truth, dare and promise* (1985) Alison Fell, the poet Denise Riley and other feminist women describe their memories of the 1960s and 1970s. Elizabeth Wilson's *Mirror writing* (1982) and Carolyn Steedman's *Landscape for a good woman* (1986) are extraordinarily rich accounts of lesbian and of working class lives. These writers use ideas and motifs from feminist theory in a remarkably challenging manner. If feminism is understood to be the theory of women's point of view then a writer's self-reflexivity, or autobiography, might be an important means of boundary crossing. In *Feminism and psychoanalysis*, Jane Gallop argues that nostalgia bears specifically on femininity.[14] Women's memories in the multiple and contradictory autobiographies of these feminists deliberately oppose the Freudian notion of a coherent unified femininity. These autobiographies show how the production of new selves combined with the deconstruction of given and stereotypical identities should be part of feminist writing. These writers often experiment with identity and consciousness multiplying narratives rather than adopting a solitary 'I'.

In *Landscape for a good woman*, Carolyn Steedman (1947-) combines psychoanalytic theory and feminism to enable socially marginal women to break through the literary frame. She explicitly positions her alternative portrait of a 'good woman' – her mother – against the gender stereotypes drawn by the male sociologists Richard Hoggart and Jeremy Seabrook. Steedman challenges the conventions of sociology, in particular its attribution of psychological simplicity to working class women. Where Vera Brittain could only envisage a 'good' mother by 'intellectualizing' motherhood, Steedman understands how, for her mother, maternity was a justifiable means of bargaining with the constraints of society and of marriage: 'Never have children dear, they ruin your life' (Steedman, 1986, p. 17). And Steedman situates her own illegitimacy in its period, a time when the rise in illegitimacy added to the 400 per cent increase in the divorce rate between 1900 and 1980 caused a substantial increase in single parent households, usually headed by mothers. Steedman deliberately syn-thesises, in a non-linear sequence, the extra literary writing of the Victorian historian Henry Mayhew, Freud's case studies, and the American object relations psychoanalyst Nancy Chodorow in order to test the boundary between disciplines, literature and autobiography while attending to the book's own composition. *Landscape for a good woman* together with *Dutiful daughters* and *Fathers* make the historically specific female experience of being non-hegemonic, (or what Steedman calls 'living on the borderland') choreograph writing form as much as provide the book's sexual politics by erasing the ontological boundary between woman author and woman reader.

In the two decades that saw the sexual revolution of the 1960s and the growth of the women's movement, Doris Lessing (1919-) made similar swerves from realism in her *Children of violence* (1964-1969), *The golden notebook* (1962), *Memoirs of a survivor* (1975) and the *Canopus in Argos* (1979-) series. Here too sexual politics, intellectual estrangement and the uncertainties of motherhood are active settings. *The golden notebook*, fabricated as it is from descriptions of women's everyday lives, attracted a large constituency of women readers. The period itself is both content in the novel, in the sense that Lessing includes a great deal of authentic contemporary detail, and structure, particularly in the way that the books of *The golden notebook* are about different ways of writing family history.

Lessing resigned from the Communist Party after the invasion of Hungary in 1956 and was a member of the anti-nuclear movement with John Berger, John Osborne and others. Her politics are bound up with her own specific position as an ex-colonial émigré from Africa and her subsequent concern for the politics of the marginalised. In *Children of violence* it is the Jewish Cohens, standing as they do on the borders of South African racism, who make the most radical political analysis in the novel. As an exile Lessing self consciously registers the ambiguities of British culture. She says in the preface to *The golden notebook* 'the essence of the book, the organisation of it, everything in it says, implicitly and explicitly, that we must not divide things off, must not compartmentalize' (Lessing, 1962, x). Similarly Martha in *The four-gated city* (1969) is an outsider to the class conventions of British culture and tests out alternative kinds of cultural identity in her different symbolic and naturalistic narratives. Martha's vision cannot be contained within the limits of realist fiction just as the character herself tries to escape her rigidly enclosed environment. Again, in *Briefing for a descent into hell*, the sea which is Watkin's schizophrenic obsession, symbolises cyclical body rhythms which subvert the rigid chronologies pitted against him by his doctors. Anna Wulf in *The golden notebook*, like Martha, sometimes accepts the conventional explanations of Marxism or Jungianism but both women baulk at the limitations of these theories and move beyond them. Anna's continual discussions with herself about her writing critique social conventions, and the way language constructs the female in fixed subjectivities. Anna sets out to record every moment and every feeling during an entire day – 17 September 1954 – and Lessing's phenomenological detail represents a challenge to existing literary conventions.

Women are Lessing's emotional centre of gravity. They are at the centre of Lessing's fiction more than any British writer since Virginia Woolf. It was racial apartheid in South Africa which first provided Lessing with a model of oppression and its impact on women. In her first novel *The grass is singing* she illustrates the boundary of white colonialism and the ensuing black male aggression and anti-women violence. The early novels of *Children of violence* disavow the typical constraints on women's lives – motherhood, the family and suburban domesticity. By making the central character of *The golden notebook* a woman writer, Lessing poses the questions of the personal and the public very directly, for example by juxtaposing on the same page Anna's political decision to leave the Communist Party with the private biological rhythm of her menstruation. The constant feature of women's identity, in the later *Canopus in Argos* series, is instability. Al·Ith even crosses species boundaries in her empathy with horses. As Lorna Sage has pointed out, the term 'representative woman' has a more sophisticated and ideological meaning for Lessing than simply 'woman' as representing a particular political belief (see Sage, 1983).

This critique of fixed gender roles is matched by an open form. Lessing's novels never have one simple and overarching structure. The golden notebook propels us into multiplicity as the four notebooks demonstrate the inability of particular political or historical representations to adequately categorise women. The Black Notebook is Anna's African biography; the Red Notebook is her experiences in, and disengagement from, the British Communist Party; the Blue Notebook is a psychoanalytic exploration of Anna's fragmented daily life and the Yellow Notebook is Anna's self-reflexive account of her creativity projected onto a fictional Ella. The golden notebook draws an analogy between a fragmented female identity and incoherent stories. The book is never continuous or complete but always in process.

In keeping with this multiple structure there is no telos of 'normal' femininity. Women characters alternate between being sociocultural models and more fluid protagonists. On the one hand Anna harshly characterises Richard's wife Marion as 'stupid and ordinary', Molly is too vulnerably emotional, older women sadomasochistically enjoy the bullying of younger men and finally, and famously, a vaginal orgasm is 'the only one real female orgasm' (Lessing, 1962, p. 186). But there is a contradictory response to gender proprieties. Ella and Julia mother each other, and, in Anna's fantasies about her mother, Lessing clearly endorses a maternal object relations which is represented in Anna's tender care for her daughter Janet sharing 'the feeling of continuity, of gay intimacy' (Lessing, 1962, p. 310). Anna celebrates dissolution; 'that's how women see things. Everything is a sort of continuous creative stream' (Lessing, 1962, p. 229). She denounces the bounded 'purpose in life' of the Communist Party because it cannot answer 'lonely women going mad quietly by themselves, in spite of husband and children, or rather because of them' (Lessing, 1962, p. 146). Anna's 'understanding' which she gains from the physical sensations of food and sickness, exists outside the parameters of conventional language, just as the juxtaposition of popular fiction and autobiography in the novel represents the boundary between memory/experience and writing/text.

Because the reading process of The golden notebook is linear yet loops backwards and forwards in intensive fictionality, it provokes a woman reader to produce, together with the text, a female identity out of these diverse fictions. Lessing claims that The golden notebook 'was not a trumpet for Women's Liberation', yet also that 'all sorts of ideas and experiences I didn't recognise as mine emerged when writing' (Lessing, 1962, viii-ix). But just as the feminism of Olive Schreiner clearly marks Martha Quest (1964), Lessing's subsequent writing – the Canopus in Argos series – reflects second wave feminism as she subverts gender stereotypes by choosing non gender specific characters and switching character identities regardless of their gender.

Science fiction is the ontological genre par excellence for feminism because it liberates narrative from the restrictions of realism and liberates women characters into new forms of perception and communication. Women characters can explore change by moving across the border of 'given' realities to an imagined elsewhere. In the late 1960s, critics like Herbert Marcuse were exposing the abstract objectivity and machine mentality of science and prepared the way for Lessing's fictional essays. The central theme of Lessing's Canopus in Argos is the dissolution of private and public, the central theme of contemporary feminism. Shikasta's Zone 3 shares childcare equally between the sexes and between biological and non-biological parents. It is a society without exploitation or hierarchy. Zone 5 is a matriarchy which depends on the powers of sensual intuition. They are clumsy novels in some ways. Feminism is somewhat subsumed into the universality of apocalypse. Yet the books have strong, autonomous women and Lessing has an articulate vision of a communal world, rooted at once in the dialectic of sameness and difference.

One of the most distinctive terms of contemporary feminism is 'feminist consciousness'. Lessing is insistent that women's thought processes are different from those of men. Consciousness has to do with the nature and place of women's power and the 'mad', according to Lessing, have available a double consciousness: current communication and future information. The grand poetics of women's estrangement is madness. Madness is a way of getting in touch with powers beyond women's 'normal' comprehension. It is not only fiction that crosses the boundary between 'madness' and 'sanity'; the hysteric in Cixous's theoretical texts also challenges the cultural boundary of normality.[15] By accepting the authenticity of her 'mad' as well as of her 'normal' selves Anna is able to complete the golden notebook. Following Woolf, Lessing assumes that the real madness of society lies in women's experiences of marriage – like George and his wife with 'the compassion of one victim for another' (Lessing, 1962, p. 97).

One of the most vivid inventions of radical feminism is a new language. Lessing's 'new' language with its mixture of autobiography, sermons and multivocal characterisation is a major part of her attack on the border of gender representation. Molly explains, "'If we lead what is known as free lives, that is, lives like men, why shouldn't we use the same language?" "Because we aren't the same, that is the point"' (Lessing, 1962, p. 413).

By the 1980s, it was clear that the British Equal Pay and Sex Discrimination Acts of the 1970s were being mitigated by a resurgence of moral conservatism combined with a government policy of public spending cuts. Yet it is also significant that, by the mid 1980s, as Anna Coote and Beatrix Campbell suggest, a new feminist culture – in writing, in the arts and in theory – was involving women in Britain on an unprecedented scale (see Coote and Campbell, 1987). Women writers participation in, yet marginality from, mainstream culture – what Margaret Homans in another context calls '(ambiguously) non-hegemonic' – was generating new kinds of subject matter.[16] Angela Carter's (1940-) career in particular offers a fascinating example of this process. The subject matter of her earliest writing *The magic toyshop* (1967), *Heroes and villains* (1969) and *The passion of new Eve* (1977) – sexual politics and the myths of patriarchy – connect it to feminism. Carter rescues definitions of femininity from Freud's limiting version of the same Hoffman tale and broaches the incest taboo by depicting Margaret's loving sexual relationship with her brother Francis. Yet, from the vantage point of the 1990s, we see that this choice of subject matter involved Carter in a major re-evaluation of psychoanalytic and literary theory enabling her to construct the magnificent bird woman Fevvers in *Nights at the circus* (1984).

Of course Carter would not claim that feminist fiction has in some way 'solved' the problem of women's representation. Indeed the prevailing tone of her fiction in the 1960s and 1970s is best summed up as an ironic pessimism. *The passion of new Eve* parodies matriarchy and *The Sadeian woman* (1979) wryly claims that 'the missionary position has another great asset ... it implies a system of relations between the partners that equates the woman to the passive receptivity of the soil' (Carter, 1979a, p. 8). *Heroes and villains* is a post-nuclear holocaust novel whose heroine Marianne rules 'with a rod of iron' in sublimated masculinity. The Eve of *The passion of new Eve* is a male forced into a sex-change operation by an underground matriarchy.

This problematising of matriarchal values is common to other feminist dystopias of the period, for example Zoë Fairbairns's *Benefits* (1979). Fairbairns's matriarchy is a community of illegal squatters whose values are only marginal in the political world outside which is busily relegating women to the status of breeders. The development of the narrative in *Benefits* depends not, as conventionally on plot, but on forms of feminist argument. The Feminist Writers Group which included Michèle Roberts, Michelene Wandor and Valerie Miner, together with Fairbairns were radically testing the relationship between feminism and the texture of writing. That newer feminist thinking is represented in *Benefits* by the younger generation of feminist women who are the only possible survivors. Carter's fairy tales *The bloody chamber* (1979) share Fairbairns's prophetic hope of new identities. The relation of sexuality to power is a central question in feminist theory. Fairy tales are specifically about power and the possession of women and so can problematise gender identities. Feminist fantasy can explore the contradictions between women's growing awareness of their sexuality and the harsh constructs which society creates to control women. In *The company of wolves* and *Bluebeards castle* Carter transforms the sexual politics of the fairy tale and the Gothic to disarm aggressive masculinity. The girl uses her sexuality as a weapon to control the wolf and Carter transformed Perrault's passive victims into positive women. The mother of Bluebeard's bride stays faithful to her daughter and their mother/daughter dyad replaces her oppressive marriage. Carter's feminist ideas about social and psychological violence to women force her into a wholly new conception of narrative. She makes use of non-naturalistic, eclectic materials (fairytales, Freud and Jung, mythology) to encapsulate and illuminate in literary shape the kind of de-colonisation she hopes women might be attempting in real life. Throughout the 1970s and 1980s, Carter's narratives investigate progressively new ideas of the contours of literature as she celebrated a carnival of diffuse female experiences.

The past ten years have been characterised by an increasing awareness of ethnic and sexual diversity among women and by the tension between the languages of non-hegemonic groups and the spectrum of concepts from 'family' to 'sisterhood' which might represent them.[17] *Nights at the circus* is fed by this diversity and celebrates the two-woman couple with a Bildungsroman about the sensual counter culture of Fevvers and Lizzie. The novel reveals a complex interaction between fiction and the ideas that have gradually developed alongside its writing in the 1980s. The six foot two heroine Fevvers is a birdwoman aerialist who performs in London, St Petersburg and Siberia. The novel incorporates a number of feminist themes. The most notable is Fevver's account of the feminist theory of the gaze – that representations presuppose a male spectator and an objectified woman (see Mulvey, 1975 and chapter four). Fevvers 'served my apprenticeship in being looked at – at being the object of the eye of the beholder' (Carter, 1984, p. 23). Carter chooses a 'women's time' for Fevvers great moment: 'For, as my titties swelled before, so these feathered appendages of mine swelled behind' (Carter, 1984, p. 24). Aware of the 'terror of the irreparable difference' being a bird woman will be, Fevvers 'births' herself and learns to fly from her brothel. The poetics of estrangement from 'the natural' resonates in Carter's continuous parody of traditional philosophy:

the penis represented by itself, aspires upwards, represented by the wings, but is dragged downwards, represented by the twining stem, by the female part represented by the rose. H'm. This is some kind of heretical possibly Manichean version of neo-platonic Rosicrucianism, thinks I to myself; tread carefully, girlie. (Carter, 1984, p. 77)

Indeed the whole novel works to contest the 'natural' with its group of Ape-men professors who mimic women's subordination with 'the mutilated patience one finds amongst inmates of closed institutions' (Carter, 1984, p. 119). Nights at the circus adopts an assertive feminist argument in Mignon's horrific account of domestic violence and Lizzie's sophisticated understanding that Fevvers is a 'symbolic exchange in the market place'. The novel continually speculates about fictionality. Fevvers makes an insouciant break with the conventions of Edwardian language by inserting contemporary critical theory into her speeches: 'The choice was, you might say, the sign or signifier'. Similarly Lizzie likes The marriage of Figaro 'for the class analysis' (Carter, 1984 p. 129 and p. 53).

Carter's desire to break the borders of women's cultural representation postulates a mixed mode of exaggerated adjectives and assertive epigrams set into a chronologically 'confused' narrative. Nights at the circus demonstrates Carter's faith in the exuberant possibilities of women's stories which can break the boundary of realism. The novel adeptly mixes narrative voices and cross-cultural experiences in a baroque challenge to conventional depictions of femininity. In addition Carter 'thinks back' to other women authors. She engages with the maternal figure of contemporary feminism – Virginia Woolf

– making Fevvers share Orlando's dream 'of the coming century' (Carter, 1984, p. 86). If Lizzie and Fevvers somewhat resemble Little Dorrit and Maggie the emotional intensity of their friendship, ('Are they mother and daughter? wonders Walser') cuts the knot of both heterosexuality and literary convention as Lizzie and Fevvers compile their collaborative autobiography. As Hélène Cixous argues in 'Conversations' changes in the sexual order will necessitate corresponding changes in poetic language.[18] Nights at the circus ends not with a whimper but with 'the spiralling tornado of Fevvers' laughter' (Carter, 1984, p. 295).

Together with Carter, Asian and Black women's poetry and fiction represents British feminism's most intense literary rescription. By writing in tandem about racism and sexism Asian and Black writers protest about the experiences of Black women in Britain in the 1980s and also project a vision of womanhood for the 1990s and beyond. By mixing non-Western images and languages from the Caribbean to India, Asian and Black feminism is a major work of Black mythopoesis. Both Debjani Chatterjee's 'I was that woman' and Grace Nichols's 'i is a long memoried woman' face the contradiction that non-Western culture is remote by distance and by time from them both and from white British readers. The poems are characterised by specific and recurrent motifs. Most obvious is Chatterjee's attention to the multiple women 'victims' of history: 'The first rebel, I was the mother of Cain ... I was that beautiful horror with snake-hair' (Cobham and Collins, 1987, p. 27)

For the Asian and Black feminist to find her own space, hear her own voice she must re-enter Asian and Black history and myth. As Grace Nichols points out:

I have crossed an ocean
I have lost my tongue
from the root of the old
one
A new one has sprung. (Ngcobo, 1987, p. 104)

If Nichols and Chatterjee prefer the broad historical sweep, Sindamani Bridglal's 'She lives between back home and home' is a more specific picture of migration and the juxtaposition of cultures. Mothers are made 'frantic' by dislocation and it is daughters who 'give mothers / A sense of themselves' (Cobham and Collins, 1987, p. 88).

Geographic mobility prevents women's lives from being swept into the flow of white patriarchal history. Yet the sum of the two moments, past and present does not produce a satisfying totality.[19] It is therefore consistent that these poems focus on the constants in women's lives which are mothers and daughters and sisterhood. For example, in 'A house' Sandra Agard suggests that 'history' is the story of her childhood home. There are many social and economic factors that argue in support of Asian and Black writers' attempts to relocate and redefine womanhood. Asian and Black women in Britain are rooted historically in three different continents but suffer a similar and double burden of occupational segregation or single parenthood. Inevitably, as Amos and Parmar point out in 'Challenging imperial feminism', the specificity of Asian and Black women's struggles will lead to a new kind of feminism since this self definition challenges both patriarchal culture and white imperialism (see Amos and Parmar, 1984). For example Nigerian-born Buchi Emecheta condemns the sexual politics of African culture in The joys of motherhood (1979) as well as in Second class citizen (1977) attacking the racism affecting migrant women in Britain.

One result of this variety in Asian and Black writing in the 1980s and 1990s is a greater attention to alternative life styles. Nowhere is this more apparent than in the treatment of sexuality. For example Barbara Burford's The threshing floor (1986) highlights the bourgeois and racist commodification of sexuality in her depiction of the homosexual, lesbian and heterosexual mores of an English country town. A final theme that informs writing by Asian and Black women across races is the motif of the journey which represents both a psychological as well as geographic mobility. Autobiographical fiction and poetry constitute a running commentary on the collective migrations of women to Britain. Joan Riley's The unbelonging (1985) depicts Hyacinth's journey to Britain and her subsequent victimisation. The novel underscores the difference between patriarchal social conditions and a more stubborn self consciousness by contrasting Hyacinth's warm memories of the blissful relations between women back home with her social and psychological 'rape' at the hands of her father and British institutions.

All feminist writing puts into question orthodox assumptions about the relationship between the text and the reader. Asian and Black women confront the issue of audience in an especially acute form. Grace Nichols (1950-) explodes parochialism with vivid, sensuality:

My black triangle
Sandwiched between the geography of my thighs
is a bermuda ... . (Cobham and Collins, 1987, p. 29)

'My Black triangle' forces white readers to acknowledge the fact of Black sexuality and secures that sexuality, metaphorically, into a place safe from contemporary racism. At one level, Nichols writes to awaken her reader's sensitivity, to shake up and disrupt the numbing that accompanies racial and psychological alienation. At another level, and as a consequence of this, Nichols addresses the gap between the dominant model of white womanhood and an Asian or Black woman.

In contrast writers like Maud Sulter, Valerie Bloom, Brenda Agard and Marsha Prescod draw their vocabulary primarily from Black English and Caribbean dialect. Taken together Prescod's 'Womanist blues' and Agard's 'Business partners' establish some important characteristics of Black feminist writing. A conspicuous strength in Caribbean culture is the verbal power of Caribbean women, the ability to move their audience with humour and a shared storehouse of puns and dialect:

Ah gwine mek she kno' mi a big ooman,
A no yesterday mi bawn
Lawd ha' massey, dem a come back,
Onoo gi mi pass, mi gawn!' (Ngcobo, 1987, p .89)

Bloom's Black British dialect is a technical and rhythmic innovation. It is a self conscious attempt to subvert the traditional language of poetry and insist on a merciless difference. These poets refuse embellishment or camouflage. They are linear poets who write free and open verse which works directly from example to example to make designs upon the world. Much of this writing focuses on the struggles between Black men and Black women: 'I say it's my body / It says it will be bad tempered for the rest of the day' (Cobham and Collins, 1987, p. 69), as well as on the divisions between Black and white men and women and between self and culture. Poems such as 'Touch mi; tell mi!' prove that Black dialect is the bedrock of Black feminism in a dazzling play with domestic slang. Asian and Black feminist poetry is invested with a structure of reality which might change the course of British literary history.

This passion illustrates one danger in the attempt to establish border crossing as a fresh feminist vision or paradigm. By claiming that 'this' is what best defines feminist strategies, we may be tempted to read selectively, omitting all the 'taboo' characteristics (of sentimentality or inferior style) which might exist as much within feminist writing as in any other writing. But Asian and Black writing represents real psychological, political and geographic crossings set into material realities. It is 'border traffic', not simply in the obvious sense of physical movement from one country to another, but also in the sense of generational crossings as younger Black and Asian British women cross cultural and economic barriers into new professions and new languages. But, as in other twentieth century feminist writing, this crossing is also an emotional term, an ideological term since location is always a place of mind as well as of geography.

As feminist literature has developed in this century, it has changed and it has changed British literature through a constant attention to mothering and to the intergeneric work. This writing gives women more mobile identities than does mainstream literature. Feminist literature, like feminist theory, exposes sexist stereotypes and celebrates woman-to-woman relationships and the mother/child dyad. The strategies of feminist writing that I have been labelling 'border crossings' are not, perhaps, as 'different' as their authors or my argument suggest. But whether we use a model of *écriture féminine* or one of translation, the point is that 'border crossing' can be the basis of a fresh poetics of feminist writing. It is a discursive and politicised lens through which to view essentialism. A poetics of border crossing would account for a women's writing that recognises the essential differences that we think we know, as well as the instabilities and variety that might be possible. One of the lessons of finding border crossing is to know that women's writing is often double voiced, that such writing will never comfortably inhabit a masterly syntactics. Feminist literature is a dynamic response to the urgent threat of patriarchal closure and the abandonment of metanarratives. Most of its concerns constitute a reversal of realist and solipsistic practices. Like the cuckoo, feminist writers lay texts of a similar hue and size but which hatch into a very different politics. They also involve a rejection of genre boundaries and of the entire misrepresentation of women in British literature at least in modern times. This challenge to the limitations of 'women' has repercussions for the stability and fixity of social and political definitions. Contemporary feminism currently focuses on the fact that we speak only through other languages, especially if we speak the language of literature, and that this is not the same as speaking the language of citizenship. My focus has been on fiction because fiction highlights the obvious incongruity of borders in an inevitable way, with its intermingling of personal history, daily experience and family time. Whether this chapter has outlined a single technique, or a whole strategy, it has tried to recognise both politics and aesthetics, working on the assumption that feminist politics is the politics of representation. Feminist literature in the twentieth century is an exciting measure of borders crossed, languages changed and images broken.

The mother country: Jean Rhys, race, gender and history

Anthropology names the first border crossing the rite of passage. This is the moment when boys become men in a journey across the border of the wilderness, or girls become women crossing the threshold into a menses hut. Border crossing signifies the detachment of an individual from one set of fixed gender categories in any given social structure and a celebrated movement into another (see Turner, 1969). Yet to be a coloured woman, a Creole, or a mulatto is to be a visual signifier of *permanent* border. Neither white self nor Black other, the Creole can only be manumitted across the boundary of colonial difference.[1]

The *Wide sargasso sea* is Jean Rhys's most complex novel of border crossing in relation to colour. It is not her only writing to chart that passage. Indeed the most consistent note in all her work is exactly the explicitly thematised interrogation of racial categories. *Voyage in the dark, Good morning midnight* and her letters and autobiography *Smile please*, all explore the moves women characters make to rewrite the colonial script, and navigate their way through the consolidated limits of imperialism. In 1907, at sixteen years of age, Jean Rhys left her own colonial 'home' for Britain, the mother country. Yet 'home' and 'mother' are ambivalent, paradoxical terms for a writer of the colonial race and class whose allegiance is to the 'mothering' experience of Caribbean culture. The Creole Antoinette and the Black Christophine struggle together in the *Wide sargasso sea*, through complex discursive negotiations, to cross the border between them. It is Jean Rhys's particular relation to 'desire' and 'difference' that dinomic of the colonial world which gives marginalised women a hearing.

At the centre of this chapter are Rhys's women of different races. These women cross the boundaries of racial stereotypes by mirroring each other and in their friendships. But how do we read this condition of border crossing as Rhys describes it, and how do we identify Rhys's distinctive version of border crossing in her fiction? These are questions which I will try to answer by interweaving, as Rhys does herself, different moments of her personal history and its historical place(s).

What Rhys constructs in her fiction, particularly in the *Wide sargasso sea* is, I would argue, a feminist anti-colonialism becoming aware of its own history. Rhys interrelates history and gender, and images anti-colonialism as her particular version of boundary crossing. Rhys's texts all have heroines struggling with ethnic and gender identity without a stable geographic or national place. The *Wide sargasso sea* lies between Rochester's England and Antoinette Cosway's island, between the opposite categories of colonisers and colonised, and between the world of capitalism and the post-Emancipation West Indies. Of course other Caribbean writers also refuse an island confine, but they often resolve the division of white subject from Black objects by placing the Caribbean into a myth of lost origins; or, like V. S. Naipaul, use a Europeanised character to patrol traditional culture with a baleful eye.[2] Gender as well as race is at issue here. In some North American literature, for example in William Faulkner's *Absalom, absalom!* the West Indian woman is the repressed subject. For example it is Eulalia Bon's sexual as well as racial characteristics which make her the feared and different dark Other. In Faulkner's novels all Caribbean Blacks, even at their best, are passive victims of sexual, economic or imperial events.

The *Wide sargasso sea* rigorously refuses this reductionism. Rhys's novel subverts the conventions of colonial romance by denying the white patriarch, Rochester, his geography. It subverts colonial history by refusing linear time. It crosses the boundary of racial difference with the mirroring of Black, Creole and white women and the choice of a Black Other as Mother. It replaces the colonial gaze with a Black semiotic vernacular.

For all their possibilities, the *Wide sargasso sea* and Rhys's earlier writing cannot create an easy ingress into fiction for minority women. There are absences inseparable from any act of emergence, an appropriate unsaid, since Rhys writes often about absence. In a letter to Frances Wyndham, Rhys interweaves her sense of absence with race and sexual politics: 'As far as I know I am white – but I have no country really now ... *Meek!!!* When I long to slaughter for a week or more. All over the place...' (Rhys, 1985, p. 172). Re-articulated by Antoinette in the *Wide sargasso sea*, the letter, now monologue, dramatises the ambivalence of racial place:

It was a song about a white cockroach. That's me. That's what they call all of us who were here before their own people in Africa sold them to the slave trades. And I've heard English women call us white niggers. So between you I often wonder who I am and where is my country and where do I belong and why was I ever born at all. (Rhys, 1966, p. 102)

As Elizabeth Nunez-Harrell points out, the Caribbean street name for the Trinidadian woman is 'whitey cockroach', a term signifying a lack, both of colour and of humanity (Nunez-Harrell, 1985). Antoinette, like her author Jean Rhys, is unable to assert a fixed and definable racial identity. The full meaning of such an identity comes from the long historical chain of colour coding used by imperialism to void miscenegation and to negate the possibility of Black and white women's intimacy. Hence all Rhys's novels are fictions about female creativity. They are about females mercilessly experiencing the racist, financial and gendered constraints imposed by an imperialist ethic, and feverishly searching for meanings to pose against monotonous masculinity. Not to enjoy the exhilarance of knowing is precisely the kind of ambivalence which is the mark of border women.

What importance does the border have as a meaningful category in Rhys's writing and in the shaping of her style? If, by nothing else, minority writers are linked by an imperative to violate, initiated by the prior violation of minority culture by the coloniser. The historical referent of the border is in Rhys's accurate evocation of gender. The alternative negotiation of borders by male and by female characters symbolise gender difference. For example, exile signifies great physical hardship for Rhys's women. In Rhys's historical reconstruction of the Caribbean and in her construction of England and Paris in the 1920s and 1930s, women like Anna in *Voyage in the dark*, cannot enjoy the detached objectivity of a masculine flâneur. Rhys's novels are boundary texts, full of signals about epistemological and ideological rupture, which group women in newly conceived differences. Rhys makes a fresh figurability of history to avoid the constraints of racial stereotype, juxtaposing her own autobiographical history with fictive moments to scan a larger horizon of literary meaning.

The question to ask of Rhys is: How does the subjective need to cross discursive boundaries, become a new literary resource? What is the relation between social and literary conventions on the one hand and racial awareness, gender and literary innovation on the other?

'When I went into it (the Roseau Cathedral) I thought it beautiful. Instead of the black people sitting in a different part of the church, they were all mixed up with the white and this pleased me very much' (Rhys, 1981, p. 79). Yet, in the *Wide sargasso sea*, Rhys's own mixture of black and white – her attempt to write across racial boundaries – is often not 'beautiful'. The tension produces a text which awkwardly rides along the edge of many styles, sometimes sliding into a clichéd vocabulary where coffee is always 'brimming' and butter is always 'melting'; and righting itself into the veracity of Christophine's doubts about England: '"I don't say I don't *believe*, I say I don't *know*, I know what I see with my eyes and I never see it"' (Rhys, 1966, p. 111).

In a discussion of the problems involved in dialogic fiction, Bakhtin says, in passing, that to understand another person or character at any given moment 'is to come to terms with meaning on the boundary between one's own and another's language: to translate' (Bakhtin, 1984, p. xxxvii). I want to express Bakhtin's concept applied to Rhys, as the crossing of two major boundaries.[3] First I want to analyse Rhys's writing by actively contesting academic boundaries, by leafing through the disciplinary catalogues of literary criticism, psychoanalysis, cultural theory and history. Finally, I want to move Rhys herself across the boundary of history, juxtaposing her childhood with the sexual politics of colonial history, and with the racial/sexual politics of the British health care Rhys experienced in the 1960s. The three histories of the *Wide sargasso sea* are its historical setting, the history of its author and the historical moment of its composition.

This chapter has a writer Jean Rhys at its centre and it is about her crossing of writing boundaries and the stories she tells us in order to cross. This chapter, then, is about meanings, about the ways in which we rework what we read to give fiction meanings. It is about the kinds of stories we can tell about fiction and the contradictions between those stories. The regenerative motor of Rhys's fiction is colour. Jean Rhys writes about white, Black and Creole women and, in a quite particular way, escapes the limits of colonised colour. She escapes, I will argue, through creating a reciprocal world of mothers and daughters of different races.

In *Smile please*, her autobiography written between 1976 and 1978, Jean Rhys describes a struggle she witnessed in the school convent between the articulation of the maternal and patriarchal law:

'Who made you?' It asked, and my chief memory of the catechism was a 'No, dear, that's not the answer. Now think – who made you?'
'My mother,' the stolid girl replied. At last the nun, exasperated, banished her from the class. (Rhys, 1981, p. 78)

An ambiguous passage in which the sense of the ferocity of the symbolic law and its consequent denial of the empirical experience of mothers and daughters is unmistakeable but displaced onto another child. In the novels *Voyage in the dark* and especially in the *Wide sargasso sea*, Rhys labours over how women can name their mothers. In Rhys's aristocracy of sensuality, there is a lyrical and careful observance of the maternal. as the crucial source of a female identity. Nancy Chodorow, in *The reproduction of mothering*, argues that women's identities develop through an identification with their mothers, real or imagined, that is interdependent and empathic. Rhys chose a particular mother figure – the Black woman nurse – to suggest a continuum of sensual warmth, that was at least a possibility for women sharing the nurturing pre-oedipal moment. Of course we must be cautious not to endow women only with affiliative qualities as if gender identity is not also, and equally, shaped by changing constructions of history and culture. Yet in Rhys's novels this affiliative moment is always a uniquely female ecstasy outside the understanding of men and their colonial prerogatives.

The lost mother is Rhys's organising motif. I want to read Rhys, to look at Rhys's recognition of race, gender and history in relation to the maternal, or, to use the good fairy of feminist theory – the semiotic. In telling Rhys's stories my sketches of Rhys's fiction, autobiography and history cannot in themselves constitute a closed, finished account of a writer. Neither can the point of the chapter lie only in the books Rhys wrote in the 1930s and 1960s. There is also the point that Black mothers occupy a very marginal space in white criticism. The only point for all of us lies in interpretation, in critical methods. It matters, then, for us to know that a feminist criticism of borders is likely to better understand the Black mother/nurse figure through the agencies of history, literary criticism, cultural theory or psychoanalysis by itself examining the borders and limits of those disciplines, own meaning making. Of course the stories that critics write in order to explain the writers they read are not the same stories. The interpretative devices of history or cultural theory are often in deep and ambiguous conflict. This chapter is placed on the border of these conflicts taking as its starting point that no single disciplinary method, of history or of literary criticism can deal with a 'difficult woman'.

Although Jean Rhys claimed to resent the nomenclature 'a woman writer' (she changed from her given name Ella Rees Williams to 'Jean Rhys' by mixing the names of her first husband [Jean] and father Rees/ Rhys, her first male protectors), she addresses one of the central questions that feminist criticism seeks to answer: What is the connection between women as material objects of their own histories and the representation of women in narrative? It is literary criticism which appears best equipped first to handle Jean Rhys's writing. Certainly from Quartet to the Wide sargasso sea, Rhys uses many different literary devices and her work is dense with allusions to contemporary, and to past, English and French literature. In addition, literary critics are now in general agreement that meanings do not lie directly in texts but in the interpretative strategies we agree to share to produce texts. Since the 1960s, with the advent of deconstructive and feminist criticism, literary studies have become aware of the issues involved in using metalanguages to colonise figural domains.[4] In the system of classifications that literary criticism relies on, imagery figures (sic) very large. Rhys's texts are littered with a residue of literary effects designed to emphasise a literary thematics of romance. Rhys's images are consistently those of journeys and consequently of borders.

Rhys began her descriptions of marginal women and their repression tentatively in her first novel Quartet (1928) where Marya Zelli tests the bounds of femininity in the bourgeois Paris of the 1920s. Rhys doubled her literary currency in After leaving Mr Mackenzie (1931) with the character Julia Martin, a similarly placed but older version of Marya. In Voyage in the dark (1935) Anna's geographical journey from the Caribbean to England is replicated by her psychic return to the 'mother' world of her childhood. In Good morning midnight (1939) Sasha's rite of passage through the abnegation of Parisian poverty is into her unconscious, her only world sans frontières. In Rhys's final and marvellous novel Wide sargasso sea, she completes her examination of women's marginality by laying claim to the 'real' story of Bertha Rochester in Jane Eyre, named as Antoinette Cosway, but equally abused by the patriarchal boundaries of mid-Victorian empire.

The Wide sargasso sea works with, and through, images and languages of border to undermine them radically and to substitute real unities between women of different races for the smoothness of border differentiation. In the Wide sargasso sea Jean Rhys makes Black Christophine the one character who might free Creole Antoinette from the stereotypes of white settler discourse by encouraging her with songs and patois expressions:

'Not horse piss like the English madams drink', she said. 'I know them. Drink their yellow horse piss, talk, talk their lying talk.' Her dress trailed and rustled as she walked to the door. There she turned. 'I send the girl to clear up the mess you make with the frangipane, it bring cockroach in the house. Take

care not to slip on the flowers, young master.' She slid through the door.
'Her coffee is delicious but her language is horrible ... '. (Rhys, 1966, p. 85)

This speech constitutes a direct and explicit representation of a Black
woman's facility with the languages of race and sexuality. In defining
and contrasting the cultural signifiers of 'coffee' and 'horse piss',
Christophine's speech is governed by the intersection of two languages. Christophine's intercession here has an obvious effect: by
switching between the syntactics of dialect, 'talk their lying talk' and
the orthography of standard address, 'Take care not to slip ... young
master', she installs difference in the discourse of the text. Christophine
constantly interweaves 'standard' and non-standard English, drawing
profoundly on a wide range of styles. The verbal dexterity of this
passage does not bespeak merely Christophine's personal skill and
authority but suggests as well that Rhys actively supports Christophine's
understanding, by allowing unparaphrased 'speechifying', that words
embody rather than merely represent the racial characteristics they
stand for. Rochester's stabilising displacement of Christophine's
dangerous 'code-switching' as 'horrible' reveals not only that he
occupies another language but that he occupies a different way of
understanding the practice and meanings of languages in the colonial
context. Christophine's speeches are always governed by the doubling
of 'vernacular' and 'standard' English. That she constantly draws
attention to the opposition of these codes rather than simply either
appropriating received English or adhering to patois, is a clear example
of Rhys's faith in the Black woman/mother as bearer of linguistic
variety and as maker of a more complex dynamic of appropriation.
Christophine's continuous bifurcation between the rhythms of the
vernacular voice and the limited colonial language is an explicitly
thematised example of Black verbal power.

Christophine's facility in English, French and patois, the trope of the
translator, represents boundary crossing. Rhys was herself a translator
before she became a writer. The activity of translation in her novels
has great social consequence as well as creative potential. Powerful
women are those who can speak across linguistic boundaries. So in the
Wide sargasso sea, Aunt Cora saves the family from the fire at Coulibri
because she can 'translate' the needs of the family into local dialect.
And it is Annette who incurs colonial incomprehension with her ability
to distinguish between 'nigger', 'negro' and 'black'. The violence of
the coloniser is both linguistic and sexual. Possessing Antoinette,

Rochester appropriates her 'I' by renaming Antoinette – Bertha as he textually appropriates the 'I' for his own monologue by taking over the narration of the long middle section of the novel. At the end of the *Wide sargasso sea*, Antoinette triumphantly recovers her 'I' by displacing Rochester's monologue although, of course, she is unable to fight the pre-existing prison of Charlotte Brontë's Thornfield. Where, in her short story 'Pioneers, oh pioneers', Rhys's coloured woman Mrs Ramage acts merely as a mediating plot device in order to motivate a confrontation between the white colonialists and Black Others, by the time of the *Wide sargasso sea*, Rhys allows Antoinette's 'authorship' to be empowered as a 'palimpsest' by Christophine's Black language of Hoodoo which helps Antoinette regain her voice. It is significant here that in the two sections of the *Wide sargasso sea* which comprise Antoinette's own narrative she speaks, not of her marriage, but first of her childhood and then of her incarceration in Thornfield – those periods when her identity is consolidated by her Creole mother and by her Black and white servants.

Let us consider the opening of the *Wide sargasso sea*:

'They say when trouble comes close ranks, and so the white people did. But we were not in their ranks. The Jamaican ladies had never approved of my mother, "because she pretty like pretty self"' Christophine said. She was my father's second wife, far too young for him they thought, and, worse still, a Martinique girl. When I asked her why so few people came to see us, she told me that the road from Spanish town to Coulibri Estate where we lived was very bad and that the road repairing was now a thing of the past. (My father, visitors, horses, feeling safe in bed all belonged to the past.) (Rhys, 1966, p. 17)

The most significant feature of this opening is the immediate positioning of Black/Creole speech as direct, authentic language dramatised in its own space (Antoinette merges her mother into Christophine with the indefinite pronoun). In addition, Rhys suggests the mirroring of Black/Creole, mother and daughter through the indeterminate use of 'she' and the association of Annette/Antoinette as 'pretty selves' by Christophine. Rhys signals both the possibility of a self-expressive Black woman and the simultaneous domination of all women caught in a colonial nexus of decaying plantations and a history which places women's past, of 'feeling safe', in parenthesis. One of the remarkable features of Rhys's style is the way in which she deploys conventional rhetorical figures very powerfully. Note, for example, the hidden metaphor 'a thing of the past' (road/childhood) reinforced by the use of repetition; and the choice of the ironic 'ladies' to signal class/race boundaries. The connotative effect of the passage overwhelms any trite denotative function.

The tools of literary criticism and its insistence that the subject is a discursive construct can take this issue into account. Certainly Rhys's books Quartet and the Wide sargasso sea are rich in imagery. Rhys is fond of evocative adjectives and adverbs ('soft rain')and heavily connoted verbs, and an iconography of colour. Anna, Annette and Antoinette are all emotional romantics and Rhys chooses coded images to describe them. For example Antoinette resembles Coco the green parrot. Turning herself into a commodified object, Annette sells her wedding ring to buy the white muslin for herself and Antoinette that will enable her to buy a second marriage to Mr Mason. Antoinette's most prophetic dream is of her future husband 'holding up the skirt of my dress. It is white and beautiful and I don't wish it to get soiled. I follow him sick with fear ... but it trails in the dirt, my beautiful dress' (Rhys, 1966, p. 60). Yet it is not easy to use, as Rhys does here, the signifiers of romance, for example 'white' or 'birds'. Such writing allows its cognitive functions to be invaded by associations. The narrative of romance, its fantasies of sensuality and female thraldom is visible in a limited iconography of colour, of 'black' and 'white' morality. Romance is both a potent and regressive account of femininity (see Modleski, 1984). Romance is both part of a politics of consumerism aimed at women and also read by women as if it represents their social aspirations (see Radway, 1985).[5]

Imperialism has always portrayed its own(ed) women as romantic emblems of white purity against the Black Other, for example in Tissot's paintings of Edwardian women luxuriating in white dresses.[6] Rhys is, on the other hand, insistent on the relation of white women to Black. A significant example is the scene of Antoinette's nurture from nightmare by Sister Marie Augustine the coloured nun who 'had large brown eyes, very soft and dressed in white, not with a starched apron, like the others had' (Rhys, 1966, p. 52).

The convent, like Coulibri, is a crucial environment in the Wide sargasso sea. In both places, the absence of racial and class antagonisms perform their enchantment in stark contrast to the masculine world outside. Both places seem to be idealised female worlds. Yet Rhys takes other paths of response away from atomised masculinity. We need to listen carefully for other frames of reference watching Antoinette entering the Wide sargasso sea recording the daily lives of those around her. A neighbour, Mr Luttrell, kills himself because he cannot 'live at Nelson's Rest? Not for love or money' (Rhys, 1966, p. 17). That casual saying is freighted with import. In the first page of the novel, Mr Luttrell, another white Creole, has chosen suicide as his response to the economic exigencies of the Emancipation Act. Annette, on the other hand, chooses to connect 'love' and 'money' in a nexus of bourgeois patriarchy, sexual politics and racial exploitation in order to survive. She 'sells' herself to Mr Mason as his fantasy of a West Indies girl 'a pretty woman ... light as cotton blossom' (Rhys, 1966, p. 29). Through the institution of marriage, white patriarchy appropriates the full bounty of nature – her plantation estate together with its flower. The opening establishes the racial/sexual constraints of Antoinette's life. Acting as a mirror of her mother, Antoinette will replicate not only her mother's name but also her mother's history by selling herself to the next patriarch – Mr Rochester. She and Annette are as similar in their appearance as they are in their histories sharing a particular way of frowning and a 'sitting posture'. Christophine italicises the sexual politics of colonialisation: 'Money have pretty face for everybody, but for that man money pretty like pretty self' (Rhys, 1966, p. 113). Antoinette's double/triple consciousness placed between Black and white cultures heightens her awareness of difference.

In literary criticism feminist critics have been working during the last decade to rescue Rhys from obscurity and restore her, not to a traditional canon, but to a parallel tradition of women's writing?[7] Judith Kegan Gardiner judges Rhys's honesty to came from her unabashed attention to heroines alienated from others and themselves because they are female, poor and sexually active; 'They are also misdefined by a language and literary heritage that belong primarily to propertied men' (Gardiner, 1982, p. 233). Yet Gardiner's detailing of sexual exploitation is a mere oxymoron of marginality. It accepts the binary oppositions: men/women, surface/absence. This stress on victimisation *per se* cannot adequately orchestrate that more complicated relation Rhys describes between the language of colonial culture and Black, white and coloured women's mimicry and desire.

It is a problem both of language and of politics. Writing about Derrida, Jonathan Dollimore reminds us that binary opposites are 'a violent hierarchy where one of the two terms forcefully governs the other. A crucial stage in their deconstruction involves an overturning' (Dollimore, 1986, p. 190). Rhys's overturning of opposite colours, in her fictional figures, cannot be celebrated tightly inside the boundary of traditional literary criticism but requires another story – the story of cultural theory. How is the Other constructed in cultural theory? How does cultural theory tell its story? Cultural theory works through processes of signification which establish race in specific ways. Repression has a meaning in cultural theory which uses linguistic instruments of authority like 'primitivism'.

The Third World women in Rhys's writing are no primitives – no monolithic constructs. The mimicry of Annette/Antoinette. Antoinette/Amélie and Antoinette/Christophine refuse the codified categories where Black and white women are opposite portraits drawn by white culture. *They* are never *She*. Amélie's song of the 'white cockroach' metaphorically emphasises the shared outsider position experienced by both the Black servant and the Creole woman. Colour plays an important part in a character's self identification of what I have called border crossing. Anna, in *Voyage in the dark*, is a fifth generation Creole who figures Creolisation as part of her sexual and cultural response to Europe. If it is the active ideology of imperialism which provides that discursive field placing the Creole on the boundary of acceptable society, Anna collapses binary oppositions. In control of the text as its narrator, she is a free woman *and* a prostitute having a personal morality which is both black and white. Rhys's use of a Creole figure has two functions. It enables Rhys to explore the relation of gender and race while, at the same time, it can *express* that relation, rather than falling into the trap of what Homi Bhabha has called a 'fetishistic identification' with black culture (See Bhabha, 1983). Homi Bhabha in his account of excess in 'The other question', has explained the ways in which the coloniser encloses the colonised in legal, psychoanalytic and historical fictions. Bhabha criticises existing cultural theories of colonialism, in particular those of Franz Fanon and Edward Said. Fanon's *Black skins white masks* and Said's *Orientalism*, Bhabha finds to be ultimately unsatisfactory because both writers believe that colonial discourse is only intent on creating a unified object – the racist stereotype of the 'lying Arab' or 'bestial African'. A colonial discourse which can only rule and conquer by such endless repetition is a discourse of *excess*. Bhabha argues, in turn, that excess reveals both a dualistic fear of, but *desire for*, the native. It is, paradoxically, the power of such stereotypes which allows disjunction (from the perspective of the colonised). Bhabha's statement of the problem is elegant.

From the direction of feminist psychoanalysis comes a similar argument. The same concern to deconstruct the stereotypes in

patriarchal discourse occurs in The enigma of woman. Here the psychoanalyst Sarah Kofman works to establish the 'truth' of Freud's
stereotypes of femininity. She asks: 'Why did he seem panic-stricken?'
(Kofman, 1985, p. 65). It is the excess in Freud's exaggerated account
of femininity, Kofman claims, which reveals his fear of women:
'Woman in general becomes unapproachable, a forbidden Mother'
(Kofman, 1985, p. 83). If the instability of women needs to be so
frequently stereotyped it might also, Kofman makes clear, be a source
of disruption. Both Bhabha and Kofman successfully link racist or sexist
activity with racist or sexist language. I have put both accounts in
tandem because both critically evaluate culture in terms of its adequacy
in expressing the experience of women and of the colonised. In
addition, since Freud's account falls on nature – on women's
irresponsible desires – his version of 'excess', I would argue, matches
the coloniser's appropriation of the native into 'bestiality'.

Feminist criticism can learn from similar formulations about race
and gender within the discipline of psychoanalysis. While it may be
objected that this is making a literary matter out of a psychoanalytic
affair, the concept of 'excess' is a way forward to understanding how
racial and sexual stereotypes are shifting states produced as much
through language as through biology.

Rhys signals a rupture with conventional stereotypes because she
demonstrates their excess. Only by expressing, and hence engaging
with, the power of colonialist language can a writer begin to produce,
as Rhys does, it seems to me, an adequate ideological critique. If we
listen to Mr Mason and Mr Rochester, informed by both Bhabha and
Kofman, we can hear how their language is both misogynist and racist.
Bhabha and Kofman agree that colonial or patriarchal ideologies
contain Blacks or women by codification. Rhys allows the 'excess' of
the coloniser to be heard. After Annette marries Mr Mason:

we ate English food now, beef and mutton, pies and puddings. I was glad to
be like an English girl but I missed the taste of Christophine's cooking. My
stepfather talked about a plan to import labourers – coolies we called them
– from the East Indies … 'the people here won't work … they are children
– they wouldn't hurt a fly.' 'Unhappily children do hurt flies', said Aunt Cora.
(Rhys, 1966, p. 35)

To impose English customs and language is a normalising act whose work
is to codify difference, to fix the Other, Christophine, outside the
boundary of the civilised. Mr Mason's strategic aim is to create a subject
space for natives through the production of knowledges about them.

The overriding romance of colonial fictions, cultural theory tells us, is one of geography. One of the great narratives of colonial literature concerns a male protagonist coming into rightful possession of his territory and 'seeding' it, twice over, marrying the white heroine and entering into a mutually redemptive relationship with indigenous natives (see Chevigny and La Guardia, 1986).[8] Rhys's courageous stand against that narrative of imperialism is abundantly clear in her letters. Writing to Selma Vaz Dias she says that her writing will be 'more an escape from time and place as we know them – or think we do', and she quotes St Teresa of Avila's moving address to the Conquistadores: 'I will find that country which is ever new and ever young. *Come with me and you will see*' (Rhys, 1985, p. 144).

Rhys continually depicts a continuum between geography and sexuality. Paris is a vivid character in her European novels and short stories because the city evokes and reflects the sexual politics of the men and the women who live there. An insistent theme in colonial writing is its tendency to abstract relationships as mappable geographic space. The map is the colonial signifier of a dominated race, its economy, and topography. It is also a trope for that other colonial geography – the body of woman. Rochester identifies his estates with his wife. At Coulibri Antoinette and the house are intimate in their iconography of fertility. The family garden is a convincing image of the power and the danger of the semiotic balanced as it is between dead flowers and flourishing orchids (Rhys, 1966, p. 16). It is the maternal space of Antoinette's childhood with its markers of nature – flowers, intense smells, and the rhythms of birds and animals. – 'Wild untouched, above all untouched with. And it kept its secret'. Rochester knows that 'what I see is nothing – I want what it *hides* – that is not nothing' (Rhys, 1966, p. 87).

Thrown out of the 'symbolic' civilised world of England, Rochester faces the wild zone of femininity. Rhys deliberately juxtaposes Rochester's fear of the environment with his fear of Antoinette's sexuality. After Antoinette is forced to bite him, Rochester finds 'everything around me was hostile. The telescope drew away and said don't touch me. The trees were threatening.' (Rhys, 1966, p. 149.) Rhys's childhood and fiction are in dynamic interaction here. Her father placed a telescope on the verandah of their home above Massacre in order to overlook the geography. We shall come in a moment to Rhys's depiction of telescopes as signifiers of the paternal eye and its limited gaze. Without his telescope, Rochester fears entanglement in nature and in his narrative he constructs an apartheid between his speech and Antoinette and Christophine's language of songs and body movement. Rochester finds safety in mappable boundaries. He possesses Antoinette's Granboise, like her body, by mentally mapping its rooms, steps and limits. Rochester refuses its romance and imposes his knowledge of boundary: 'The barrier of the cliffs and the high mountains. And the barrier of the sea. I am safe' (Rhys, 1966, p. 27). It is the possibility of blurred boundaries on the honeymoon island which causes Rochester's terror and demonstrates the limitations of a monocular patriarchal gaze. It is Rochester, not Antoinette, who is speechless, whose mind has blanks 'that cannot be filled up' (Rhys, 1966, p. 64).

Questions about the representation of identity, difference and race are interestingly at issue. Collapsed into colonial writing are two myths about Black identity. The first is that all natives are childlike and the second myth is that all natives are lazy. An awareness of these forms of racism informed Rhys's story 'Overture and beginners please':

Winks, smiles. Is it 'honey don't try so hard' or 'honey don't cry so hard?' 'How should I know?' 'Well, it's a coon song, you ought to know'. But when I discovered that although they never believed the truth, they swallowed the most fantastic lies, I amused myself a good deal. (Rhys, 1987, p. 69)

What Rhys reveals in her account of racism in an English public school in the story is the boundary of its language. Such racism works, can have effectivity, only in constant excess, either through paternal metaphors of the child or the extremity of 'coon'. Yet, although the game of linguistic fantasy is a complex form of pleasure/unpleasure for a Creole girl, it does secure her a brief psychic space.

The fetishism of the Other, cultural theory argues, is at its most transparent when the coloniser substitutes natural or generic categories (of emotion, or deviancy) for those that are socially determined. Mr Mason fears Annette is 'always at one extreme or the other. Didn't you fly at me like a little wild cat when I said nigger. Not nigger, not even negro, Black people I must say' (Rhys, 1966, p. 171). Similarly, Rochester's equation of Black/women's emotions with insanity is profoundly in debt to a nineteenth century cultural framework in which notions of gender influenced definitions of madness. As Elaine Showalter points out in The female malady, it was in the nineteenth century that 'the dialectic of reason and unreason took on specifically sexual meanings' (Showalter, 1987, p. 8).[9] The Manichean bifurcation of black = emotion, white = sanity are the extremes of the colonial script. Deconstructive cultural theory takes the biography and the book to be each others 'Scene of writing'. In her letters Jean Rhys experiences no bifurcation but rather connects her motive for writing – the figuration of 'the vanished West Indies of my childhood' with her own body 'this is the first time I've felt half alive' (Rhys, 1985, p. 133).

Interviewed for the *Paris review* Rhys said 'I was a bit wary of the black people I've tried to write about I gradually became even a bit envious. They were so strong … They had lovely dresses … They had swarms of children and no marriages. I did envy them that' (Vreeland, 1979, p. 230). In the crude taxonomy of values that Rhys describes – strength, spectacle and sexual freedom – it is possible to hear the voice of a white woman's desire. Nor is the *Wide sargasso sea* homogeneously subversive of colonial thought. It embodies some recognisable colonial tropes, namely that of the Caribbean as the infallibly good and free place. With the Black Tia, Antoinette is free to boil 'green bananas in an old iron pot and eat them with our fingers out of an old calabash' (Rhys, 1966, p. 23). But rapidly Rhys historicises colonial experience and works to examine how that experience contains women in particular. Antoinette gradually loses her land, her dowry, her freedom and finally her sanity to Rochester. Rhys gives to the nurse Christophine, the most radical insight into this racial and sexual economy: 'These new ones have letter of the law. Same thing. They got magistrate. They got fine. They got jail house and chain gang. They got tread machine to mash up people's feet. New ones worse than old ones' (Rhys, 1966, p. 26).

Both Mason and Rochester fear the 'promiscuity' of the native body and take Annette and Antoinette away from their 'coloured' relatives. To Mason and to Rochester the sexuality of Annette and Antoinette is a sign of racial miscenegation. Both Mason and Rochester simultaneously fear, and ambivalently desire, the taint of race. In the colonial psyche the black/white female cathetus is expressed in the sexual bifurcation white goddess/black she-devil ('Magdalene'/'nigger'). Rochester's search for the 'true' history of Antoinette is an attempt to transfer white responsibility for miscenegation on to Black 'history':

One afternoon the sight of a dress which she'd left lying on the bedroom floor made me breathless and savage with desire. When I was exhausted I turned away from her and slept, still without a word or caress … if she was a child she was not a stupid child but an obstinate one … her mind was already made up. Some romantic novel, a stray remark never forgotten. (Rhys, 1966, p. 93)

The association of the Otherness of a coloured woman with a feared lack of sexual control has a long term history in Victorian literature written by men, for example in Pierre by Herman Melville and Blithedale romance by Nathanial Hawthorne.

Rochester tries to contain female sexuality by denying Antoinette access to speech and hence to recognition in the symbolic. Since the Other might transform the rational patriarch into a 'breathless savage' she must be entirely knowable as a child. Among Rochester's progeny in Rhys's exploration of atomised masculinity is Mr Mackenzie in After leaving Mr Mackenzie who treats women as sexual objects existing outside his self-protective moral code. Mackenzie's world of Blacks, Creole or coloured women is chaotic, uncontrollable and can only be fixed in the Manichean allegory of intelligence/random thoughts, father/child, subject/object. Similarly, in the Wide sargasso sea, Rochester's gratification is impaired by an alienation from his own unconscious desires. So that Rochester's narrative remains pertinately nameless. He is identified only as 'a younger son' while women's names are eternally in play. Women name each other easily and constantly without compromise. The historical crystallisation of Rochester's identity is in doubt. Daniel Cosway, the bastard son of Antoinette's father, is a hideous parody of Rochester's lack of a close father.

Rochester, in his section of the novel, constantly tries to 'name' his position, and the past. Rochester's imagined and actual letter to his father, and his reduction of Antoinette to a 'child's scribble' are then desperate attempts to reinscribe the father as telos. Yet the power of patriarchy is swamped by the categories it needs to tell its tale, so that Rochester desperately swarms in the subjectivity of his pronouns, first objectifying Antoinette as 'she' and then moving to an intersubjective 'you' in order to maintain his power of designation. So that it is clear that simply to amass the many 'languages' of the Wide sargasso sea cannot by itself answer the question of its effect, especially its effect on a woman reader. What we seem to need to understand Rhys's complex discursive subversions, it appears, is some way of talking about her fiction which is neither the 'imagistic' practice of literary criticism nor the continual 'performativity' of cultural theory.

Rhys said that she began and could finish the Wide sargasso sea because of a dream of giving birth. Explicitly evoking the pre-oedipal bond between mother and daughter in her autobiography, Rhys progressively develops the theme in her fiction that the nature of women is determined by the maternal. Rhys makes constant recourse to what we might conveniently call the psychoanalytic. A psychoanalytic account of Rhys's writing is clearly needed. My debt to psychoanalysis is clear in the language of this chapter, for I use a vocabulary of repression, oedipal relations, and the scopic drawn from Freud's original conceptualisation of femininity and masculinity and pursued by feminist psychoanalysts ever since. Rhys too moves through tropes of displacement and a psychoanalytic symbolism that occupy strategic positions in her writing. Rhys's heroines display the Freudian characteristics of femininity – 'passivity', 'narcissism' and 'masochism' – combined with low self-esteem. Rhys's aim in deploying these models of femininity is to show how the social inscription of women is marked by these characteristics of alienation and inadequacy and, in turn, she aims to give women a more positive language and gender identity gained from knowledge of the maternal.

Certainly Antoinette's character and situation reveal the imperative for the maternal bond, for example she tries to live with Rochester in a pre-oedipal sensuality at Grandbois. Antoinette is prepared to cross psychic boundaries. She finds pleasure in becoming an Other in mirroring and reflecting Tia. Similarly in *Voyage in the dark*, it is the Black Francine who nurtures Anna through into womanhood with her clear and honest descriptions of Anna's first period. The representation of mirroring and mothering allows Rhys to rescue women from the allegorical closure of the colonial imaginary. The iterative nature of mirroring structures the narrative of the *Wide sargasso sea* so that characters and scenes can only be apprehended through *other* characters and scenes just as the novel itself mirrors *Jane Eyre*. Rhys adapted the symbol of the mirror from her source text where mirrors are also crucial to meaning, for example in the scene where Jane perceives Bertha (reflected in a mirror) as her mother. Fleeing the burning Coulibri Antoinette is hit by Tia's stone: 'I looked at her and I saw her face crumple up as she began to cry. We stared at each other, blood on my face, tears on hers. It was as if I saw myself' (Rhys, 1966, p. 45).

Yet transference is also the repetition of paternal prototype relations, of unconscious desires in the oedipal relation. If Rhys, psychoanalytically, comes to grips with the ambiguities of white women's desire for, and dependence on, the Black Other woman, desire itself has a contradictory nature. There is also the female desire for the father which is the theme of Antoinette's psychic and physical need for older men. Jane Gallop sums up the daughter's desire for her father as 'desperate' (Gallop,

1982, p. 70). In *Speculum of the other woman* Irigaray argues that the only redemption of her value as a girl would be to seduce the father.[10]

Rhys tells us in her autobiography that 'I probably romanticised my father, perhaps because I saw very little of him'. This sentence sums up a network of issues; issues of desire for father-figures, of literature, of invisible patriarchy. The signifier 'romance' is the sign of the intricate tangle of masochistic relations into which Rhys thrusts not only Antoinette and Rochester but also her other heroines and their patriarchal lovers. Rhys, like Charlotte Brontë, matches this desire to literary precedents. Both writers adapt *Paradise lost* to establish Rochester as simultaneously threatening and desirable. Masochism informs their shared obsession with apocalyptic sexual encounters. For Rhys, the struggle reaches back into adolescence. As she states in her autobiography, 'Satan existed … he could be a very handsome young man, or he could be so ugly that just to see him would drive you mad'. The Satanic paternal contributes to a masochistic regression in *Good morning midnight*, where Sasha ends the novel in a swoon of sadomasochist desire for 'his mean eyes flickering'. But in the *Wide sargasso sea*, Rhys brilliantly stays the 'omnipotent' power of the daughter's desire for seduction with the contrary fantasy of maternal nurturance. For example, Antoinette takes no simple, 'primitive' delight in Rochester's domestic violence, rather it is revealed only, and significantly, by Christophine: 'I know more than any doctor. Undress Antoinette so she can sleep cool and easy, it's then I see you very rough with her, Eh?' (Rhys, 1966, p. 151). Christophine, the Black nurse, recuperates Antoinette with the skills of transference from the anxiety of the daughter's desire. Freud's term for transference 'uberzetzung' is, in German, the word for translation, or the replacement of disturbance by the person of the therapist.

On the other hand, Rochester suffers a schizophrenic split between physical activity and mental detachment as a result of his response to race and to sexuality. He rapes Amélie, but then distances her as excess since 'her skin was darker, her lips thicker than I had thought' (Rhys, 1966, p. 115). Rochester has the same dichotomous relation to the 'body' of Grandbois which he can encounter only when numbed by alcohol. The sense that a better understanding of sexuality can occur in maternal surroundings inspires the scene where Antoinette crosses the boundary of menstruation into womanhood among the red flowers in the wilderness of Coulibri. The juxtaposition of the contradictory psychoanalytic paternal and maternal makes the *Wide sargasso sea* into, not an incoherent text, but an extraordinarily accurate representation of the contradictions of femininity. The *Wide Sargasso Sea* is able to express that yearning for a maternal bond which emerges in the Antoinette/Christophine relationship, by fashioning a story which displaces the paternal heterosexual romance plot in order to displace a 'colonised' femininity. Rhys's writing centres, emotionally and thematically, on the sensuality of women and on the bonds between them. In the fine story 'Let them call it jazz', Selina is succoured in her imprisoned marginality by a deep identification with a same sex role model. 'Liberated' from a white father and fair coloured mother, Selina imitates her grandmother because 'she's quite dark and what we call "country-cookie" but she's the best I know' (Rhys, 1987, p. 169). *After leaving Mr Mackenzie* emphasises, and prescriptively stresses, the importance of women's friendship in Julie's gorged satisfaction with her female companions.

Racial/sexual difference is often described as if it is uniform. In Rhys's writing, difference is multiform. Through her Black mothers and white fathers, Rhys sets up a psychoanalytic articulation of difference and contradiction which escapes the misrepresentations of colonialism. It may be colonial patriarchy which brings Antoinette to Thornfield and fixes her into the ideological order, or disorder, of madness. It is not Jean Rhys or her readers.

The most thorough example of the syncratic possibility of self/ Other identification informs Rhys's preference for the voice over the scopic gaze. The authority of colonial writing depends on its repeated recognition of the *visible* difference of the Black Other, for example when Rochester displaces his guilt by signifying Amélie as more visibly (and bestially) black. Jean Rhys herself experienced the specular seclusion of the colonial world during her girlhood in Dominica. In Bakhtian fashion the colonial gaze could be overturned at carnival when 'we could watch from the open window' (Rhys, 1981, p. 52).

The antagonism of the Look to the Other is the position of domination. Rhys recasts the positions of dominant and muted in songs, folk singing and stories. The iteration of the feminine in the *Wide sargasso sea* and in her other books is in its voice(s). Rhys's desire to speak difference erupts in the several Black, Creole and white voices which actively break the specularity of colonial knowledge. In her short story 'Temps perdi', Rhys describes how Caribbean women 'carried on the old language and its traditions, handing them down from mother to daughter. This language was kept a secret from their conquerors' (Rhys, 1987, p. 157). Anna Morgan in *Voyage in the dark* strongly identifies with the Caribs, the indigenous people of the West Indies and she makes equally careful distinctions between the languages of Black, Creole and white.

Yet, as Hélène Cixous and Catherine Clément argue so acutely in *The newly born woman*, each time there is a repetition of memory, a return of the repressed, it will be in a specific cultural and historical context. Fictional representations of difference must carry the impress of history. Woman's identity may be malleable but malleability itself is differently established in different times. To unpick Rhys's representations, to understand her tactics better, we need finally to read the story of history.

Now the telling of history elevates politics and the social. What I should do is to write the history of post-Emancipation politics and the social history of Jean Rhys. I should proceed by an exhaustive listing of events and their *conscious* literary representations. But Rhys is dead and, unlike David Plante in his book about Jean Rhys *Difficult women*, I do not want to make Rhys difficult. Rhys is an indirect historian but she is not an ahistorical writer. Rhys does give conscious attention to public history. She carefully delineates, with dates and exact cultural objects and vocabulary, the historical moments in which her short stories and fiction are set. For example *Good morning midnight* contains little political detail about its period but does have a great sense of the economic fears that were a part of 1930s history, and Rhys's 'The insect world' is a graphic account of blitz life during the Second World War. Like a good postmodernist, Antoinette vents her hostility against (is 'mad about') the *teleological* unfolding of family history. She translates British history into childish songs: 'A Benky foot and a Benky, for Charlie over the water' (Rhys, 1966, p. 148). Antoinette turns patriarchal history into the aberrant texts which it cannot repress.

Like Antoinette what I need to do, aberrantly then, is put an account, which is more or less a historical sociology of the 1840s (the moment of Antoinette) against an account of Black British women in the 1960s (the moment when Bertha became Antoinette). There is no question of direct influence at issue. We do not know exactly how much Caribbean history Rhys studied, but her letters reveal a great interest in, and knowledge about, the Caribbean. Nor, of course, can criticism any longer make simple one for one analogies between autobiography and fictional representations. The customary allision of literature and history is effected when critics uncritically rewrite novels as historical narratives, as if literature could *directly* represent an external social world. Yet this allision does not satisfy the question of writing movements. Part one of the *Wide sargasso sea* is set in 1834, the year after the Emancipation Act which replaced slavery with 'apprenticeships'. Yet in a strong sense the *Wide sargasso sea* is intelligible only in relation both to its own contemporary history of the 1960s and from the point of view of Rhys's personal history. We need to speculate about the *Wide Sargasso Sea* in the context of the dominant ideologies of race and sexuality of the 1830s and 1840s, and of the 1960s to understand how the text finally crosses and criss-crosses the boundary of historical representation.

Rhys felt herself to be in and out of history.

Eventually I got back to being a Creole lunatic in the 1840s. Quite an effort. Sometimes am almost there, sometimes I think I'll stay there!! ... the Creole in Charlotte Brontë's novel ... attacks all and sundry – *off stage*. For me (and for you I hope) she must be right *on stage*. She must be at least plausible with a past. (Rhys, 1985, p. 151)

The word Creole itself personifies imaginary history. It originated from the Spanish *criar* (to imagine) and *colon* (a colonist). In general terms, *Creole* can refer to European settlers or to people of mixed race living in the colonies. Very briefly, the Creole Caribbean of the 1830s and 1840s was a society of bankrupt post-Emancipation white plantationers who saw 'their' blacks in animal guise, 'their noses flat like Dutch dogs' and whose girls decline very fast from puberty 'until they grow horribly ugly. They are lascivious' (Brathwaite, 1971, p. 182).[11]

The epistemic violence of the colonial world is savagely misogynist: 'It is quite common for an attorney to keep ... thirty or forty doxys'. Women most of all must not cross the boundary of white and black but accept linguistic and sexual apartheid. Otherwise 'we may see ... a very fine young woman awkwardly dangling her arms with the air of a negroe servant ... the Creole language is not confined to the negroes. Many of the ladies ... speak a sort of broken English that is very tiresome if not disgusting' (Brathwaite, 1971, p. 301). The description leads to Hester in *Voyage in the dark* who berates Anna for sounding exactly like a nigger while they are living in Dominica: 'I tried to teach you to talk like a lady and behave like a lady and not like a nigger and of course I couldn't do it' (Rhys, 1969, p. 65). In terms of the colonial/Creole order the action by British law in emancipating the slaves from 1833 allowed Caribbean racial groups to enter society carrying with them their cultural backgrounds. Creolisation in this sense was an aspect of white control which was, necessarily, intensely specular:

Sambo: child of mulatto and negro
Mulatto: child of white man and negress
Quadroon: child of mulatto woman and white man
Mustee: child of quadroon and white man. (Brathwaite, 1971, p. 295)

The hierarchy of colour continues through 120 possible graduations. The frontier quality of Caribbean culture has often been noted in the sense of the harshness of post-emancipation economic life. It was also, and mainly, a man's world because the Deficiency Law was 'peculiarly oppressive to white females possessing small properties' or Annette at Coulibri (Brathwaite, 1971, p. 147). Adding to the economic crisis, the British government withdrew its protection of Jamaica's sugar market in 1846.

A close reading of these observer accounts of the 1840s Caribbean, when the system of apprenticeship was finally abolished, serves to remind us once again that writing is always a form of sexual politics and that sexual politics, no matter how specifically historical the context, is always constructed. Victorian travellers described the Caribbean as if it were a displaced paradigm of the dangers in, and their fears of, gender and class in Victorian England. The Caribbean highlights the subterranean shifts and fissures in the British social terrain, as Britain was settling to support the material practices of imperialism.[12] Colour, or what G. Lewis calls a 'multilayered pigmentocracy', structured Caribbean class position, and its genetic values inevitably associated the status of women with blood and family history. The novel is set at that crisis point in Caribbean history when the white Creole in particular was most at risk of loss of place. Jean Rhys hoped to seize the 1840s as an intact object of knowledge. Writing to Diana Athill in 1966 she promises that 'it (the Wide sargasso sea) wouldn't take long ... I mean all the action to take place between 1834 and 1845 say. Quick!' (Rhys, 1985, p. 297).

Fortunately the novel is not that unitary historical text. The heterogeneity of its various narratives, its various locations, its complex mirroring of characters and its open ending provide Rhys with the space in which to express, and to negate, that complex interdependence of capitalist imperialism, sexual relations and race in relation to women. Daniel Cosway explains to Rochester the relation between mixed marriages, Annette's identity and Emancipation economics: 'Then comes the glorious Emancipation Act and trouble for some of the high and mighties. Nobody would work for the young woman and her two children ... She have no money and she have no friends ... We all wait to hear the woman jump over a precipice ... But no. She marry again' (Rhys, 1966, p. 96).

In addition to its colour-coded history imperialism depends on a firm belief in evolutionary time. Traditionally anthropology arms imperialism with science by placing Western linear time in opposition to 'primitive' cyclical time. As Johannes Fabian argues, the subjectivity of the Other's time is permissible only inside the autobiography of the ethnographer who constantly qualifies the marginal culture. (See Fabian, 1983).[13] Anthropology exists in the ethnographer's time and exiles the native to the continuous present tense. Similarly, David Plante battled with Jean Rhys's sense of 'monumental' time: 'One grey day in late March we tried to organize the bits of her life chronologically ... "Come on Jean, when did you and your husband stay at ... and for how long?" She raised herself from the pillow. "All I can remember is the sea". "Try!" I said' (Plante, 1983, p. 32).

The *Wide sargasso sea* replicates a similar masculine 'excess' in the winding course of Rochester's imperialism. Rochester disparages the way in which Baptiste refuses to recognise the economic benefits that imperial history can give to ownership: '"Plenty rum", he said. "Is it really a hundred years old?" He nodded, indifferently. A hundred years, a thousand years all the same to le bon Dieu and Baptiste' (Rhys, 1966, p. 16).

Rochester's commodity chronology is disrupted by the songs of Antoinette and Christophine which call on a potent alternative of dream and memory. Rochester fears the strength of 'women's time': 'Someone was singing "Ma belle ka di", or was it the song about one day and a thousand years. But whatever they were singing or saying was dangerous. I must protect myself' (Rhys, 1966, p. 149). Similarly, in 'Let them call it jazz', it is the songs of women prisoners in Holloway prison which enable Selma to metaphorically 'jump' the gates of the jail. Antoinette, frightened that Christophine is ageing, is able to blot out demographic distance with anthropomorphic memories. 'All this was a long time ago, when I was ... sure that everything was alive, not only the river or the rain, but chairs, looking-glasses, cups, saucers, everything' (Rhys, 1966, p. 37).

Antoinette's account of history is a phenomenology of physical details. The world of everyday concrete objects has more explanatory value, for her, than the past which Rochester unravels. So, for example, Antoinette's Proustian memory of her mother's death triggered by drinking chocolate with Sister Marie Augustine is more potent and vivid than the event in itself. By the end of the novel Antoinette rejects colonial time altogether by imposing a unitary world where word equals thing: 'Nights and days and days and nights, hundreds of them slipping through my fingers. But that does not matter. Time has no meaning. But something you can touch and hold like my red dress, that has meaning' (Rhys, 1966, p. 193).

Antoinette thinks that time should represent the power of female sensuality – with looking-glass, rain and red dress. She asserts her own physical history – her memories of the island – against Rochester's historical prison. The red dress represents her real name. Red is the colour Antoinette chose when she embroidered her canvas at the Mount Calvary Convent and signed, along with her name, a place in her own time: 'Antoinette Mason, née Cosway, Mount Calvary Convent, Spanish Town, Jamaica, 1839' (Rhys, 1966, p. 44). Rhys makes Antoinette speak out the animated subjectivity of physical reality over the colonial boundary of history.

The *Wide sargasso sea* is not the only book in which Rhys plays with chronology. Rhys's other texts also confidently dialogue with the past in the light of the present. In *After leaving Mr. Mackenzie* the detail of rooms reflects women's history. The descriptions of Julia's room, her wallpaper and her bed, indicate her feelings and anxieties. They are textualised images of the existence of her past – made up of maternal memories when her mother had been the warm centre of the world. 'You loved to watch her brushing her long hair; and when you missed the caresses and the warmth you groped for them' (Rhys, 1971, p. 106). This is a phenomenology of the maternal espoused in a vocabulary of the body – of hair, gestures and warmth. Julia's mother, a Brazilian by birth, 'sickens' in England for the sun and her invalid existence cannot offer Julia the reciprocal support which Antoinette enjoys with Christophine. Anna Morgan is the history of *Voyage in the dark*. The potency of her recollections is the only real event in the novel. As in the *Wide sargasso sea*, Rhys retreats from chronology to emphasise the physical, intending to disrupt patriarchal history through the figuration of a feminine and alternative story. We watch Anna's history on a screen of double exposures. Anna continually superimposes the memory of her childhood onto her contemporary history by describing the West Indies with the immediacy of the present tense in contrast to the third person account of English experience. The introduction of Anna's memories is far more than a device to create plot contrasts. These textual tactics, of a confused chronology and disembodied dreamlike states, specifically occur with Anna's memories of her mother and of her servants. So that, as Anna drifts into prostitution and loses control over her body, her memories of the Caribbean have to darken. Past and present continually struggle against each other. The tension in Anna's mind between them shows how Rhys's women characters need to stand outside the boundary of the contemporary and how a woman's maternal history draws a truer picture of her identity than external chronology. Anna finds the meaning of experience in her reflections, specifically in her memories of Francine, the Black servant girl. Significantly, throughout the novel, Francine is portrayed as a mother. She nurses Anna by cooling Anna's head with a palm leaf in an episode which foreshadows Christophine's nurturing care in the *Wide sargasso sea*: 'It was she who explained to me, so that it seemed quite all right and I thought it was all in a day's work like eating or drinking' (Rhys, 1969, p. 68). And Francine's knowledge about women's bodies (she explains here about menstruation to Anna) and about women's language (her singsong rhythmic 'nigger-talk') represents a now lost sensuous, semiotic past. *Voyage in the dark* gives us women's history as an epistemological alternative to linear chronology. Like Monique Wittig in her fiction as well as her theory, Anna chooses childhood as a form open to history.[14] One understanding of dreams is that they are active dramas of events passively felt in childhood (see Miller, 1983). In the *Ritual process* the anthropologist Vincent Turner explains that movements in and out of time, through dawn and dusk, are characteristics too of liminality, of 'threshold people' (see Turner, 1969).[15] Rhys rewrites 'time' to challenge the effacement of threshold women as historically muted subjects.

The *Wide sargasso sea* is Rhys's own intertext of childhood and adulthood. For example, the landscape of Coulibri resembles Rhys's birthplace Dominica not the less equatorial Jamaica where the novel is ostensibly set. Rhys's family history is the plot of the *Wide sargasso sea*. In October 1837 James Lockhart, Rhys's great-grandfather died leaving his widow (significantly called Jane) to manage his plantation. In the Black riots which followed a colonial census the house was burnt down (see James, 1978).[16]

Jean Rhys describes in her letters how she was also constantly pressured by contemporary history. Trying to explain that tension to

Selma Vaz Dias she says: 'If you do talk about my short story will you remember that they were all written during the war and in London. That explains a lot. One couldn't imagine any end to that time' (Rhys, 1985, p. 66). The *Wide sargasso sea* provides points of concentration, what we might call historical symptoms of resistance, to the different configurations of race and gender that Rhys experienced. These configurations are her cognitive experience of the 1840s, and her *affective* experience of childhood and her likely encounters with Black women in the early 1960s. In the novel these configurations may, or may not, inspire a writing of resistance but, I would argue, it is the juxtaposition of these experiences which enabled Rhys to actively alter traditional representations of race.

Rhys wrote the *Wide sargasso sea* in an epistemological crisis specific to the early 1960s, a crisis occasioned by the break up of the British Empire and the need in Britain, for fresh thinking about the Black subject, specifically the Black female subject. 'Race' is a concept used to classify and its reference point is always physical appearance. In the 1960s race was spoken in a new public voice, forced into speech by the Nottingham and Notting Hill riots against Black immigrants in 1958. The Conservative Party discussed the possibility of using 'Keep Britain White' as an electoral slogan as early as 1955 (see Gilroy, 1987). The 1962 Commonwealth Immigration Act 'legalised' English racism and the 1964 Smethwick election returned a white racist MP Peter Griffiths. A fresh vocabulary of the enemy within, of white men and of the sexual contagion and disease of Blacks was named as such by Enoch Powell in his famous 'Rivers of Blood' speech. In other words, the period during which Rhys was writing the *Wide sargasso sea* was a period in which a truly 'popular' language of race and nation flowered in Britain (Gilroy, 1987, p. 47). Notions of Black sub-citizenship and Black people as objects of social reform were already current in the post war period, drawn from debates about Indian independence, but the path travelled by racism in the late 1950s and early 1960s, was strewn with a taxonomy of the Black body and specifically of gender. The Eugenics Society, in 1959 argued that miscegenation was impossible to unmix and much racist writing was striking for the way in which images of race were gendered.[17]

Equally the vibrancy of Christophine, Antoinette's nurse, and the strange excitement of their interdependence also have a relation to the elderly and alcoholic Rhys's dependence on, desire for, or distaste of, Black nurses in the many nursing homes and hospitals she attended while writing the *Wide sargasso sea*. Jean Rhys was intensively rewriting the manuscript from the 1950s until its publication in 1966. During these years her husband, Max, was often in hospital and Jean herself was hospitalised in Exe Vale Hospital and Surrey Hills Clinic for several months, and continuously had medication for a heart condition. These were also the years when Britain's hospitals were radically transformed by the recruitment of West Indian nurses.

From 1944, the National Health Service and the Ministry of Labour, working in consultation with the Colonial Office, set up a recruiting system with offices in Jamaica and Trinidad. It is notable that subsequent restrictions in immigration were not applied to unskilled ancillary labour where West Indian women were concentrated (see Mama, 1984). Nursing was the main occupation for Black women and in addition 78 per cent of ancillary workers and 84 per cent of domestic workers were also from overseas. In 1964 Jean Rhys was 74 years old and Max was 80. In 1964 Jamaican women were seen as providing one crucial source of cheap labour to enable the National Health Service to meet the demands of Britain's changing demography. It was migrant, Caribbean women who catered for the ever increasing numbers of geriatric men and women in nursing homes and hospitals throughout Britain.[18]

In *The Paris review* Rhys dramatises her psychic separation from the first Black nurturer: 'At the start I hated my nurse. A horrid woman. It was she who told me awful stories about zombies and sucriants, the vampires' (Vreeland, 1979, p. 230). The early stereotype reveals something of Rhys's desire for, but initial defence against, her relations with older Black women. By *Voyage in the dark*, Rhys could use directly the names of the significant Black women she knew as a child. In later encounters with Black nurses Rhys more adequately addresses the demands of her dependence and desire. At first, with Max in hospital, she felt 'Oh Lord: If only they'd let us alone ... the nurses aren't very nice ... the matron and most of the nurses are dreadful he says and they are beastly. I saw how they treated him when I was there' (Rhys, 1985, p. 222). But, by the time of her own hospitalisation in St Mary Abbotts, Rhys was too weak to 'separate' from care. Although the following two months in geriatric wards made her 'not mad about the welfare state' her letters also reveal Rhys's deep need to more accurately signify the Black woman in her fiction: 'I've made the black woman, *the nurse*, [my italics] too articulate. I thought of cutting it a bit ... (but) there's no reason why one particular negro shouldn't be articulate enough' (Rhys, 1985, p. 297).

The hospital is the place of Rhys's desire for a Black mother/nurse. Homi Bhabha hints at the symmetry of darkness with a maternal imaginary. Darkness, he suggests, signifies a desire to return to the fullness of the mother (see Bhabha, 1983). In Rhys's text this is visible in the extent to which the Caribbean woman of the 1840s is flooded with maternal images. 'When I was safely home I sat close to the old wall at the end of the garden ... Christophine found me there when it was nearly dusk, and I was so stiff she had to help me up. She said nothing, but next morning Tia was in the kitchen' (Rhys, 1966, p. 23). Later Christophine takes care of every physical detail of Antoinette's existence.

'I wake her up to sit in the sun, bathe in the cool river. Even if she dropping with sleep. I make good strong soup. I give her milk if I have it, fruit I pick from my own tree. If she don't want to eat I say 'eat it up for my sake, *doudou*' ... I let her have rum. (Rhys, 1966, p. 154)

The scenes are nodes of allusions to the nursing required by a geriatric alcoholic. David Plante describes a similar moment with appalling clarity: 'She (Jean) fell in the bathroom last night, getting up to pee. It was a struggle, I had to roll her on to a blanket and drag her back to bed' (Plante, 1983, p. 52). The *Wide sargasso sea*'s emotional strength derives in part from the impression it gives of the total loving care of a Black to a Creole woman.

The equation patient = child, which creates the fictive term 'childlike' often accorded to the characteristics and identities of patients by most medical thought, provides another metaphorical space in which Rhys might see the Black nurse as 'mother'. In 'The sexual division of labour', Eva Gamarnikow describes how the ideological identification of good nurse with femininity is signified as motherhood (Gamarnikow, 1978). Add the category Black to this equation and the representation becomes specific to post-war British health care. It is the imaginative engagement with Black women, through her childhood, in her adult illness and in reading about the Caribbean, which enables Rhys to develop a complex expression of race and sex. Black 'Other', in Rhys's writing, is not the colonial's Other but characters like Tia who is Antoinette's alter ego and Christophine who evokes the maternal. Rhys places the psychodynamics of mother/daughter relations in historicised narratives.

Rhys is disarmingly casual about her accomplishment:

The big idea – well I'm blowed if I can be sure what it is. Something to do with time being an illusion I think. I mean that the plot exists – side by side with the present, not behind it, that was what it was – is. I've tried to do it by making the past (the West Indies) very vivid. (Rhys, 1985, p. 24)

Rhys continually writes the marginalised woman back into history not simply by celebrating marginality but by rewriting history itself. She 'remembered the last part of *Voyage in the dark* written like that – time and place abolished, past and present the same – and I had been almost satisfied. Then everybody said it was "confused and confusing"' (Rhys, 1985, p. 253). Rhys actively replaces chronology – linear history – with maternal memory, dreams, and process.

The attraction of the mother is not reliably constant. Rhys never once describes in her autobiography a scene where her mother and herself share warmth and understanding. Nor is the mother always a Black mother. Grace Poole's narrative also hints at the reciprocal voice, in this case one which speaks across class boundaries rather than across boundaries of race. Grace Poole's vocabulary is specifically that of a servant but where, in Charlotte Brontë's *Jane Eyre*, Poole is an unsympathetic reactionary invocation of a working class woman, Rhys's Poole has an authentic voice. She echoes and shares Antoinette's concerns. Grace Poole's introductory monologue to the final section set in Thornfield, mirrors Antoinette's dreams both in its vocabulary of 'darkness' and 'shelter', and in its ideas. Rhys openly revises a classic nineteenth-century novel by adopting the point of view of its marginal character. Yet by choosing to represent psychic mothering in the *Wide sargasso sea* through the 'mother' text *Jane Eyre*, Rhys gives powerful attention to the literary, as well as to the representational, mother. Rhys's fiction, then, is the historical romance of the mother. Rhys wrote, as all writers write, to possess what is irretrievably lost. Surrogate mothers, usually Black servants, function in many women's texts and lives as alternative role models to white patriarchs. The warmth which develops between white women and Black servants is heightened when the Black woman acts as a receptacle for the white woman's fantasy of being mothered. Other writers have shared Rhys's negotiation of that desire. For example Lillian Hellman explains that, 'my own liking for black people maybe came a few days after I was born when I was put into the arms of a wet-nurse Sophronia ... It was she who taught me to have feelings for the black poor ... and she gave me anger, an uncomfortable, dangerous and often useful gift' (Hellman, 1978, p. 33).

Where Lillian Hellman conflates, somewhat unproblematically, the representation of desire with patronization, Adrienne Rich is more honest and more radical: 'I had from birth not only a white but a black mother. This relationship, so little explored, so unexpressed, still charges the relationship of black and white women ... We have been mothers and daughters to each other' (Rich, 1976, p. 253). Rich understands that when a white woman identifies with a Black Other this risks dependence. Black and white women have to steer between the Scylla of the white woman's 'infantilisation' and the Charybdis of the Black woman's 'childlike intellect' the rocks created by patriarchy and racism. Such is, I believe, the moment of Rhys's text. *Reciprocal* dependence binds Antoinette with Tia and with Christophine and informs the discursive and political effect of the *Wide sargasso sea*. A similar sentiment of interdependence structures *Voyage in the dark*. Anna seeks to recapitulate the mother/child dyad and, in her memories, bifurcates between the sensual nurturing of Francine and the morality of a white stepmother Hester. Rhys makes the important statement here that Anna's pain is only relieved by her memories of women 'mothering' her during a period of her history which predates her heterosexual encounters.

In 'Three women's texts and a critique of imperialism', Gayatri Spivak acknowledges that Rhys allows Christophine to be 'first interpreter and named speaking subject' (Spivak, 1986, p. 271). The essay contains Spivak's usual subtle and sophisticated placing of texts in economic as well as in critical theory. Spivak however judges the novel to *refract* the project of imperialism because Antoinette, and the 'commodified' Christophine, are finally caught in an imperialist hegemony. If Rhys does mediate historical events through women who remain inevitably marginal in dominant society, there are ways in which Rhys invites the reader to circumvent that domination. What Spivak downplays is the recognisable socio-psychological trope, namely that of mother/nurse that enables Christophine to be that intelligent, articulate spokeswoman for oppressed women.

Christophine is a visible role model of the Other, self-made into self, in the full density of otherness with her powerful language and the medical power of obeah. Christophine links Antoinette to a more complex knowledge made up of magic, earth gods and Arawak history. There is a strong focus to Christophine throughout the novel, which begins with the opening description of her specialness and continues in Rhys's sympathetic portrayal of an alternative and purer Arawak mythology for example in Christophine's song, 'ma belle ka di maman li' which deliberately places the maternal in a Black and patois voice. It is Christophine who both makes and tells Antoinette's history. In the *Wide sargasso sea* Rhys with vehement pleasure celebrates an articulate Black woman, Christophine, who is authentically subversive of patriarchal history *because* she is positioned on the boundary between races, between languages and between histories. Christophine, Antoinette, Tia and Amélie retrieve the maternal from its nexus of misogyny and racism. In *Gynesis*, Alice Jardine points out that it is in the nature of the 'European ensemble/confronted with systems of production and belief foreign to its own', to colonise or retreat into its own boundaries (Jardine, 1985, p. 92). The space outside of the conscious colonial subject has always connoted the Other, either/or female and Black. As Jardine observes, this space carries 'feminine connotations' which intersect the female body with maternity (Jardine, 1985, p. 88).[19]

Jean Rhys challenges the boundaries of such 'systems of production'. In the *Wide sargasso sea* the reciprocity of Black women and white women, as mothers and daughters is a microcosmic reversal of the failure of culture and history to consolidate a progressive new identity of women. Jean Rhys fissures colonialism with discrete breaks: first she disrupts paternal history with the maternal semiotic by replacing chronology with a 'women's time' of maternal imagery and memories; second she plays out differing Creole and Black voices to refuse the specular aesthetic.

Of course, although her writing makes a monumental effort to subvert the colonial script it necessarily raises in its very strategies some problematics of boundary crossing. For example, the pre-oedipal is inevitably implicated in a nostalgia for lost origins which cannot, by itself, provide the grounds for a counter discourse. There is an inevitable tension, too, when constructing a new 'history' of women, between 'women' as a discursively constructed group and women as material subjects of their own history. Again, linguistically, discursive formations of marginal women might be misheard as articulating a limited scale. It is not possible for Rhys to fully replace the taxonomy of colonial racism with a white/Creole/Black discursive feminine.

What then are the maternal/gender theories of boundary crossing? As we have seen, Nancy Chodorow, in *The reproduction of mothering*, argues that female children do not accept any boundary between themselves and their mothers because mothers cannot represent 'difference' for girls in the same way that mothers represent all that is not masculine for boys. The other significant theory of the maternal is the one proposed by Julia Kristeva, in *Desire in language*, where she defines maternal imagery as the semiotic subtext of symbolic language. Plato 'intuitively' understood, Kristeva suggests, that there is 'a *chora*, receptacle, unnamable, improbable, hybrid, anterior to naming, to the one, to the father, and consequently maternally connoted' (Kristeva, 1980, p. 133). The chora is the place of orality, sensuality and 'laughter'. Rhys took that further journey across the frontier of the imperial dominative terrain. Rhys's project is to break the boundary of 'race', as constituted in paternal symbolic language, by working towards a warm and incestuous understanding between women of different races in mother/daughter dyads.

What is really meaningful in her writing is not just its radical content – an attack on the racist misogyny of colonial men – but its portraits of authentic Black and Creole women subjects addressing the instability of difference. Her work is charged with the conditions of its creation. It does not present a unified category 'woman' but represents the multivocal and personal narratives of different women of different colours. 'About my book. It is done in the way that patchwork would be done if you had all the colours and all the pieces but had not yet arranged to make a quilt' (Rhys, 1985, p. 162).

Simultaneous translators: Zora Neale Hurston and La Malincha

The bilingual writer lives in countries of contradictions because, of course, language is the key instrument in the construction of national as well as of individual identities. To translate from one set of meanings into another is to experience the suspension of one's maternal tongue and therefore in a sense one's gender and cultural significance. For Black writers who do not wholly inhabit the dominant language, the construction of identity is a complex linguistic process. A Black American woman experiences that difficult task of writing herself into two symbolic orders: American English, the language of white power and Black American, the language of subjectivity, of Black power and solidarity. Thus, although at least, the bilinguist can 'enter' translation as a liminal space in order to avoid the stifling boundaries of any single culture, she may, in the activity of translation, evade political boundaries altogether. Her pluralism may have no place.

Bilingualism is often devalued as the necessary skill of transient peoples. Yet bilingualism is a creative process because it talks of differences and living transformations. It is the epitome of border crossings. In a period of critical displacement and cultural migration the techniques of bilingual writers are worth tracing in order to unpack the taxonomy of the traditional canon. Traditionally white cultural criticism favours ethnocentricity by arranging and categorising literature in 'developed' countries by singularity, and painting everywhere else a generalised 'colour'. Edward Said, in *Orientalism*, specifically opposes this monocentrism in the 'name of formerly colonized peoples' and asks criticism to question available systems of difference precisely to envisage ways in which cultural specificities may provide an escape from the uniformity of the Other (Said, 1979, p. 25).[1]

Women often write about translations precisely to avoid the binary we/they division of colonialist and colonised. Maxine Hong Kingston's *Woman Warrior* is a good example of the special power 'talk-story' gives to women wishing to appropriate a larger world. What makes the activity of translation a feminine, even feminist, aesthetic is when women writers, such as Maxine Hong Kingston and Zora Neale Hurston celebrate the language of their early childhood and therefore, in some respect, fall in with Cixous's idea of a 'maternal' language. What Cixous describes, in The newly born woman, are the maternal images available to female children through their mother affiliation. In addition bilingual writers display those complexities of displacement which can provide criticism with new structures of meaning. Such writers often share with critics the same political problem – one of negotiating a new literary aesthetic under the pressure of changes in class, race and gender roles.

Zora Neale Hurston is such a writer. Writing about the Black South for a Northern white audience, Hurston is a translator who avoids either wholly positive or negative definitions of Black women and Black men. The triumph of Black women's orality is inscribed in the straggly, disordered, miscellaneous modes of Hurston's writing career. Similarly Hurston deliberately refuses the boundaries of 'literary' Black speech in her subversive love of double descriptions ('low-down'), and verbal nouns ('funeralise').

Only recently has her work begun to receive the attention it deserves. Contemporary reviews of Hurston's books were hostile. In his review of For their eyes were watching God, Richard Wright misogynistically helped to destroy Hurston's literary status (see Wright, 1937). The New Yorker called Mules and men 'disorganised', and The Saturday review thought it a 'curious' mixture of remembrance, travelogue, 'sensationalism' and anthropology. Not surprisingly the book did not sell well. The mixture of political analysis, Black culture and Haitian history appeared superficial to contemporary reviewers because such discourses are 'extraneous' to literature, and they are similarly regarded within some current criticism to be impure and full of dangers. Darwin T. Turner, in particular, attacks the shifting narrative voice of For their eyes were watching God and attacks Hurston's attempt to define independent Black women across the border limits of race and gender representation. For example Turner's dismissal of Hurston is couched in gendered terms when he refers to her work as 'artful, coy, irrational, superficial and shallow' (Turner, 1971, p. 90).

From the 1920s Hurston was a member of that large and dominant movement in Afro-American literature known as the Harlem Ren-aissance[2]. Blacks who had migrated to the North were vexed with the urgency of finding a fresh identity. The invocation of the 'New Negro' and the precise specifying of a Negro identity was undertaken by Alain Locke who celebrated the new psychology and the new spirit of the masses in the journal The new Negro, founded in 1925. Locke claimed that the struggle to become urban workers generated in Harlem negroes a consciousness that Black was as much a zealous identification as a colour of skin. Harlem was constituted as the place where Negroes could take on a new Black identity supported by their numbers and by the creative activities of musicians, writers and artists. W. E. B. Dubois and other Black thinkers believed in the solid chain binding art with politics. This would shackle culture to the notion of 'Négritude' creating a progressive new identity of Black people settled on positive characters set in a backdrop of their oral history. It was taken for granted that even if such an identity did depend on white audiences it must not relegate the Negro to exoticism. With Langston Hughes, Zora Neale Hurston founded the journal Fire! which published a now substantial realm of Black writing and was claimed by Alain Locke as one of the voices of the 'talented tenth' who intended to express their 'dark-skinned' selves on top of the mountain (see Cooke, 1984, p. 32).

Yet women writers were not considered to be major figures in the 'high stepping' Harlem Renaissance which did feel free, as Barbara Christian has pointed out, to celebrate Black male sexuality (Christian, 1980, p. 40). When the writer Dorothy West went to New York in 1926 she encountered the explicit misogyny of Black male writers who were busily silencing women: 'I went to the Harlem Renaissance and never said a word. I was young and a girl so they never asked me to say anything' (Washington, 1987, p. 344.) Zora Neale Hurston was not alone in believing that this deployment of Black culture was losing touch with its women and with its Black roots. Her witty term 'niggerati' for the Black literati reveals her longing for a more fluctuating 'difference'.

So that while male writers in the group like Langston Hughes, W.E. Dubois and Alain Locke were articulating a canonic Negro aesthetic, Hurston's energy went into her travels throughout the South where she collected a very different mixture of Black folklore, songs, sermons and social rituals. Clearly, while the Harlem Renaissance provided Hurston with inspiration and publishing outlets, it also confounded her with its hierarchy of ethnically 'right' social issues and critical rankings of literary form. Harlem writers were wary that mass culture and commercialism might contaminate the 'essential' Negro and his pure folk culture. Hurston rejected the images of Negro men and women being established by the Harlem Renaissance, for example Carl van Vechten's highly eroticised 'addiction' to photographing young Black men. Where Hughes and others were celebrating the spiritual force of Négritude, Hurston believed that the strength of Black community women came from struggle and otherness.

The notion that only the skilful dramatisation of multiple languages can capture the voices of those outside the 'literary' order is vindicated dramatically in Mules and men by Hurston's success in capturing the translation techniques and language games of rural Blacks. As the only Black Southerner in the Harlem Renaissance, Hurston knew that the accurate representation of Black culture resided, paradoxically, not in 'role models' but in rhetorical reversal and inversion because these played so large a part in the production of Black speech and humour. As Henry Gates argues, these techniques are 'fundamental' to black artistic forms, from painting and sculpture to music and language use' (Gates, 1988, p. xxiv).

Mules and men collects together stories, hoodoo rituals, songs, proverbs and sermons together with Hurston's autobiographical insertions:

'Zora, Ah'm gointer tell one, but you be sho and tell de folks Ah tole it. Don't say Seymore said it because he took you on de all-day fishin' trip to Titusville. Don't say Seaboard Hamilton tole it 'cause he always give you a big hunk of barbecue when you go for a sandwich. Give ole John French whut's comin' to 'im.'
'You gointer tell it or you gointer spend de night tellin' us you gointer tell it?' I asked.
'Ah got to say a piece of litery.' (Hurston, 1978, p. 51)

Hurston's account here of 'untranslated' Black vernacular conveys racial difference. Her selective syntactical fidelity not only displays difference but also demonstrates the importance of language in bearing any racial concepts such as 'received'/other. The role of the returning Black interpreter is a profoundly awkward one. 'The Negro offers feather-bed resistance. That is, we let the probe enter, but it never comes out' (Hurston, 1978, p. 4). Hurston has arrived from the dominant American academic/literary world and so already, by leaving New York, acknowledges the impossibility of living completely in that linguistic terrain. Yet her role entails ambivalence caught as it is between a knowing ethnography dedicated to preserving 'local colour' and cultural displacement. 'If I had exalted myself to impress the town, somebody would have sent me word in a match-box that I had been up North there and had rubbed the hair off my head against some college wall' (Hurston, 1978, p. 4).

Hurston does not build up her Black community with the textual conventions that govern ethnographic writing. She is not that fabulous figure – the participant observer. Hurston reveals her close ties to her Northern education but simultaneously refuses any power over her informants which is the usual concomitant of academic knowledge. The use of untranslated words foregrounds racial distance while at the same time, of course, the narrator is rapidly bridging distance by simply bringing the two languages together. Yet by choosing to translate or not to translate, not even to contextualise Black usage for example 'gointer' and 'match-box', Hurston demonstrates the fundamental importance of Black meaning making in its own place unmediated by any 'higher' standard American.

Walter Benjamin, in *Illuminations*, argued that 'all translation is only a somewhat provisional way of coming to terms with the foreignness of languages' (Benjamin, 1969, p. 75). For example, at least since the Second World War, translation has become an almost accepted description of the work of anthropology. One of the commonest techniques in anthropological writing is translation. The most consistent form this takes is the symbolic. That is to say the anthropologist translates a culture as if it were a collection of texts, choosing its most symbolic practices so that parts come to stand for the whole, for example Clifford Geertz's Balinese cock-fight. But, as Benjamin hoped, Hurston gives voice to her culture, not in mimesis or reproduction but as the outcome of dialogue, of multiple voices. She does not preside over and control the production of a text but admits to the value of the prior object – the folk tale – which is the primary and independent originator.

Hurston invented, in the book, an exceedingly potent method of telling Black tales without interposing a distanced narrator. Similarly in *Jonah's gourd vine*, Hurston purposefully describes an African heritage of drums and 'ju-ju'. The novel is redolent with evocations of African religion which beats 'upon the o-go-doe the ancient drum' (Hurston, 1971, p. 311). Hurston vividly depicts how it is the precisely double voiced, signifying the nature of Black language ranged against a dominant white culture which is a locus of epistemological power[3].

Yet, even by 1942, critics of Hurston could still dismiss her attempted reconstruction of 'literature' by refusing her particular way of writing. Hurston's editor Robert Lippincott deleted two chapters of *Dust tracks on a road* because he felt that Hurston's political opinions were irrelevant in autobiography. The book dovetails childhood memories with folk tales, and is a circuitous account of Black life in comparison with the resonant racial protests in other books of the 1940s, such as Richard Wright's *Native son*. Hurston writes another story. Where Wright and Ralph Ellison deal directly with racial violence, Hurston's schooling in anthropology and intimate knowledge of small town communities shape her reluctance to formalise Black protest and her preference for describing the culture of nurturing and women's friendship. Hurston's attention to maternal roles, her dramatisation of Black humour rather than explicit radical argument places her outside the sociopolitical continuum of other Black writing of her time. Within the Harlem Renaissance's agenda of racial issues, sexual oppression, and Hurston's literary depiction of it, inevitably suffered. Similarly Hurston's rich mixture of the folk allegories of rural Southern Blacks with sharp political analysis was truncated and adapted to meet the demands of white editors and readers.

Thus Hurston was caught between two writing worlds – between the artistic priorities of the Harlem Renaissance and the exigencies of white publishers and their white readers. In *Dust tracks on the road* Hurston ironically refers to this overarching double bind when she describes her student image at Barnard College as 'Barnard's sacred Black cow' (Hurston, 1984, p. 169). It is Hurston's slipperiness, the way she dramatises herself as the marginal Negro woman who gains an apparent 'accidental' success, which creates her ambivalent narrative voice. Hurston's writing is often called apolitical because it does not neatly reconcile race, sexual politics and gender identity just as Hurston, in her own life, could not easily buy her way into a stable persona.

Not surprisingly the writing of women like Zora Neale Hurston, who transmuted between cultures and refused to let her race dictate her politics, has not been a promising hunting ground for critics. Even Robert Hemenway, Hurston's most sympathetic critic, prefers her skilful fictions and hides from her forays into white values. Yet, from the thirties to the sixties, Zora Neale Hurston wrote novels, short stories, and journalism as well as autobiography, became America's first Black literary ethnographer and opens up, more than any other writer in the Harlem Renaissance, a broad range of forces within which Black culture was at a particular moment constructing itself.

There are several reasons why Hurston's path of response to the constraints of Black representation eluded critics. Pluralism can be critically inscribed as political anaesthesia. Most Marxist and even postmodernist critics prefer writers who deal actively with historical specificities not with polyglot humour, writers who can ironise religion yet who have a firm sense of the mappings of race, class or chronology.[4] Yet the first person narratives in many of Zora Neale Hurston's books are good examples of marginality in its major key. Hurston often uses a simple past tense, avoiding a specific 'world view'. She loved the paternal figures of Moses and Herod, and equally anathematically, refused to be a spokeswoman for Black rights. Perhaps understandably Hemenway characterises this as Hurston's 'inchoate challenge to cultural identity' (Hemenway, 1977, p. 100). Clearly this misses the point(s).

Henry Louis Gates, examining the autobiographies of Frederick Douglas in 'Race', writing, and difference, comes to the conclusion that a crucial aspect of Black autobiographical writing is its positing of fictive Black selves, 'arbitrary in reference' (Gates, 1986, p. 123). Similarly, Hurston employs plethoric and efflorescent characters and a syntax remarkable in its linguistic complexity. Hurston refuses the vulnerability of 'race' by producing a dramatic mixture of folk tale, autobiography and anthropology in order to make an ambitious critique of the fixed categories of American ethnic identity. Mules and men is, in any sense one thinks of, an exciting fresh record of living Black history, Hoodoo religion and their interaction:

The way we tell it, Hoodoo started way back there before everything. Six days of magic spells and mighty words and the world with its elements above and below was made. And now, God is leaning back taking a seventh day rest. When the eighth day comes around, He'll start to making new again. Man wasn't made until around half-past five on the sixth day, so he can't know how anything was done. (Hurston, 1987, p. 193)

Hurston translates the values of Hoodoo both by narrating its history and by introjecting its difference into the syntax of her text. For example, her narrators are like mediums who have their own spirits. By refusing to articulate Black difference in traditional genres like the protest novel, Hurston could expose the limits of those genres in styles of writing they had not encompassed.

As Gloria T. Hull observes, in her book about the Harlem Renaissance, Color, sex and poetry, it is clear that women writers felt 'tyrannized' by its critical rankings and canon (see Hull, 1987). Hurston admits the degree to which the lived effect of Black female identity is not easily flagged but she is passionately conscious of the density of Black women's language. In *Mules and men* Hurston creates different languages which carry social as well as aesthetic messages. Hurston's focus, on the connection between language and experience for rural Black Southerners, emphasises in her writing the context of Black representation. That is to say the stories reproduce in their form and vocabulary the economic and community parameters of Southern rural life. They tell of the hardship of work and of the omniscience of white patriarchy. They are coherent, pointed accounts. The text overcomes the limitations of narrative causality by interweaving a ceaseless dialogue between the storytellers and narrator which becomes an open ended phenomenology of Black rural lives.

Consider, for example, the opening chapter. Zora begins her quest for Black culture by returning to her 'native' town, Eatonville, Florida:

I hurried back to Eatonville because I knew that the town was full of material and that I could get it without hurt, harm or danger. As early as I could remember it was the habit of men folks particularly to gather on the store porch of evenings to swap stories, even the women folk would stop and break a breath with them at times ...
AS I CROSSED THE MAITLAND-EATONVILLE TOWNSHIP LINE I could see a group on the store porch. I was delighted. The town had not changed. Same love of talk and song. So I drove on down there before I stopped. Yes, there was George Thomas, Calvin Daniels, Jack and Charlie Jones, Gene Brazzle, B. Moseley and 'Seaboard'. Deep in a game of Florida-flip. (Hurston, 1979, p. 4,9)

The opening autobiographical account is by now an expected entry into any ethnography. Most describe the situation in which ethnographers find themselves and their reasons for going there. Most are emblematic personal descriptions which invariably tell of the ethnographer's difficulties in learning the language and overcoming hostility, casting the ethnographer as a mystified, sometimes naive observer, as for example in accounts by Clifford Geetz, and Evans-Pritchard, who presented his famous study *The Nuer* as a demonstration of scientific abstraction. Hurston has no (objectifying) academic expertise but describes Black Southerners as specific persons with real names. A conspicuous sign of this in the passage being the shift from a personal narrative in the past tense to a particularised description of Black vocabulary and experience – 'Florida-flip'. Hurston does not adopt the conventional fixed vantage point of a detached authority describing a single or unique performance but 'hurries' and is 'delighted' by the continuation of 'habits' she so loved as a child.

The visit reverses the traditional return of the educated woman to her pastoral home. To begin with, this is an evening arrival which is relatively rare in ethnographical writing (see Pratt, 1986). It does not promise a new dawn, the coming of light. It tampers with judgment and any ethnic or rhetorical narrator expertise. As 'Lucy Hurston's daughter' Hurston meets no townsfolk hostility. 'Hurston' crosses the boundary of a detached narrator by gradually becoming shaped by the speaking subjects which she describes, just as the reader is attracted to a shared intimacy with Hurston's people. The chapter is typical of all the chapters in *Mules and men*. It is important to note that the narrator 'Hurston' is in no way a competent ethnographer but is portrayed as a vulnerable but not naive woman.

'Hello boys', I hailed them as I went into neutral ... 'You back home for good, I hope.'
'Nope, Ah come to collect some old stories.' (Hurston, 1978, p. 9)

The boys agree to take Hurston 'woofing' to a 'toe-party' but repeatedly ponder the choice of location, of place, by telling mythic stories of the dangers and perils slaves experienced in earlier journeys. For example in one such case a slave John drowns in a great storm. Arriving in heaven John bores the angels with his version of 'de big flood'. In conclusion, the story problematises the transparency of oral experience. John, telling his tale to an old man with a crooked walking stick discovers that to 'Ole Nora' (Noah), John's exaggerated manipulation of reality is inadequate. '"You can't tell him nothin' 'bout no flood"' (Hurston, 1978, p. 15).

The cycle of John and 'Ol Massa' stories emerged in the South after the civil war. The stories are characterised by John's vehement pleasure in outwitting his master who is revealed to be a foolish white patriarch. In Hurston's 'John' stories the paternalism of white patriarchy is fully rejected – alligators formerly 'pure white all over' become black and it is a woman Big Sweet who tells the best story. The Afro-American folk tale serves to remind us that authentic Black self representation is not essentially there as some given entity but emerges as part of an expertise in translation requiring, as translation does, an understanding of audience. What is remarkable about the chapter is not Hurston's keen eared rendering of Black speech *per se*. Such expertise after all might be said to be a feature of the racist Brer Rabbit stories. The force of the tales, as Hurston recounts them, lies in the *process* of narration as much as in the content of the narrative. Broadly speaking, each chapter is a story about translation. The arguments between Calvin, James and the narrator about the veracity of storytelling become messages about language both in the stories they choose to tell and in the organisation of each chapter in that Hurston gives much more space to these debates than to the ostensible aim of her journey – the documentation of Black township life.

The text contains a great deal of phonetic transcription and Hurston tries to encapsulate the linguistic spontaneity of her rural friends as part of the 'plot' of her time in Eatonville. The point is that her choice of form is not a prior event but emerges out of the joint activity of the narrator and her friends. The emphasis is on a co-operative storytelling which passes from participant to participant in a polyphonic text. Local dialect is not some exotic and framed miniature of Black culture but incorporated immediately into the narrator's voice which changes and adapts to the linguistic needs of her friends. At first the recorder uses standard literary syntax but does not fully conform to it. Literally 'I' goes into 'neutral' and the local 'Ah' is substituted. The first person pronoun is always indexical. It is too 'free'. Symptomatically Hurston prefers the contextualised 'Ah' even the collective 'we' such a rare pronoun in conventional ethnography.

With pointed precision Hurston is allowed to enter into the body of a narrator only by deliberately lying about the value of her clothing and car, in other words by an explicitly untruthful account of herself. The narrator, and her translation, frame spatially the intertexts they display. The strong 'Ah' speaker merely sets the stage. It is the mélange of speaking voices which trigger off the production of meanings. Hurston makes an innovative tension out of hybrid forms and dialect voices. *Mules and men* is a book of multiple stories told in many dialects. The multilayered text depicts people who, lacking a comfortable past, themselves dramatise the problems of realism in order to subvert the authority of their white owned history. Hurston allows the choice of Afro-American colloquial expressions, and intonational rhythms to come from within the Black community.

Hurston's finest writing, *For their eyes were watching God*, similarly focuses on the performative values of culture. *For their eyes were watching God* is specifically about the power of Black women to transform their own lives and those of others through storytelling. Janie, the protagonist, presents her autobiographical story to her friend Phoeby. The woman listener, as a supporting audience, 'provokes' Janie into a language of metaphors marked by women's humour and expressions. This is not some intertext in Hurston's longer tale to her readers but the whole 'plot' of the novel. Janie's ability to create her life by learning to control her men with insults and hyperbolic and metaphoric speech is the story of Janie's growth. Not surprisingly, the narrative can displace the narrative of slavery which dominates Mules and men. For their eyes were watching God focuses on Janie's life which Hurston depicts as a generalised Black female history set in the American South. The novel begins in the home of Janie's grandmother. It opens with the grandmother's story which is the story of all slaves in the South. What Janie learns in the space of the novel is to refuse the closed brackets of her grandmother's social ambition, who marries Janie to Killicks, just as Janie learns to break with the definitions of femininity given by Black men.

Janie's childhood name of 'Alphabet' is replaced in turn by the names of her three successive husbands – Killicks, Starks and Woods. Janie moves from her first husband Logan Killicks to Joe Starks and finally marries and 'kills' her third husband 'Tea Cake' Woods. Janie's marriage to the farmer Killicks, as his name implies, almost 'kills' her youthful spontaneity. Once Jody takes her to Eatonville, he 'starkly' limits her role to being that of a wifely symbol of his bourgeois storekeeping success. When Tea Cake enters her story, Janie escapes with him into an 'irresponsible' Afro-American itinerant existence. The emergence of a new female identity is highlighted each time by the metaphor of clothing. Throwing away her apron, Janie elopes from Killicks with Starks. Yet although the discarded apron symbolises Janie's freedom from physical subordination, marriage to Starks brings with it the head-rag with which Starks covers Janie's hair and which stands for the social constraints of a 'Victorian' marriage. In widowhood, Janie triumphantly renounces such fixed gender determinations, and with Tea Cake, chooses to wear overalls which she wears back to Eatonville after his death 'wid her hair swingin' down her back like some girl' (Hurston, 1986, p. 10).

Janie escapes the gender roles defined by others and the hegemony of a white economy by discovering a language of emotion, which she learnt from Tea Cake, but only fully displays in a pleasurable translation of its effects to another Black woman – Phoeby. It is in the episode of Janie's trial and courtroom speech that Hurston demonstrates Janie's fluent trajectory from private to public forms of address. Janie makes an easy passage from one voice to the other. She carefully calibrates her life with Tea Cake as it might be differently seen with the eyes of a white judge and jury, and with the baleful eye of Black masculinity and with the true 'blue' eye of an independent Black woman in a racist world where 'Tea Cake couldn't come back to himself ... He had to die to get rid of the dog' (Hurston, 1986, p. 278). Janie is able to tell her story in a plurality of voices speaking both in an intimate and inspired way which made the jurors 'all leaned over to listen while she talked', and, simultaneously, in a public 'testifying' manner because 'first thing she had to remember was she was not at home' (Hurston, 1986, p. 278).

I have no doubt that Hurston's bilingualism is eminently 'feminine'. That is to say, while not all, many women writers (and hence their women characters) focus on the activity of translation as a way of subverting patriarchal culture. Translation is often the conscious subject of women's writing. There are diverse examples. Jane Eyre 'translates' herself from Gateshead to Thornfield and can finally violate all 'textual' limits when translating the visible world to a sightless Rochester. In To the lighthouse, Mrs Ramsey translates the abrasiveness of her husband into a less cruel rationality and the indecisions of her son James into imagination. Esther, in The bell jar, longs to abandon herself inside the Russian translator at the United Nations. The heroine of Margaret Atwood's Surfacing, as we shall see, is similarly caught on the border of maternal and paternal linguistic terrains. According to Nicole Ward Jouve, in translation, 'You escape from definition, from the law which rules and partitions women, which prevents femininity from coming into being. Translation = no man's land = woman's land?' (Ward Jouve, 1986, p. 46).

Hurston's mobility is represented substantially and subjectively throughout all her writing. The supposed oppositions which characteristically structure her writing – Black/white, gender opposites within the Black community, the polarisation of rural South and urban North, work and its concomitant folk culture/intellectual polarity were substantial forces whose synthesis could not easily be attempted. Hurston skates across these in translation rather than adopting an easy passage from rural Black to universal woman. Every ungrammatical noun is the stuff of psychic difference. Each shift in narration contributes to the sexual politics of each book. The extraordinary slippiness is inspired as much by Hurston's awareness of a white readership as by the cultural heterogeneity of a Black community. As Gloria T. Hull intriguingly points out, Afro-American dialect verse in the nineteenth century was the exclusive prerogative of *male* poets. The vernacular was too unfeminine for women writers to use since it could not match their conscious understanding of a white Victorian ideology of femininity (See Hull, 1987).

It ought to be remembered that throughout the 1930s and early 1940s most Blacks did not have access to higher education and segregation severely restricted their economic progress. Hurston's translation necessarily had to bring Black culture into a continuous textuality which can only display, but not resolve, the racial and psychosocial constructions of Black women[5]. This is not a question for women of 'preferring' one kind of writing to another but what amounts to, in effect, for women placed between two cultures, a movement from one language to another so as to throw into crisis any facility in naming. But nor is it a simple celebration of difference.

These contrasts might be said to represent that more overtly political difference between a feminine pluralism and a masculine singularity. Like Bertha, women who are not allowed to identify their difference linguistically, go mad. Where Thornfield imprisons Bertha's sexuality, Eatonville allows Hurston to celebrate her sensuality in a vivid vocabulary: 'My laughing acceptance of Pitts' woofing had put everybody at his ease ... They put me on the table and everybody urged me to spread my jenk:' (Hurston, 1978, p. 70.) Hurston refuses to privilege a particular stable version of Black culture by privileging Black orality in itself.

B. Mosely looked over at Mathilda and said, 'You just like a hen in de barnyard. You cackle so much you give de rooster de blues'. Mathilda looked over at him archly and quoted:
'Stepped on a pin, de pin bent
And dat's de way de story went.' (Hurston, 1978, p. 38)

Humour is frequent in ethnography but it is usually marked by a narrator's punning collusion with his readers. Here Mathilda's irony subverts the 'transparent' intent of the text – the documentation of Black humour, emitting a contradictory message of female linguistic dexterity which is displayed over and above the subversive Black discourse as a whole. The element of tone is a significant generator of these messages. Although fewer of the tales are told by women, the verbal battle represents the complexity of female language in relation to Black male custom because Mathilda colludes in Black values as well as challenging them.

In *Mules and men*, language is more significant than characterisation. Hurston does not assume that the language of literature is the language of authority, but exposes a tension between different manners of speaking. What is at stake in Hurston's use of Black dialect is not simply the expressive possibilities of metaphor but a power struggle between women and men considered as the power structure of Black literary identity. So that although Hurston never renounces heterosexuality, she makes a persistent attack in her writing on the inadequacies of marriage and husbands. A compelling example is the story 'Sweat' in which marriage brings only undeviating physical hardship and emotional pain to Delia the protagonist. Hard at work as a washer-woman supporting the adulterous Sykes, Delia creates her own woman's culture by cultivating her garden and attending Church. When Sykes tries to kill Delia with a rattlesnake she springs his trap and he dies, killed by Delia's metaphoric appropriation of the patriarchal symbol. (See Hurston, 1987.)

In Hurston's writing the prevalence of domestic metaphors may be seen as a way to place women's domesticity within the realm of the creative. Hurston uses such metaphors to articulate the sexual politics of Eatonville because metaphor best captures the connections and differences between the word and the object or person which the word is designed to signify. Often these domestic metaphors are combined with irony and humour. In Mathilda's story the woman has a set of keys to lock up her kitchen, the bedroom and the child's room. Woman, metaphorically as it were, has power over food, sex and reproduction. Cooking and mothering link literary with biological creativity. In addition, Hurston's metaphors frequently as here depend on meanings in other prior texts like folk tales, showing how no text can exist in and of itself.

In *For their eyes were watching God* Janie's metaphorical 'double' killing of Tea Cake – first by talking endlessly rather than tending to his wounds and second shooting him like a rabid dog, is a far more vivid resolution to the narrative than a single violent moment could be. The final frame of the novel is a grand metaphor of female power over the production and exchange of meanings. Janie translates her story to Phoeby and so gains a descriptive purchase over her own socialisation.

In their book *Conjuring*, Marjorie Pryse and Hortense J. Spillers argue that the tradition of Black women's writing is itself a matrix of literary discontinuities (see Pryse and Spillers, 1985). They point out how

Black women writers must write not only against the symbolic values of the canon but disarm that tradition by speaking to particular community histories in order to create a counter tradition, a counter myth. To pursue Pryse and Spiller's theme, it is Hurston's rendition of community speech which enables her to walk freely into a new literary landscape. In *Mules and men* questions of literary representation are always functions of locutionary address. In her rapid passage in and out of dialect, Hurston makes the process of translation pose the question of representation. 'A toe-party! What on earth is that?' 'Come go with me and James and you'll see.' 'But, everybody will be here lookin' for me. They'll think Ah'm crazy – tellin' them to come and then gettin' out and goin' to Wood Bridge myself'. (Hurston, 1978, p. 11).

The switching of modes of address in the whole passage is extreme. Hurston speaks first as an educated outsider, with her distanced and grammatically exact interrogative, but instantly adopts the Black personal pronoun. The pronoun structure is not intact. 'Ah'm' collides with an unphoneticised 'everybody'. And the pronoun structure is doubly unstable with Hurston's use of non-standard speech patterns to dramatise what can only elsewhere in the book be described as a feminist ideology. From a broad perspective it is clear that Hurston's strength lies in the linguistic tension between self and others that underscores all her writing. So what should a white feminist critic do with this? By what new critical criteria could Hurston's work be judged?

The question of how to evaluate all this is not an easy one. Admitting the impossibility of mapping in this space a full critique of Hurston's writing career I want myself, like Hurston, to consciously refuse the ethnocentricity of much sociolinguistics. I want to approach Hurston very tangentially, to search for her identity by looking at her writing through the life of another female translator, La Malincha, an Indian who learnt to control the Spanish Conquistador Cortés in her own ensemble of linguistic moves. La Malincha, the mistress of Cortes the conqueror of Central America, who in turn conquered his language, is a resonant figure in Chicana theories about women's identity. La Malincha's story is a metonymy of the power of spliced languages and the struggles of women of colour.[6] In other words to explore the theme of linguistic identities we can, like Hurston and La Malincha, adopt an approach which Bakhtin and Todorov have ambitiously formulated as 'dialogism' or intertextual criticism.

As I described in detail in the Introduction, according to Bakhtin all social groups speak languages based on a shared morality and beliefs, but individual consciousness can only be constituted when an individual's group is in dialogue with another group (which is often constructed as Other). Consciousness, to Bakhtin, is a kind of inner dialogue in itself – a process linking the psyche with the voices of social Others. A useful idea is Bakhtin's definition of the 'polyphonic' novel. In this genre, he argues, there is no singular culture or language but an open-ended creative dialogue between different ages, different dialects and different cultures. Bakhtin's examples are Dickens and Dostoevski whose words and forms 'belong to no one' (Bakhtin, 1981, p. 259). The practice of feminist criticism similarly should not be a monologue attempting some abstract version of textual reality. Bakhtin's notion speaks to the situation of women who cross the borders of racial difference and ethnic languages – Black women like Zora Neale Hurston and Indian women like La Malincha.

What interests me in Todorov's *Conquest of America* is the recognition that any critical effort has only very provisional starting points. This is clearly not the place to elaborate Todorov's theories, but they can better help us understand how Hurston survived the limitations of Black exoticism in the same way that La Malincha survived the Spanish Conquest. Todorov's critical interest is in the categories by which one culture – Spain – conquered the Other cultures of Central America. Todorov seeks to connect the activity of language with the activity of conquest. He starts from the conviction that the Spanish conquest was made possible precisely through language, since the Spaniards could take military control of America because they could take linguistic, or symbolic, control of new situations. Spain won America, Todorov argues, because the Spaniards were able to improvise, where the Aztecs, Incas and Mayans could deal with new experience only when it fitted their elaborate cyclical codes. Todorov shows the Indians to be imprisoned by the concepts they produced since they could not, linguistically, account for the generative features of Spanish militarism.

In *The dialogic principle* Bakhtin tells us the same story: 'The past is preserved, not in the unconscious, not even a collection one, but in the memory of languages, genres, rituals' (Bakhtin, 1984, p. 32). Language functioned, during the conquest, as a material means of control. Vasco de Quiroza wrote that the Spaniards transformed Indian faces into illegible books: 'They produced so many marks on their faces, in addition to the royal brand, that they had their faces covered with letters, for they bore the marks of all who had bought and sold them' (Todorov, 1984, p. 137).

I am doing Todorov and Bakhtin an injustice in thus excerpting briefly from their considerable body of work but I hope to have indicated how powerfully responsive these approaches are to understanding the role of women translators. Todorov concludes that the relation of knowledge to power is not contingent but constitutive: 'I feel the need ... to adhere to that narrative which proposes rather than imposes; to rediscover ... the *complementarity* of narrative discourse' (Todorov, 1984, p. 253 [My italics]).

It is not easy to make, as Todorov does, such a radical assault on critical habits but if criticism is to be at once practice and the deconstruction of practice we could at least collapse historical linearity by juxtaposing two women translators, the sixteenth century La Malincha with the twentieth century Zora Neale Hurston. The 'contamination' of Hurston's literary texts with the extra literary narrative of La Malincha, dead long before, acknowledges difference. It suggests a criticism which belongs neither to history nor to literature although it can partake of both, I hope, in a deliberately 'complementary', or postmodern manner.

Hurston's ability to cross over, to translate, discomforts even a Black feminist critic. In her introduction to I *love myself when I am laughing*, Mary Helen Washington asks: 'How did this celebrant of black folk culture become, in later years, a right-wing Republican, publicly supporting a staunch segregation decision?' (Washington, 1979, p. 9). Washington clearly wishes to believe in the solidity of a 'Black woman' but is surely wrong to feel that Hurston's foxiness is a late imposition on an otherwise blameless feminist career. We might agree with Washington that Hurston is denying the *political* message of Black language and hence the social mediations that must necessarily shape folk literature. Or it might be better to listen to Hurston herself. In a passage describing her hero Moses, Hurston writes, 'He had crossed over, he felt as empty as a post hole for he was none of the things he once had been. He was a man sitting on a rock. He had crossed over'. (Hurston, 1978, p. 194). Hurston's Moses is able to win power because he can blur together linguistic elements which had previously been held apart. The elders of the tribes of Israel 'done took notice' that 'Moses is getting so he talks our language just like we talk it ourselves'. What is significant is that Moses functions as a generalised metaphor for translation – demonstrating that linguistic power comes from an ability to combine an uncertain background with the acquisition of high caste Egyptian rhetoric. Similarly, in *Jonah's gourd vine*, John Pearson is stigmatised by miscenegation and lacks formal education yet has the power of spiritual tongues.

Dust tracks on a road goes further: 'The Light came to me when I realised that I did not have to consider any racial group as a whole. God made them duck by duck and that was the only way I could see them' (Hurston, 1984, p. 235). It is Hurston's delight in a concept of a *constructed* Blackness rather than a genetic race which gives her the strength to translate a complex Black language full of slang, inherited codes and expressive metaphors. Hurston claimed an identity in the Black community as its self appointed cultural translator. 'But they told stories enough for a volume by itself ... An't Hagar's son, like Joseph, put on his many-coloured coat and paraded before his brethren and every man there was a Joseph' (Hurston, 1978, p. 21). The use of biblical rhetoric has been a common resource for many Black writers. But Hurston does not stay within the limitations of an inherited tradition. This is not the language of a typical Black *informant*. By moving from Black to Hebrew to white styles of speech Hurston gives a linguistic freedom to her subjects. They are not objectified Others in a limited Black space. In her folklore field notes, Hurston explains how Black people, with no access to the written word created their own linguistic routines. She dramatises the predicament of people caught between understanding the complexities of white speech and yet needing to reject its simple Black stereotypes. Hurston describes the figurative operations at work in folklore with its use of verbal nouns such as 'looking', intensified descriptions such as 'kill-dead' and action nouns such as 'sitting chair' (see Hurston, 1976). She explains that the Black preference for dramatic and visual language stems from an ability to think in hieroglyphics. Through this strategic description of the metaphoric heart of folklore Hurston establishes the linguistic inventiveness of rural Blacks as a complex 'theory'. As Barbara Christian points out, 'my folk, in other words, have always been a race of theory – though more in the form of the hieroglyph, a written figure which is both sensual and abstract, both beautiful and communicative' (Christian, 1989, p. 226). As such, Black language makes full use of metaphor in a system of cultural cognition. The vividness of the language is heard in Big Sweet's compact with Hurston. 'Do your fighting for you. Nobody better not start nothing with you, do I'll get my switch-blade and go round de ham-bone looking for meat'

(Hurston, 1984, p. 188). Big Sweet dramatises the relationships between women and sexual and linguistic power, just as Hurston learns from Big Sweet to gorge us with sexual innuendos.

Here is La Malincha.
Peter Martyr D'Anghera calls her:

Marina of Painalla, an Aztec girl whose mother had some years previously sold her to some Indians of Xicalango in order to secure the girl's inheritance to a son by her second husband. Marina was taken to Tabasco and finally fell to the share of Portocarro when the female booty was divided among the Spaniards. (D'Anghera, 1912, p. 359)

Aguilar has it that 'she was given the name Marina in Christian baptism' (de Fuento, 1963, p. 237). Today Mexicans use the term *Malinchismo* derogatively to mean an abject preference for foreigners or things foreign since the Spanish conquest was made possible partly through the mediations of a translator — La Malincha. In Hispanic literature her name has become a symbol of betrayal, a voice who spoke for Cortes rather than for the Indian nations.[7]

That two disparate and chronologically distant women translators should be similarly attacked should not surprise us. Nicole Ward Jouve tells: 'When you translate the absolute status of nouns, the "Name-of-the-Father", is shaken. Exchanges between words are no longer 'full', that is, guaranteed by the law of the Father, the law of significance' (Ward Jouve, 1986, p. 45). Andres de Tapia described La Malincha's linguistic skills in similar terms:

The Indian women referred to is Malincha, who became Cortes's mistress and the mother of his bastard son Martin Cortes. Her native tongue was Nahuatl, but in Tabasco she learned the Maya language. She and Jeronimo de Aguilar communicated in Maya, which he translated into Spanish for Cortes. In addition to her charms and linguistic abilities, Malincha possessed a shrewdness that helped the Spaniards in many a knotty situation. (de Fuento, 1963, p. 215)

D'Anghera has it alternatively:

Knowing the language of the coast tribes which resemble that of Yucatan, she was able to communicate with Aguilar; Aztec was her mother tongue, and when the envoys from Montezuma appeared, it was speedily discovered that only through Marina could Cortes negotiate intelligibly with the Mexicans. Marina was thereupon promoted to the commander's tent, where she remained during the entire Conquest, her importance daily increasing. (D'Anghera, 1912, p. 35)

Bernardino de Sahagun prepared a substantive account of this period since called The Florentine codex in which he categorised Indian culture using the paintings (codices) of native informants. The Codex reveals dramatic evidence of La Malincha's skill: 'Later addressing the rulers of all the cities about their gold. Then Marina spoke to him: "The Captain (Cortés) saith, Is this all? The Captain saith, Ye will find all two hundred pieces of gold". She measured off the size with her hands; her hands described a circle' (de Sahagun, 1982, p. 122).

Both La Malincha and Zora Neale Hurston created narratives which were composed during performances. Such narratives are subject to continuous composition and enabled La Malincha to create rituals where Indians could 'speak' homage to Cortés and enabled Hurston to depict characters who have stepped beyond the law of the Father, beyond linearity, with its claims to evolutionary progress and its devaluation of 'women's time'. As Jack Goody points out, in The interface between the written and the oral, his study of oral and literate cultures in West Africa, typically oral cultures fudge time. 'Only literate societies have to wrest the month away from the moon' and introduce the concept of era and the tool of chronology (Goody, 1987, p. 132). Translation makes a critical break with conventional ideas about history, and history's narrative conventions. One of the greatest messages in For their eyes were watching God centres on Janie's ability to subvert patriarchal time with 'women's time', as she predicts in the opening of the novel: '"Now, women, forget all those things they don't want to remember, and remember everything they don't want to forget. The dream is the truth. Then they act and do things accordingly' (Hurston, 1986, p. 9).

Janie gives her past a special reconstructed present tense allowing time in the novel to be more fluid. Or, as Julia Kristeva in 'Women's time' forcibly argues, 'female subjectivity would seem to provide a specific measure that essentially retains repetition and eternity from among the multiple modalities of time' (Kristeva, 1982, p. 34). In her recovery of folk tales Hurston chooses to position the key times of her women characters as performances which occur outside of economic relations. Being 'out of time' depends on narrative dexterity. The 'work' of storytelling replaces the work of farm labouring and rural production. Similarly, storytellers are placed in drinking 'jukes' outside of the fixed time of diurnity.

When Hurston first began collecting her stories in 1927 not a single American university possessed a department of folklore. Franz Boas's enlightened accounts of cultural relativism, Primitive arts and Primitive

religion, appeared only in 1927 and 1937 respectively. As a student of
Boas, Hurston was encouraged to make a close study of myths, songs,
oral traditions and the psychic understanding peoples may have of
their culture as well as of the more conventional artifacts and rituals.
But she did not embrace Boas's mode of 'rescue' or 'redemption'.
Hurston refuses the typical stance of the recorder of a vanishing race.
She recognised that the value of Black folklore and its vast web of
spirituals, sermons and folk tales lay in its difference from a white
aesthetic. Hurston was 'fired' by her belief that Black oral culture was
soaked in the passionate consciousness of oppression and spiritual
animism not the exotic primitivism claimed by white devotees of
Harlem.

In 1931 Hurston published her account of Hoodoo in The journal of
American folklore and was given almost the entire issue to develop what,
in effect, was the first important representation of 'conjure' and
Hoodoo myths.[8] Such work obviously heightened her consciousness
of how narrative could be a moment caught between two cultures and
two periods. On the one hand her stories are a careful account of Black
history, on the other they give us often violent descriptions of mythical
powers for a Black future:

> The Queen of Sheba was an Ethiopian just like Jethro, with power unequal
> to man. She didn't have to deny herself to give gold to Solomon. She had
> gold-making words ... so she made Solomon wise and gave him her talking
> ring. And Solomon built a room with a secret door and everyday he shut
> himself inside and listened to his ring. So he (my emphasis) wrote down the
> ring-talk in books. (Hurston, 1978, p. 195)

Like La Malincha, Hurston shows us how men will inevitably try
to appropriate translation in 'books' or in battles. Of course we must
remember that the division between literature and orality is never a
question of a simple binary shift. The very existence of writing leads
to the creation of oral stories which would not be possible in a purely
oral culture. Hurston's Eatonville had its school-house and if the Incas
relied on a mnemonic of knotted cords (quipu) the Mayans had a
complex system of glyphs. Yet La Malinche escaped her slavery among
the Mayan-speaking peoples by learning to translate. Similarly Janie,
in For their eyes were watching God creates multiple stories which gradually
displace the 'slavery' of her three marriages.

After talking her husband to death, Janie returns to her community,
bearing seeds like Demeter, in a conscious metaphor of women's

creativity. 'Translating' herself from marriage to marriage Janie offers her story, in friendship, to another woman as the place in which sex-roles are parodied and appropriated. 'The light in her hand was like a spark of sun-stuff washing her face in fire. Her shadow behind fell black and headlong down the stairs. Now, in her room, the place tasted fresh again'(Hurston, 1986, p. 285). References to taste and smell are very rare in ethnography. Hurston, here in her fiction, *and* in her ethnography, refuses the predominant metaphors of transcription in favour of sensual environmental sensations.

If one close tie between Hurston and La Malincha is their pivotal position between, for Hurston, white bourgeoisie/Black culture and, for La Malinche, Spanish aristocrats/Indian culture, another is their dependence on male figures. Men occupy an ambiguous position in Hurston's narratives seeming to be respected heroes, for example Moses, yet men's patriarchal families are never signs of order. Certainly La Malincha's acceptability within the Spanish force depended on her ability to negotiate the class boundary of Spanish lineage. As an Indian aristocrat she could fit congenially into a Spanish hierarchy, just as much later, the claim of family lineage to Pocahontas signifies historical status for many Americans.

Hurston ridicules the 'white ancestor hounds' in Dust tracks on a road 'who rushed down the coast and descended from Pocahontas. From the number of her children, one is forced to the conclusion that Pocahontas wasn't so poky after all' (Hurston, 1984, p. 202). One could argue that for all their radical form, Hurston's texts *are* conservative because they rely on, and even admire, past or contemporary male figures such as Herod and her own white patrons. 'I had one person who pleased me always. That was the robust, grey-haired white man who had helped me get into the world. He was always making me tell him things about my doings, and then he would tell me what to do about things' (Hurston, 1984, p. 40). Again, when the anthropologist Boas offered a taxonomy for Hurston's ethnography she thought him 'the greatest anthropologist alive' and 'king of kings'.

Bernal Diaz in his chronicle of the Spanish Conquest describes La Malincha as a woman of remarkable beauty and superior character who called Cortés 'her King of Kings'. Yet, in seeking to translate for men La Malincha and Hurston look as well for the experience of *active appropriation. The Florentine codex* unwittingly, but very graphically, depicts La Malincha as twice Cortés's size. And it is Hurston's apparent conservatism – her use of the conservative trope – the aristocratic figure – which places Black speech inside of legitimacy.

Hurston works to reclaim Moses for African folklore and conjure. He is depicted as an authoritative and protective patriarch invested with compelling sexuality. All Hurston's fictions embody notions about masculinity which give men like Moses, Herod and John Pearson in *Jonah's gourd vine* the mark of incestuous desire. *Jonah's gourd vine* makes a sustained account of the theme of incest. John Pearson is a fictional recreation of Hurston's Papa whose sexual prowess she describes exuberantly in her autobiography. Fiction provided Hurston with a safe space for the dramatic enactment of the enchantment of her incestuous longing and a means to stay its seduction. In *Jonah's gourd vine* Hurston portrays John Pearson's duplicity – a minister of the Church who is a persistent adulterer – as an understandable battle between Christianity and Afro-American manhood. Yet, as Hortense J. Spillers argues in her subtle analysis of incest motifs in the writing of Alice Walker and Ralph Ellison, 'we might tentatively look at the situation this way: moments of African-American fiction show Father-Daughter incest or its surrogate motions as an absence, not an overdetermination' (Spillers, 1989, p. 49). Hurston embraces her desire in order to cancel out the Father's power. John Pearson, like his successor Moses, must discover, and humbly learn, his limits.

It is interesting to note that, according to Bernal Diaz, Cortes's dependence on La Malincha earned him her name from the Aztecs: 'He was given this name because Dona Marina, our interpreter, was always in his company, especially when ambassadors arrived and during talks with chiefs, so they called Cortes "the captain of Marina" in their language, or "Malincha" for short' (Diaz, 1956, p. 116). But what makes Hurston's or La Malincha's enormous effort to reorganise language from a woman's viewpoint valid and effective? If the actions of La Malincha and the texts of Hurston appear to rely on male eschatology, they take a shifty and invidious path through masculine taxonomies. For example, Hurston's characters are not defined primarily by their motives, that is to say psychologically, but syntactically according to their verbal reflexivity. They learn how to manipulate language only by constant negotiation. 'The words do not count ... the tune is the unity of the thing' (Hurston, 1984, p. 197).

In *Mules and men* the stories are told directly apparently at random without classification and the text's structure derives from each character's free association with another not from an intervening narrator. The effect is almost 'Bakhtinian' with the characters coming forward like so many authors 'as subjects vested with full rights' (Bakhtin, 1984, p. 103). Hurston narrates in different identities, abruptly shifting pronoun from first to third person and the referents which they identify. It is the narrator not the characters who suffers ambivalence. Significantly Black women's invective has more authority, has 'full rights', than the more conventional male folk humour. 'Strong stories of Ella Wall, East Coast Mary, Planchita and lesser jook lights around whom the glory of Polk County surged' share an equal space with well known ballads like 'John Henry' (Hurston, 1987, p. 62). Indeed Hurston intervenes much less in these moments dramatising in full the stories of her female characters without the disturbing effect of authorial footnotes which do appear as comments on Black male 'bookooing' and 'woofing' and male sexual innuendos. Hurston makes another bold stroke by discovering Black rural life through the words of women not, as traditionally, through the words of elders. In oral societies, by and large, there are two recognised forms of knowledge. One is the codified knowledge passed down by the elders of a tribe while the other is the more creative language of inspiration, of hysteria and female Shamanism.

Hurston transforms the Black-woman-as-object into Black women subjects. In For their eyes were watching God, Hurston liberates Janie from an intervening narrator. The liberation is registered by a shift in epistemological control when Janie controls the subject matter of her own past and present experience. The impact of her interior monologues, her dreams and unconventional metaphors performs its enchantment on her readers as much as on Phoeby. Janie is free from the oral disability imposed by traditional realism and might become free, Hurston hints, from the 'disability' of heterosexuality. What Hurston radically demonstrates is that the question of a Black woman's identity is part of the specific linguistic situation in which she might find herself. It is Hurston's rapid changes of pronoun and referent and Janie's acquisition of rhetorical skill which enact the acquisition of self-identity. This is why Hurston continued to record the oral transmission of Black folk tales when American publishers valued the literary. Obviously to record, and then to translate, rather than to fictionalise makes the teller of the tale an indispensable part of the telling. Similarly, by retaining some control over the manner of telling, Black women render their status more secure.

Mules and men and For their eyes were watching God refuse eternalised Others and homogeneous Black figures in order to actively refuse the monologic simplicity of ethnographic narratives. Hurston's intimacy with Black women may be an obtained effect, but the self-denigrating 'Hurston' fully dramatises the dialogic quality of Black women's lives. Before this is dismissed as a too easy generalised romance of female friendship we must see it wedded to what Hurston calls elsewhere 'a restrained ferocity in everything. There is a tense ferocity beneath the casual exterior that stirs the onlooker to hysteria' (Hemenway, 1977, p. 114). Hurston's 'ferocity' comes with the conjuring of Hoodoo. This gave her the confidence to privilege magic and myth. Some Hoodoo doctors, like Mother Catharine, celebrated a woman-centred holism. 'Mother Catharine's religion is matriarchal. Only God and the mother count. Childbirth is the most important element in her creed' (Hurston, 1986b, p. 56). Hurston dedicated her life to Marie Leveau the goddess of Hoodoo and, in New Orleans, studied with Kitty Brown and Eulalia because these mambas 'specialised in Man-and-Woman cases' (Hurston, 1978, p. 197). Hoodoo offered Hurston narrative symbols which helped her to subvert realism.

La Malincha represents the same alien rupture in the discourse of the Spanish Conquest. Columbus, Todorov tells us, perceived names only when they could be identified with things. Proper names served only for denotation, and not directly for human communication. So, for example, Columbus named the first islands he found for God, the second for princes and only gave the names of appearance to subsequent acquisitions. 'The entire dimension of intersubjectivity, of the reciprocal value of words (in opposition to their denotative capacity) of the human and arbitrary character of signs, escapes him' (Todorov, 1984, p. 29). If we compare the letters of Cortés we find the same disparity. After the seige of Tacuba Cortés carefully itemises arms, soldiers and field pieces while ignoring the Spanish women who fought alongside their men and nursed them. When travelling on the road, were found 'many loads of maize and roasted children' (de Fuento, 1963, p. 107). Cortés's mode of narration can find no adequate vocabulary to express such a surreal moment. D'Anghera reminds us of La Malincha's more interactive relation to a natural environment. As a 'native' the pages on which she wrote 'are made of the thin bark of trees of the quality found in the first, outer layer' (D'Anghera, 1912, p. 40). This is a form of graphics known in anthropology as 'tutorial Shamanism' which often draws pictographs on birch-bark scrolls to act as prompts and mnemonics in story-telling (see Goody, 1987).

The rural mnemonic is the means by which Hurston, too, arrives in a natural world. But where the conventional ethnographer uses a version of 'natural history', the Black storytellers in Mules and men operate language as if it were a natural object – figurative expressions are taken from the natural world as in 'plough up some literary'. Before such an account of two diverse women begins to seem overdetermined let me demonstrate what I mean by a closer reading of a single textual moment:

There was a lot of horn-honking outside and I went to the door. The crowd drew up under the mothering camphor tree in four old cars. Everybody in boisterous spirits.
'Come on, Zora! Le's go to Wood Bridge. Great toe-party goin' on. All kinds of 'freshments. We kin tell you some lies most any ole time. We never run outer lies and lovin'. Tell 'em tomorrow night. Come on if you comin' – le's go if you gwine.'
So I loaded up my car with neighbors and we all went to Wood Bridge. It is a Negro community joining Maitland on the north as Eatonville does on the west, but no enterprising souls have every organized it. They have no school-house, no post office, no mayor. It is lacking in Eatonville's feeling of unity. In fact a white woman lives there. While we rolled along Florida No. 3, I asked Armetta where was the shindig going to be. (Hurston, 1978, p. 15).

The language appears too explicit to require much analytical effort yet the scene is a beautiful miniature of Hurston's subtle signification. 'Zora' is a dramatised narrator who can both translate Black speech as an intact spatial unit and slide into conventional anthropology with her catalogue of 'no schoolhouse, no post office'. Although the difference of Black culture is clearly addressed it is not distanced in narrated 'asides'. Yet neither is the narrator 'Zora' artificially minimised. For example, Hurston adopts the immediacy of apparent note-taking, 'Everybody in boisterous spirits'. She does not suppress the possibility of multiple viewpoints and simultaneous perspectives. Hurston uses many different occasions, from 'toe-parties' to 'jooks', to represent the experiences, the plurivocalism of Black culture like La Malincha's multiple languages.

Black syntax is made comprehensible but it is not objectified as 'evidence' of Otherness since the narrator is equally 'boisterous'. Hurston signals to the reader that political lines will be drawn since she describes how a white woman creates disunity, but lulls her reader into accepting them. And it is significant that we begin from a maternal metaphor of the 'mothering camphor tree'.

One major feature of Hurston's community as it emerges in her writing, is its unique oral culture. The community voice acts as a major strategy in Hurston's writing because it is a means of empowering women. Mathilda in *Mules and men* and Big Sweet in *Dust tracks on a road* are not so much *observed* with men in the public space. Instead Hurston makes a direct correlation between a woman's *linguistic* power and her sexual politics. Big Sweet verbally lashes her male co-worker with vicious epithets and derogatory abuse. The episode substitutes an illiterate, but linguistically competent, Black woman for the author and substitutes a collective Black dialect for a distanced American/English. The power of the communal voice refuses the isolation of the signifier 'heroine' against an exotic background of motley Blacks. Neither does the narrative privilege an active masculinity. The expansive and volatile Big Sweet undercuts the psychoanalytic casuistry which is so often woman's narrative lot, in favour of an astonishing verbal dexterity, just as she is prepared to engage with men in physical as well as verbal battle with her flick knives and steel. Similarly, in *For their eyes were watching God*, Janie's life is *empirically* unverifiable but offers a considerable version of the effect of Black women's veracity. The novel is a disquisition on the efficacy of language to bring about change on the scale that Southern racism and sexism would demand. Of the forms of social narrative which are delimiting Hurston pinpoints several: Janie's Nanny, as we have seen, models the story of slavery; Janie's second husband Joe's 'big voice' merely replicates white patriarchy. Hurston underlines Janie's need to find a language beyond delimitation and beyond mimicry by allowing Janie to forge her own account of Black womanhood.

It is a technique coming somewhere between ethnography and personal diary and it is very typical of Hurston's oeuvre. Reviewers in the Harlem Renaissance often demanded the 'whole truth' about the Negro ignoring Hurston's subtlety in preferring process over content. Hurston must have seemed wilfully double-edged. It was because, as she wrote to Carl Van Vechten on Thanksgiving Day in 1934, writing 'must be done by individuals feeling the materials as well as seeing it objectively. In order to feel it and appreciate the nuances one must be of the group' (Hemenway, 1977, p. 207).

What does this rhetoric signify? Let us say that it is a deliberately stylised disarticulation of coloniser language from the perspective of the colonised Black woman. Alice Walker responded empathetically to Hurston's feminist aesthetic: 'Dr. Benton said: "She was so intelligent!

And really had perfect expressions. Her English was beautiful" I suspect this is a clever way to let me know Zora herself didn't speak in the "black English" her characters used' (Walker, 1979, p. 310).[9]

It is rare indeed in earlier oral history to find stories *about* women told *by* women *to* women. In the Thirties the Federal Writers Project began what developed into a major collection of Black oral narratives, of first person accounts of slavery.[10] But though, with women's greater longevity, most ex-slave 'informants' *were* women, their FWP 'interviewers' were a random mixture of men and women and were not, necessarily, Black, working class or Southern (see Botkin, 1945). Hurston was 'of the group'. The ethnography of *Mules and men* reveals Hurston's conscious and unconscious collaboration with a multiple and collective women's world admitting to the complexities of Black adjustments. Unlike other twentieth century ethnographies, for example Laurens van der Post's *The lost world of the Kalahari*, Hurston refuses to praise in Black women characteristics of passivity, anti-materialism or cheerful, willing 'hands'. Hurston makes her heroines experience her own learning process in establishing themselves as storytellers. It is important to note in this context that Janie identifies storytelling as the means by which she can survive only *after* she identifies sexism as if feminism was an important part of linguistic skill.

It is also significant that Janie tells her story in Phoeby's domestic orbit. The domestic is a major trope. The most famous and often quoted passage from *For their eyes were watching God* is the one in which Hurston represents Janie's conscious and unconscious mind as a cupboard of shelved dishes crashing to the floor. As a discursive strategy the domestic functions as a textual sleight of hand, which is inherently subversive because it startles the reader with a metonymic referent for interior thought from an area not usually found in the language of psychoanalysis. The domestic metaphor of the cupboard or the domestic space of Phoeby's verandah is a springboard from which female imagery jumps into literature. Significantly, Hurston refuses protection from men in Polk County but, as we have seen, chooses Big Sweet 'to put her foot on a person'. As her landlady points out 'tain't a man, woman nor child on this job, going to tackle Big Sweet' (Hurston, 1984, p. 157). And Hurston's claim to sisterhood is on the grounds of a shared and strong identity: 'You sho is crazy! ... I gave her one of my bracelets. After that everything went well for me' (Hurston, 1984, p. 188).

There is, even so, a problem with this advocacy of translation as a potentially feminist aesthetic. Wilson Harris, for example, claims that such unconscious synchronicity is the'womb of all cultural space' (See Harris, 1983). To return to my beginning, what is problematic is that its narrative features – a use of self referential devices, making the process of writing part of the content – are now common, for example in postmodernist writing by men as well as by women. Yet I would argue that Hurston's 'collisional montage' (to use a postmodernist term now much in vogue) – the personal diary married to specific incantations – validates very well the perceptions and languages of independent women. I hope too that my intertext between the voices of La Malincha and Hurston creates a similar montage so that feminist criticism might open up the boundary of literary history.

In *Mules and men* the strength of a woman's tongue may be 'all de weapon a woman got' yet storytelling in Eatonville is a radical venting of sexual antagonism. It was a power that Hurston learned from her mother: 'Mama exhorted her children at every opportunity to "jump at de sun". We might not land on the sun, but at least we could get off the ground. Papa did not feel so hopeful' (Hurston, 1984, p. 20).

The activity of translation is a chance of entry, engaging with and contesting the narratives of our social world. Translating enables women to decode a repressive ideology and tropologically investigate the function of language as a colonising/sexist practice. Only by juxtaposing the implicit contrasts that inhere in the process of translating can we separate writing practices and connect them discursively in order to call into crisis the patriarchal codes they contain.

A final coda:

Towards the end of her career Zora Neale Hurston hoped to discover an ancient Mayan city. She felt that as a Mestizo herself, 'I am getting hold of some signs and symbols through the advantage of blood' (Hemenway, 1977, p. 305). Working on this project from 1945 to 1948 Hurston visited Central America and applied for a Guggenheim grant so that she could 'translate' her discovery of an unknown group of people into a cultural moment' as important intellectually as the finding of the tomb of Tutankarkam'.

She wrote her Guggenheim proposal while living in a small town on the coast of Honduras.

The town was called Puerto Cortés.

Going through the green channel: Margaret Atwood and body boundaries

The history of the female body is a statute of limitations bounded by our fear of pregnancy, of rape and of loss of femininity. Women's bodies are shaped by the boundaries of male stereotypes and they are coded by the rules of fashion and by social expectations. Our bodies are frequently further divided into bounded erogenous zones. There is a long and deep rooted tradition, as the anthropologists Sherry Ortner and Gayle Rubin argue, which identifies women with the body and nature, opposed to the identification of men with culture. While biology is never static but interacts with psychic and social factors, the idea that a woman's body should have 'finite' limits was most fully and forcibly expressed in Victorian Britain. In the nineteenth century tight laced bodices disciplined and deformed the bodies of Victorian women. Such clothing signalled to Victorian society the submissive roles that middle class women were expected to perform and ensured the continuation of 'feminine' behaviour by constricting women's bodies and physical movement. The Victorian era, as Sally Shuttleworth argues, witnessed an unprecedented medical regulation of female reproduction (see Shuttleworth, 1990).

Feminism has long struggled with society's dualistic control of gendered bodies in campaigns associated with birth control, abortion and body images. The materiality of women's bodies and the provision of a space in which to discuss them outside of patriarchal representations has become even more urgent with increasing sexual violence. While it might be true that social institutions contribute to the regulation of all bodies, male and female, most institutions, particularly hospitals, schools and the courts are not neutral with respect to gender. They force women to perform in different ways from men. The contemporary preoccupation with fashion and appearance affects women far more powerfully than men. And it may be, as American psychologists and philosophers such as Jean Baker Miller, Nancy Chodorow and Carol Gilligan claim, that women do have a radically different 'bodily' ethics from that of men.

Outside urban society, women's bodies, as Annette Kolodny has described with reference to frontier narratives, become metaphors for land; or women's bodies are taken to be signs of moral or social disease, for example the scarred body of Lucy in *Dracula*. Similar fears produce in the twentieth century, massive and multiple technologies of reproduction to ensure the constant monitoring and control of woman's biology. Metaphors from banking, management and masculine bureaucracy abound in contemporary science and in its huge material investment in the medicalisation of the body (see Jacobus, 1990). Woman's body is disciplined and segregated, coded and appropriated by science whose rhetoric merely serves as a summary of fears and contradictions in contemporary society.

Paradoxically, women often rupture these boundaries of objectification by a mirrored reversal of such body identities. Over time, this resistance has taken many positive forms, including celibacy, hysteria and anorexia. By such means women can become, in Michele Jamal's terms, 'shape shifters' or Shamans of their own bodies by changing body language as part of a move to a more 'feminist' identity (Jamal, 1987). Hence, currently, feminist theory is awash with analyses of science, anthropology, language and literature, looking for compensatory discourses of women's bodies. In contemporary feminist theory the biological body is celebrated as much as it was mourned.

Yet although feminist theory has undertaken many analyses it has not, as yet, created a language which can demystify the cultural rhetoric of femininity. It is in feminist fiction, particularly in the writings of Margaret Atwood, that new accounts of the female body, and its potential cultural representations, amount to a feminist rewriting of culture. Of course it would be invidious to claim that Margaret Atwood is writing only, or even in the main, about women's bodies. In her work she explores a wide range of cultural myths about nationalism, political power and gender identity. She is interested in a range of philosophies, including Sufism (*The handmaid's tale*), existentialism, and Greek mythology. She explores a wide range of literary forms including Gothic romances. Utopian fiction and poetry. And she is a major literary critic. Atwood has also written in a variety of styles, mixing pastiches of women's magazines, 'annotated' texts, fairy tales and direct narrative. And Atwood is acutely aware of the contradictory meanings in literature. The main place where myths and male and female points of view conflict explicitly is in her fiction. Like all fiction, Atwood's novels can be read on many levels, for example Surfacing is both a detective novel and a ghost story. Yet Atwood's novels have strong didactic feminist elements one of which is her concrete, material analysis of the female body.

Atwood's suggestions as to how women's bodies may be viewed as objects of power and particularly objects of resistance is a crucial element in her work. What Atwood specifies in many novels and poems is the way in which female bodies entail a different form of oppression and create different forms of resistance to the bodies of men. Margaret Atwood describes the sexed particularity of the female body in culture and she constructs a new and feminist corporeality.

How a writer writes across the border of representation in order to depict a female physique without suffering an intractable 'return to nature' is the question which Margaret Atwood answers so vividly in The edible woman, Surfacing, Bodily harm, her poems and criticism. Her writing turns between the poles of specularity and anorexia scored by the chromatics of hysteria, all of which evoke 'shamanistic' motifs of biology and of power in the natural world. Atwood is very conscious that the grammar of women's and men's bodies, like the operations of literary meaning making, entails sets of expectations based on rules and on types. To read body language is similar to reading or deconstructing literature. Both bodies and books rely on structures and boundaries of implicit meanings. Atwood writes about the gap between women's bodies and the language used by culture to describe them not as simple difference but as an example of the political boundary between 'woman' and her choice of representation. I will be pursuing in chapter six the anthropologist Mary Douglas's insight that the limit of the body is never merely physical but symbolically reproduces social fears. Suffice it to say here that Douglas agrees with Atwood that the boundaries of a woman's body represent the limits of social power.

Margaret Atwood's writing then leads us straight to the key question of feminist criticism: What assignations of nature and espousal of the body can women's writing make without risking the old binary division of nature/culture?

The critical theory most obsessed with the politics of the body is postmodernism. Postmodernism focuses for the most part on the interplay between discourses of power and physical representations.

Following Baudrillard, postmodernism stages the body as the site where politics control subjectivity, where health and reproduction are manipulated by the complex biotechnology of late capitalism. Epistemologically, the body is at the centre of a grisly and false sense of subjectivity. (see Kroker, 1988, p. 21).[1]

The experience of body politics, for men as well as for women, emanates from a confrontation between subjectivity and definitions of gender in relation to the 'natural'. The identities of Atwood's women, in particular the protagonist of Surfacing, are determined by their ability to work with the raw material of nature against the destructive intensity of hunters and despoilers. And yet Atwood avoids the disgrace of nature and its exclusion from the sphere of the social. Atwood parodies cultural definitions of the natural, for example by humorously deflating Ainsley's holism and Lucy's femininity in The edible woman while at the same time associating women, specifically mothers, with the eventfulness of the natural world in recurrent images of amoebae and fetuses. Atwood's writing does more than earnestly evacuate the natural 'Other'. It simultaneously challenges the terms of body politics and intervenes within them to articulate a feminist account of female identity. Atwood's women do not dissolve their civilised identities when faced with the wilderness but dissolve the value of a metaphysical Western identity altogether.

By the 1940s and 1950s Canadian literature became an identifiable field of study in its own right. Canadian literary nationalism is best defined by a consistent attention to the wilderness. Nature enjoys a long tradition of privilege in Canadian writing but it has a complicated dialectic. Nature is both integrally part of a Canadian landscape of national identity and also a quite distinguishable source of individual identity. The critic Northrop Frye, Atwood's university tutor, set out in his writings to define the parameters of a new national literature for Canada in the 1960s. Frye recognised that the value of Canadian poetry lay in its glorious dramatisation of myth and 'primal' nature. Indeed Frye's central metaphors were often drawn from biology, for example the title of his major book is Anatomy of criticism (1967). It was Frye's criticism that encouraged Atwood to underpin her accounts of women's experience with Native American myths and an imagery of landscape. In a larger sense, Frye's examples enabled Atwood to endow the feminine and the wilderness with images of intelligence and strength rather than with images from romanticism.

This is the central argument of The edible woman and of Surfacing. These are two narratives which have female heroines who, at the beginning, are unable to adequately represent their own or other people's bodies. For both women marginality has become a condition of their being. Marian MacAlpin, of The edible woman, is a market researcher whose work floor at Seymour Surveys lies, emblematically, between the upper (male) executive suite and the lower (male) machine rooms. Marian's job is equally emblematic of gender difference. Like many women, Marian services capitalism from her positional aporia by translating questions designed by the male psychologists of Seymour Surveys into everyday and comprehensible language.

Atwood shows a woman torn between unconscious feminist questions and the stereotypical answers which society often provides. Marian is an independent professional graduate but the body discourse of opportunity which a pre-feminist Toronto offers her is that of marriage and maternity. Marian's visit to her friend Clara, who is expecting a third and unwanted child, provides a dramatic opening to The edible woman's precise articulation of body politics. The date – Labour Day weekend – metaphorically draws the anatomy of Marian's tension and the vocation she will need to reject. Ainsley, Marian's roommate, has also chosen maternity, albeit a more up to date, if equally limiting task, of bearing a fatherless super-baby. The competing imperatives of family life and single parenthood bring on the onset of Marian's anorexia. With obvious intent, Marian's anorexia emerges at the point when she rejects her fiancée Peter while they eat steak together in a restaurant. The maternal iconography of the cow which presents itself in Marian's mind forces her to a diet of salads. In The madwoman in the attic, Sandra Gilbert and Susan Gubar describe a very similar scene in Castle Rackrent, whose heroine is forced to eat pork and sausages, as 'metaphorical rape' (see Gilbert and Gubar, 1979, p. 149).

The themes of The edible woman are developed metaphorically and have to do with the connection between male violence, cannibalism and hunting. Meat has begun to signify to Marian the grotesqueries of marriage and masculinity. The difference between the men and the women in the novel is that while the women may be limited by their romantic ideas of femininity, the men enact very openly their fantasies of violence and weaponry in the pursuit of women. Peter, an apparently average and financially successful middle class male, has a collection of aggressive armaments – guns and cameras. Like Sylvia Plath's The bell jar, which The edible woman resembles both in its plot and choice of metaphors, the heroine's psychic boundaries are symbolised by food which stands for the female body as the object of masculine aggression and attempted cannibalism by marriage.

The escape from Peter during the evening of their engagement party is all the more striking by its contrast to this atomisation. Marian is helped by Duncan who is her anorexic double. Like Marian, Duncan contests the gender categories open to him and prefers his directionless, childlike, surreal existence as a graduate student in English literature to a bourgeois masculinity. In the episodes structured around Duncan and his roommates, again centring on meals, Atwood dramatises the dysfunction of heterosexuality by highlighting the exchange value of food. Finally the novel returns to Marian's point of view and her now conscious rejection of circumscribed stereotypes. Marian bakes an enormous pink cake, cast in the form of an 'intricate baroque' woman. When Peter, in horror, refuses to eat, Marian gorges in a triumphant cannibalism of the female stereotype.

Femininity then, has a vocabulary of repression, of stereotype and of victimisation. Social representations of the female body do not coincide with a woman character's perception of her body and its possibilities. In fact the two are usually entirely at odds. It is this conflict which is the major feature of Atwood's novels. Hélène Cixous argues that it is in writing that the Other to femininity can be expressed: 'Writing is the passageway, the entrance, the exit, the dwelling place of the Other in me' (Clément and Cixous, 1986, p. 56).[2] It makes sense, I think, to see the development of Atwood's women characters and their dissolutive acceptance of the natural world as a move towards Cixous's theme. This move is also shaped by Atwood's desire to make her writing very accessible and her desire to make the form of her writing in itself be a metaphor of body politics. The novel Surfacing also concerns the tension between social, national and body boundaries. The protagonist of Surfacing has spent her adult life living in a marginal career on the metaphorical border of her family memories. The novel turns metaphor into metonymy when the narrator, together with her three friends, crosses the linguistic border between Ontario and Quebec 'with its sign that says BIENVENUE on one side and WELCOME on the other', in order to solve the mystery of her father's disappearance (Atwood, 1973, p. 11).

The linguistic border serves also as a boundary between culture and nature. Contrasts are set up continually in the novel between the 'natural' world of the wilderness and the unnatural 'civilised' world of urban life. Indeed the novel only begins when David the film maker,

Anna, David's wife, the narrator and Joe her lover choose to leave the 'last or first outpost' of the city to travel to the protagonist's island home or 'foreign territory'. The journey that follows has the same emblematic and enforcing symmetry. The car radio underlines the marginality of the protagonist with its dial always and equally 'between stations'. To crack the cultural code, to solve the paternal mystery, means the narrator has to make another journey across the boundary between her childhood past and her present friendships. The protagonist's cognitive mastery over the dead paternal function – finding the corpse of her father – is made possible only when she crosses the final boundary between animal species and human by acquiring the body language and pictographs of Shamanism.

Atwood links the marginalisation of women with the marginalisation of Native spirituality and opposes both to the colonial men in the novel who attempt to render women and native Americans completely silent. The fact that Atwood is criticising both the body politics of society and the patriarchal cast of narrative cannot be overemphasised. It is not surprising that these issues take shape as a contrast between masculine totems and taboos and female folk imagery. Men's misuse and women's use of nature in Surfacing is specifically gendered. American hunters string up a dead heron as a 'totem' of their acquisition of new territory. To the narrator, an illustrator of folk tales, the jay bird is the full Freudian essence of a totem because the bird stands for her re-incarnated mother.

Not surprisingly, the protagonist's sketches which she draws to illustrate the story of the King 'who learned to speak with animals and the fountain of life' got 'no further than a thing that looked like a football player' (Atwood, 1973, p. 84). Atwood interpolates this descriptive aside and others like it to illustrate her contention that it is only women, not kings nor men who can ever genuinely attend to nature.

In accounting for Atwood's extraordinary attention to the natural, Jean Baker Miller's analysis of female identity in Toward a new psychology of women provides useful propositions. In Miller's view, attributes of femininity are not biological givens but are products both of culture and of our conscious or unconscious interaction with culture.[3] Miller argues that these female attributes which so often seem to come from subordination, for example women's 'passivity' or 'caring' roles, might be transformed into more positive female characteristics in a better structured world. Miller addresses the question of essentialism

with brilliant clarity. Because a maintenance of the body and the supply
of its comforts have traditionally been the task of subordinates, that
is women, we are 'carriers' of experience that men have refused to
integrate into their lives (Miller, 1976, p. 23). So that while the
repression process is the 'arena' between the two goals of sexual
difference, it is also a space where women have won some survival
skills. Techniques of affiliation learnt from our servicing roles are not
symptoms of repression, Miller suggests, but are skills and strengths
'learnt in imprisonment' which can help us subvert patriarchal
boundaries.

Traditionally it is women who are assigned to those realms of life
concerned with the natural world, for example in maternity or in the
preparation of food. But since no one grows without experience of
these kinds of sustenance, women have a different, and much greater
understanding of growth enhancing functions. The implications for
literature of Miller's revision of female psychology are staggering. Her
nascent redefinition of female passivity as a form of practical power
contains the undeveloped germ of a radical feminism. That Atwood
is familiar with these ideas is indicated both by her choice of themes
and by her vocabulary. In each novel Atwood undertakes a reassessment of the stable signifiers of female identity by inventing narrative
strategies, especially those involving natural imagery, that begin to
transcend the boundaries of women's anatomical expression.

To celebrate as uniquely female powers such activities as the
mother's conversations with birds, without perpetuating female
stereotypes, involves Atwood in efforts to represent her women
characters in alternative signifiers of mother/daughter dyads and to
give them women's memory and women's time. The end of *The edible
woman* illustrates Miller's contention that women's actions cannot be
defined as activity in the masculine sense of the term because women
often avoid direct expressions of physical power and do not make a
direct pursuit of their goals. Because Marian's cake making has
successfully destroyed the possibility of marriage with Peter, Atwood
has no qualms about giving a male the work of narrative closure.
Duncan finishes the cake and the book: '"Thank you," he said, licking
his lips. "It was delicious".' (Atwood, 1969, p. 287).

Among the narratives of femininity constructed by society, a
teleology of nature is usually given to to women. One major question
of second wave feminist theory is: 'Is female to male as nature is to
culture?'. Sherry Ortner, in her essay of the same name, argues that

women are universally considered to be secondary to men in any culture, in every country. There is an equally universal and symbolic identification of women with nature while men are universally associated with culture and its products. These two identifications are connected. It is woman's body, Ortner argues, because it is continually involved in 'species life', which places her in nature (see Ortner, 1974).[4]

One of the problems then for the feminist reader might be Atwood's invariable identification of women with nature. The protagonist of *Surfacing* is magically and immediately intimate with the daily behaviours of animals and birds and the survival routines of wilderness living, even after years of absence. She survives only by destroying 'culture' in the form of clothing (except for useful camouflage). She unproblematically prefers an animal like treatment of bodily wastes to the city's 'white zero-mouthed toilets' (Atwood, 1973, p. 117). This denial of 'civilised' routines recalls Miller's point that women's experience of the body (in patriarchy) is with its dirty or uncontrollable aspects (Miller, 1976, p. 22).

The violation of nature by an encroaching society is, for Atwood and for her women characters, paradigmatic of the violation of women by men. In *Surfacing* culture is a detritus of used beer cans despoiling the fruit and vegetable bounty of nature. By choosing nature over culture, the protagonist appears to choose negatives, refusing Anna's constructed femininity, discarding city clothing and finally retreating from cooked food and spoken language. Yet if *Surfacing* summarises these essentialist motifs, Atwood works them ambiguously testing their limits and crossing their borders. She circumvents civilised language by countering with alternative languages – Native American rock paintings and the language of dreams.

One of Atwood's most intelligent tactics for refusing a binary division of nature/culture is her use of paradox and exaggeration. The short story 'Polarities' in *Dancing girls* takes an inventive stance toward binary givens by addressing the equation woman = nature = body from the point of view of a man. The protagonist of 'Polarities' is Morrison, a chauvinistic misogynist academic who spends his time searching for girls with 'ungroomed, seedy breasts'. At the same time Morrison is uneasy in his own body and with the world. Atwood subtly hints that Morrison's denial of commitment and his choice of sexual stereotypes are ways in which he shrugs off both problematic experiences and the narratives which describe them. Finally, Morrison's attraction to a drug traumatised graduate assistant foregrounds and shatters the woman/nature/body equation because Louise is not a phallocentric sex symbol but an exaggerated image of the after effect of male rape fantasies, 'A defeated formless creature on which he could inflict himself' (Atwood, 1982, p. 73).

The same interrogation of binary opposites, the same use of exaggeration and inverted stereotypes is there too in The edible woman. Ainsley's desire for holistic motherhood is wittily deflated by being placed against the 'natural' childcare routines of Clara and Joe with 'a real nature child, he just loves to shit in the garden and wears his potty as a crash helmet' (Atwood, 1969, p. 34). Ainsley regurgitates the banal maxims of mothering magazines: '"Every woman should have at least one baby". She sounded like a voice on the radio saying that every woman should have at least one hair dryer.' (Atwood, 1969, p. 40). The parodic deflation reveals Atwood's tongue in cheek concern to dismiss an easy essentialism in favour of a more complex account of female representation.

The handmaid's tale is clear sighted on what is essentially the same issue. It is a passionate attack both on women's traditional roles and on the threat of gender stereotypes implied by essentialist feminism. In this novel women's natural function – maternity – is treated as being at the same time an aspect of feminine strength, holism and utopian possibility and also as an expression of punitative domination. The story is presented as if it was archive material in a future society. Offred, is the handmaid whose role is to breed and therefore to provide the reproductive 'natural' resources of totalitarian Gilgead. Her life is controlled by patriarchal biblical forces which form the basis of a society covering half of the United States. Offred's victimisation, which is a psychological as well as physical victimisation, is gender differentiated. Gilgead is an 'unnatural' place poisoned with radioactivity and patriarchal fanaticism. It denies women their bodily continuum by prohibiting eroticism on pain of death and outlawing pleasure. The female population has been categorised according to traditional jobs. All women are colour coded to their reproductive or non-reproductive functions.

The handmaid's tale is a powerful dystopia of body boundaries made and patrolled by patriarchal culture. Women's power is located solely in their fertility which is colonised by men. Atwood challenges this exaggerated exploitation of women by heterosexuality and thereby attacks the current faith in the nuclear family. The novel speaks to current contradictions between the 'liberated' everyday language of sexuality and the concomitant media fear of sexually transmitted diseases. Atwood's elaboration of these contradictions matches Jean Baker Miller's argument that such social contradictions are symptoms of transition. In Gilgead each woman can know alternative psychic and mythic constructions of nature and the body but only if these are embedded in individual consciousness or in the family histories of differing women or, in Offred's case, survive only in the novel's appendix. The novel ends with a section called 'Historical Notes' in which pretentious academics in the year 2195 speculate about the manuscript 'The handmaid's tale'. By ironising this masculine academic rhetoric, Atwood convinces a female reader that institutions like the family, and speculations about them are ideologically constructed but continually in a process of social change.

It is not easy to delineate, perhaps even to cherish, female qualities that have historically been those chosen for women and to bring these qualities boldly into culture. Excessive addresses to categories of women and nature are also caught up with conservatism. Yet Atwood's writing does carry propositions about women's memory, mothers, women's language, nature and the body that begin to provide a hermeneutics of border crossing. Looking through her work we see how Atwood returns again and again to rituals of body transformation from anorexia and Shamanism. Shamans are the religious group in particular who cross the boundary of the human species into animals, plants and the sky in order to recuperate natural powers into an individual psyche and hence into culture.[5]

The specifying of female Shamanism is, of course, problematic. Shamans can equally be men and women. In some cultures, for example the Meratus Dayaks of South Kalimantan, Indonesia, Shaman healers are almost all men (see Tsing, 1990). In addition women are sometimes understood to be incompatible with the spiritual world, but at other times are its primary human representatives. In many novels, by men as well as by women, the artist figure often has a special knowledge and could be said to represent a 'seer' or Shaman.

Yet contemporary feminists have found a way of escaping the patriarchal cast of religions through similar symbols and rituals – of witchcraft and the Goddess religion. For example, in Gyn/Ecology, Mary Daly suggests 'the task for feminists ... we eject, banish, depose the possessing language – spoken and written words, body language, architectural language, technological language, the language of symbols

and of institutional structures – by *enspiriting* our Selves' [my emphasis]
Daly, 1978, p. 348).

In many ways Shamanism expresses a number of cultural feminist
themes: one is a concern for spiritual affirmation in feminine terms
such as intuition; another is the attention to body imagery associated
with the feminine such as water; another is the interest in matriarchal
imagery. Atwood tries to root a female sensitivity and a female ethics
in Shamanism because this source can provide cultural symbols for the
social and environmental changes which concern Atwood. Atwood's
understanding of nature is analoguous to cultural feminism because
she identifies women with ecologically holistic views in opposition to
men's culture symbolised by hunting, meat eating and urban anomie.
Atwood's heroines possess myth and magic because they, and Atwood,
share a concern for the psychological and ecological survival of
women. For example the heroine of *Surfacing*, by changing her body
to lose her social identity, is able to identify her parents with Native
American totems in her visions. Similarly in *The journals of Susanna Moodie*,
Susanna Moodie transforms herself into animals and has double visions
while in the wilderness. Atwood's women often find their identity
through worshipping their mothers and grandmothers in a form of
ancester worship.

Atwood, with Shamanistic intent, takes women's struggles with
food and with daily survival away from medical or social languages
into one of myth. Like Cixous's sorceress, Atwood goes in the direction
of 'animality, the plants, the inhuman'. Both Atwood and the sorceress
have 'an exceptional capacity for language and an exclusion correlative
to it' (Cixous, 1987, p. 153).[6] This is not to suggest that a feminist
body politics is a politics of the sorceress but in Atwood's world
masculinity has ceased to regenerate itself. Only by stepping outside
white, male, hierarchical society into these alternative narratives can
women survive. Atwood's poems are clear sign posts on this path. In
her poems heterosexual relations are marred by violence. Men touch
women to etch female bodies into a colonised geography with 'a sense
of desperate forays' (Atwood, 1981, p. 55). Women are frequently
dismembered while men become 'glass towers' (Atwood, 1971, p.
32). In 'Christmas carols' an aborted woman is 'a ripped sack'
(Atwood, 1981, p. 56). To kill one's child is to kill the circulation of
your representation.

The novels transmute into metonymy many of these themes. A key
example is *Bodily harm* where Atwood focuses particular attention on

the violence of heterosexuality. Rennie Wilford, the heroine of *Bodily harm*, is a journalist who suffers both institutional and individual invasions of her body. She is scarred by male violence. Her lover, Jake, forces her to participate in bondage games. An operation for breast cancer which is conducted by a male surgeon is followed by mysterious attacks on her person. Paradigmatically, Rennie's work represents a similar inscription of the violence of male desire when she is made to review sadistic pornography for a feature article in her journal. Escaping to the Caribbean, Rennie is arrested and forced to watch physical atrocities while in prison. The title of the novel and its epigraph, which is taken from John Berger's *Ways of seeing*, point to Atwood's keen interest in theories of male sexuality. Berger has done much to transform our understanding of cultural representations and sexuality. In *Ways of seeing* he argues that the social power of men extends into the violence of their gaze – 'men act and women appear'. In *Bodily harm* the narrative voice constructs its own version of the ambiguities of sexuality and the potential violence of masculine displacements. *Bodily harm* shifts in vocalisation from the authoritative 'I' to a third person disjunction – between Rennie's being and the 'real' world. Rennie's experiences of medicine, prison and media misrepresentation, serve to demonstrate to her the connection between sexual violence, masculinity and language. The theme of the novel is, in short, inexorable. Atwood obdurately argues that the particular formulation of desire in patriarchal capitalism depends on the persistent habitation of women in medical, psychological or physical 'bodily harm'.

The edible woman submits this panoptic fear to a further imagery of dismemberment. The novel abounds with everyday violence. In Peter's white, medicalised apartment, Marian, psychologically if not literally, is in terror of 'losing' her body. The apartment is constructed from shiny surfaces and tiled floors which provide Peter with a 'beetle-hard internal shell' (Atwood, 1969, p. 58). The absence of tactility is matched by an absence of egress. The glass apartment building has no buzzer system and its 'raw' wires dangle like 'loose nerves'. Atwood constructs a dramatic statement to illustrate the omnipresence of male violence in its home decor. Peter's living room contains only two isolated pieces of furniture but he has a pegboard full of weapons. When Peter forces Marian to have sex with him in the bath she has 'a fleeting vision ... the bathtub as a coffin' (Atwood, 1969, p. 61). Marian can read the semiology of a male environment within its boundaries but has to jump out of its demarcations, by running away, in order to escape its power. Atwood's women characters while inside patriarchy best begin their process of self-definition by exercising skills of disassociation and psychic withdrawal. This is not to say that Atwood characterises Marian, Rennie or the protagonist of Surfacing as impotent feminine sensitivities. Rather Atwood makes plain that women must gain internal, psychic autonomy as a preliminary and essential event before body boundaries can be crossed. All Atwood's women characters experience a disjunction between what they observe, what they think about their observations, and what is, or what might be, actually occurring around them.

In The edible woman, Marian lies passively in Peter's bath tub. She refuses to be a female 'eye' and 'deliberately refrains' from looking at Peter 'in case he felt threatened' (Atwood, 1969, p. 62). By the same token, Marian learns to 'repress sharp comment' and cries without sensation. With the gaining of internal autonomy, Marian can actively transgress. In an absurd, a-contextual protest, she hides under Peter's bed. By defying Peter, Marian begins to identify her body. 'I had realized by this time what my prevailing emotion was: it was rage' (Atwood, 1969, p. 79). Marian's is an assertive, and political, repossession of her body.

A later novel, Cat's eye (1989), also reveals Atwood's focus on processes of socialisation and on the way women might re-present the body. The novel is set in the classic Atwood place – on the border of a dangerous ravine the only vestige of the former wilderness biting into a bourgeois Canadian city. The heroine, Elaine Risley, who returns to her hometown Toronto for a retrospective exhibition of her paintings, has crossed another border. The line of diachronic history is the border Elaine violates as she criss crosses through the stereotypes of femininity of post World War II, through 1950s teenage culture, the sexual misuse of liberated women in the 1960s to the commodified 1980s.

Elaine, like Marian in The edible woman, makes a celebratory re-vision of women. She resists stereotyping, not so much in the context of her everyday life, but in the images and metaphors she can create in her paintings. Crucial here, is the cat's eye of the novel's title, a blue marble, which Elaine incorporates into her last painting – a visionary and transcendent virgin floating across the ravine (or border) holding the mystic cat's eye. Elaine superimposes her woman's 'eye' on the firmament of men.

Surfacing marks a similar deflection. The novel's beginning, or generative moment, has the protagonist rehearsing her autonomy by preventing tears with the inducement of displaced somatic pain. 'Anaesthesia, that's one technique: if it hurts invent a different pain' (Atwood, 1973, p. 13). The protagonist deconstructs and nullifies male violence by parody and exaggeration: 'Women sawn apart in a wooden crate ... a trick done with mirrors. I read it in a comic book, only with me there had been an accident and I came apart' (Atwood, 1973, p. 108). The heroine has a repertoire of responses, drawn from childhood memories, to counter everyday stimuli whose effects, if not their causes, are clear. Any routine body exercise, whether it is driving a car or swimming, is performed well only if individuals do not need to attend consciously to body sensations. In Atwood's fiction, violent acts are always denude of narrative logic or individual motive. There is only an epistemology of body parts. The protagonist 'rehearses' emotions but her body is a collection of independent zones each with its own vocabulary of 'incandescent molecules ... the insides of my arms were stipples with tiny wounds' (Atwood, 1973, p. 111). Female appearance is outlined by the religious iconography of stigmata.

In the larger world it is patriarchy which suffers from amnesia and cannot articulate satisfactorily with its own physical realities. In *Surfacing*, Atwood describes the horrors of medicalised childbirth which 'sticks needles in you so you won't hear anything' (Atwood, 1973, p. 92). There is a similar, and key, passage in *The edible woman* set in a hairdressing salon. Here Marian leans back 'against the operating table, while her scalp was scraped' (Atwood, 1969, p. 216). Atwood's deft transformation of the 'safe' zone of women's leisure and beauty routines into a reflected metaphor of the violence of male dominated institutions dramatises the political implications for women of continued amnesia. In Atwood's vision amnesia signals women's alienation from the 'feminine'.

In all of Atwood's novels women's sexual and psychological alienation is described and inscribed through the agency of clothing. The discarding of clothing is, of course, a general metaphor for the defiance of sex roles in many women's books. Esther throws hers from the heights of a New York hotel in *The bell jar* and the heroine of *The awakening*, like *Surfacing*, removes her clothes in order to swim naked and free. The protagonist of *Surfacing*, explicitly associates clothing with the social script of femininity. She both gives, and gives up, her clothing. She leaves a sweatshirt as an offering to the gods on a ledge feathered by reindeer moss close to the site of her father's pictographs. Learning that such tokens can only be partial emblems, she slashes her clothing, carrying one of the 'wounded blankets' which she needs 'until my fur grows' (Atwood, 1973, p. 177). During this episode: 'I untie my feet from the shoes … I take off my clothes, peeling them away from my flesh like wallpaper. They sway beside me inflated, the sleeves bladders of air' (Atwood, 1973, p. 177). The description in the passage recalls life saving routines where children learn to inflate their clothing so that their bodies can 'surface'. The interface between the protagonist's 'self' and 'nature' is the surface of the body – a boundary whose crossing enables her to cease to 'appear'. The passage is characteristically postmodern. External reality is all surface. Only an anthropomorphised Native American blanket can suffice as cover.

A surface which is self reverential and has no interior is, of course, the portrait of woman in patriarchy. Feminist theory has conclusively proved that the fetishisation of woman's body as surface would be the limit of the logic of the male gaze. The female body has its signification within the boundary of the camera 'shot'. The power of the male gaze underpins the institutional representation of women. Laura Mulvey in 'Visual pleasure' has described how media images presuppose a male spectator and, in turn, enable men to distance and objectify women (see Mulvey, 1975). Mulvey's argument has been crucial to film theory because it explained the connections between gender identity, forms of representation and viewing or reading. Yet as Deidre Pribram and others argue, this early psychoanalytic work (and Mulvey has of course refined her ideas in relation to a more diverse notion of spectatorship in 'Afterthoughts') implies an unyielding patriarchy. If women are always to be the passive objects of a male gaze, or subconsciouly act out the role of passive object then it is difficult to envisage an alternative to this aesthetic.

Yet Atwood does forge an autonomy for women from a specific and profound struggle with the dynamics of the 'gaze'. In Surfacing, David is rapidly turning Canadian nature into 'Random samples', the title of his film 'straight out of Depression photo essays' (Atwood, 1969, p. 252). Reality only caricatures film. David thinks that his camera exists to confirm or to deny the identify of women. The camera is a masculine weapon. As Donna Haraway points out, technologies of visualisation in late capitalism constructed popular versions of nature for an urban American immigrant public and yet reveal the deeply predatory nature of a photographic consciousness in which the camera stands for hunting practices. (see Haraway, 1989).[7] In The edible woman, Peter poses Marian for his camera against a backdrop of guns. Marian realises that 'once he pulled the trigger she would be stopped' (Atwood, 1969, p. 252). The hegemony of the gaze is particularly pervasive in Atwood's short story 'A travel piece' where contraceptive pills begin to control women's vision, coating women's eyes with 'vaseline', just as they already control women's reproductive powers.

An important moment of boundary crossing in Atwood's writing occurs when women characters reject the male gaze and begin to name their bodies in a fluid negotiation with the natural. During the last decades other women writers have been writing about their bodies in similar and intimate detail. The language of the body, in the poetry of Anne Sexton and Adrienne Rich, relies on an anatomical imagery which admits no boundary between body parts and social events. Atwood's essay 'An end to audience' describes precisely what is at stake. Writing is 'discarding your self, so that the language and the world may be invoked through you ... writing is also a kind of soothsaying, a truth-telling. It is a naming of the world, a reverse incarnation: the flesh becoming word' (Atwood, 1982, p. 348). All of Atwood's themes are here – the discarding of a social self, the association of truth-telling with Shamanism, and the identification of a language of the body.

The main part of this enterprise Atwood creates in her novels Surfacing and The edible woman where women characters' excursive mobility is sustained by an expressive vocabulary which refuses to equate the body with spectacle. Atwood seizes on the materials of anorexia and bulimia to enable her characters to reject stereotypical femininity. Atwood makes admirable use of feminist theories of eating disorders. As Atwood presents it, anorexia is a phenomenon which threatens the stability of gendered subjects because it takes the female subject into a zone beyond social representation. In anorexia hunger has a contractual existence mediating between desire and the body, and this comes to replace patriarchal social relations.

While there is a great deal of medical confusion as to what anorexia actually is, with some notable exceptions, the emphasis in traditional medicine has generally been on the negative, destructive aspects of the 'disease' represented by women's 'unnatural' aversion to food. This traditional psychoanalytic model is a problematic one because it is based on Freud's theory that femininity is achieved through the neutralisation and transference of somatic experience. Historically anorexia has been both fetish and taboo. Charlotte Bruch defines anorexia as a series of areas of disordered perception (see Bruch,

1976). In this sense anorexia has no independent cognitive function (as it does for Shamans) because anorexics, Bruch and traditional psychiatry would claim, cannot make a cognitive interpretation of body stimuli.

In contrast with this, feminist theory argues, 'it is important to understand the symbolic meanings of body states for anorectics ... In anorexia what we see are women trying to change the shapes of their lives by trying to change the shapes of their bodies' (Eichenbaum and Orbach, 1982, p. 90).[8] Feminist theory has given anorexia a new epistemology. Anorexia is a language of power which is defined and constructed through activities of the body. Susan Bordo argues that there are strong links between spiritual asceticism and anorexia. The imagery of anorexia, she points out, includes Christian imagery with its dualistic construction of the thin body and the fat soul (see Bordo, 1985). My own analogy will be with Shamanism which more accurately possesses the same metaphorical natural powers as those represented in Atwood's novels. Nowhere is this better illustrated than in The edible woman where Atwood allows Marian to construct her own anorexic rituals which are seen from the inside in narrator monologues, and therefore from Marian's point of view. The physiological characteristics of many Atwood women resemble those of anorexia nervosa. Most heroines negotiate a peculiar, but explicit, series of somatic denials. Kim Chernin, in her book about anorexia The hungry self, has argued that if we follow the implications of such food imagery far enough we 'restore women to a tradition of sacred power' (Chernin, 1986, p. 199). For example the protagonist in Surfacing tears the layers of domestic wallpaper from her body to return to the gods of the wilderness and in so doing creates a new language of the body.

Anorexia has always been an issue of interpretation. The subject/object (a woman's body) is both an isolated self-chosen representation and yet one determined by her social class and family history. The contradiction is most apparent in the mirroring of women in Surfacing. The narrator might succeed in erasing the violence of social representation by changing her body. Her mirror image in that novel is less fortunate: 'Behind the counter there's a woman about my age but with brassiere-shaped breasts and a light auburn moustache' (Atwood, 1973, p. 25). The storekeeper is one in a lineage of freak Madames, the last 'had only one hand'. Atwood deliberately positions the 'normal' narrator soon to become 'freak' (in traditional psychiatric parlance) against the 'freak' villager whose abnormality also has no place, at least in open conversation. The mirroring of narrator and freak is a deliberate tactic to avoid the double bind. Freak women, like Shamans or anorexics have to be de-specularised. Their bodies do not, or cannot, find any function as normal sexual spectacles. All three belong to the category of the grotesque in the arranged order of the female body. Freaks do have a narrative which is the interpretable, knowable narrative of abnormality. Freaks are fixed in the genus of the Other. Together with anorexics and Shamans, the freak is herself the text of the body. Mired in an imagery of abnormality, Atwood is saying, how can women express the body? Atwood's purposeful answer is to refuse a fully causal model of anorexia. If the onset of anorexia represents a fallout from male violence, Atwood gives no causal explanation for the particular *representations* of anorexia. A physiological discourse of the anorexic body which derived *entirely* from social explanations would be merely a reflection model. It could not contain the lyrical, quasi-hallucinatory exploration of their bodies in which Atwood's women find themselves so capable.

Catherine Clément and Hélène Cixous envisage this new language in *A newly born woman*:

If there is a self proper to woman, paradoxically it is her capacity to depropriate herself without self-interest: endless body. That doesn't mean that she is undifferentiated magma; it means that she doesn't create a monarchy of her body ... Woman does not perform on herself this regionalization that profits the couple, that only inscribes itself within frontiers. Her libido is cosmic. (Clément and Cixous, 1986, p. 87)

Clément and Cixous describe narrative closure in texts written by means 'the death of women' because such texts finally inscribe the boundaries which women can no longer muddle and confuse. The vocabulary of the body which is prevalent in current writing by men, Clément and Cixous argue, is either economic ('interest'), or colonial ('regionalization'), or legal ('monarchy'). To free the representation of women's bodies from bourgeois androcentricity, they claim, will necessitate a critical transformation of vocabulary. Both Atwood, and Clément and Cixous, explore hysteria, freakishness and anorexia as embodied vocabularies of negotiation, which can articulate woman's body and escape social constraints. For example one of the consequences of anorexia is the suppression of menstruation. The suppression of menses and the power this gave women over their reproductive bodies led Victorian physicians to their anxious notions of female pathology. Female 'hunger' always signifies a desire for social change.

In The edible woman Marian dispenses with causal models for her anorexia. She gives up steak but eats high calorie jelly. She refuses fish but eats high-calorie peanut butter. Marian withdraws from meat, vegetables and eggs but not in any dietary ordained decreasing of protein or carbohydrate intake, for example by systematically refusing starches and high calorie foods. Marian has motives for her pattern of anorexia but they are not causal. Her physiological desires are drawn to the tactile, aesthetic, somatic nature of food as a subjectivity in its own right. 'She became aware of the carrot ... they come along and dig it up, maybe it even makes a sound, a scream too low for us to hear, but it doesn't die right away.' (Atwood, 1969, p. 183.).

The boundary between women and the food 'objects' of nature begins to disappear. Marian's refusal to eat represents not only her rejection of a culture which treats women as edible objects but her new understanding of nature. Surfacing presents the same mystical episte-mology derived from food choices: 'Red foods, heart colour, they are the best kind, they are sacred' (Atwood, 1973, p. 178). Kim Chernin makes a similar reassessment of anorexia in The hungry self: 'It is as if we are trying to remind ourselves, through our obsessive over evaluation of food, that we have been starved of this positive sense of an inherent female creative power on the basis of which we could elaborate a new and meaningful social identity' (Chernin, 1986, p. 197).

Note how Chernin deftly transposes the characteristics of anorexia, of 'obsession' and 'starvation' to society itself. Chernin implies that it is the anorexic condition, not society, which can best sustain the variability of organic development. Marian starves to survive. Her anorexia is not an oxymoron of marginality but a re-evaluation of her somatic ability. In Shape shifters the Shaman Jamal suggests, 'many women realized that the reason they were progressing so rapidly with the introduction of mystical practices was because of their women's bodies, not in spite of them' (Jamal, 1987, p. 9). Atwood's poems 'Pre-amphibian', and 'The settlers' from The circle game, The animals in that country and 'You did it' from Power politics are emphatic about the continuum which exists between women's bodies and the environ-ment. These poems centre on the transformation of humankind into an animal state. In 'Progressive insanities of a pioneer', the pioneer learns to accept the internal wilderness of the body made potent with the metaphoric power of animals.

Atwood's women assume Chernin's 'creative power' and Jamal's 'mysticism' either through their reproductive capacity or by sanctifying the animal within the flesh. The protagonist of Surfacing learns painfully to see that her abortion was 'an animal hiding in me as if in a burrow and instead of granting it sanctuary I let them catch it' (Atwood, 1973, p. 145). The violence of abortion triggers the narrator's first critical response and semiotic jouissance. She remembers being a fetus and how she enjoyed looking through the walls of her mother's stomach. Anorexia teaches her skills of perception and cognition so that she can ensure that her pregnancy will be the fetus of an animal god. Like Huichol Shamans eating the hearts of birds in order to fly, Marian and the protagonist of Surfacing cross over the boundaries of their bodies by metamorphosing into animals. In her study of animal rights, Josephine Donovan has identified a long tradition in women's writing which explicitly identifies women with animals. In Radclyffe Hall, The well of loneliness, Ellen Glasgow, The sheltered life, Willa Cather, A lost lady, Virginia Woolf, Flush as well as the often cited Susan Glaspell, 'A jury of her peers', Donovan argues that women's attitudes towards animals are quite different from the aggression and sadism that characterise a masculine treatment of animal life (see Donovan, 1990). Similarly Atwood makes plain that by investigating specific animal analogies or metaphors (her particular favourite is the dinosaur) women can recover the source of archaic language and come to know themselves. To some extent to have a woman narrator as the only competent survivor embraces the logic of an adventure story. Yet by choosing wilderness women as literary emblems, Atwood both dramatises, and heightens, the contradiction between conventional notions of womanhood and the freer possibilities of particular literary representations. In other words, Atwood has removed the narrative boundary between animal and woman, at least in print, and replaced boundary with complementary and metamorphosis. The protagonist of Surfacing is able to visualise her mother as a jay bird precisely because she herself has acquired the power of a Shaman – has crossed over.

Against this background a further question emerges. Might there be other ways of reading Atwood's metaphors of boundary crossing than anorexic and Shamanistic practices? While such isomorphism of imagery obviously implies affinities and similarities between Atwood's and shaman women it is worth testing such sorority momentarily against another alternative explanation.

Feminist myth critics offer another reading of the natural order and

its representations in writing by women. They argue that metamorphosis, or what they term transformations of the personality in fiction
and in myth is a renewal of identity by immersion in the unconscious,
specifically Jungian unconscious, not the gaining of consciousness
through environmental adaptation. Annis Pratt's *Archetypal patterns in
women's fiction* in particular, searches out mythical archetypes to match
to fictional women. She describes nineteenth century writers such as
Mary Wollstonecraft and the Brontës who take as their theme the battle
between a heroine's sense of self-identity and the cultural constructs
which society imposes on women. A writer's reshaping of mythic
material discloses, Pratt argues, a reservoir of meanings which can
escape cultural structures. However myth theory is not without its
difficulties. What the re-use of myth does not do, and what
Shamanistic rituals must do, is to create *activity*. Shamanism specifies
a relationship between the *body* of the performer and the content of
performance. From a feminist perspective, one major problem is that
myth criticism offers no critical vocabulary in which to analyse
Atwood's descriptions of women's bodies as inhabiting the realm of
Native American spirituality, and her depictions of the blending or
interfusion of species. In Native American traditions all creatures are
thought to be sentient cognitive beings occupying a unitary field with
humans. Recognising this hybrid – women/animals/cognition, in
Surfacing and *The edible woman*, Atwood fuses the anorexic body to the
shaman body. The oscillation women characters make between animal
and civilised worlds helps Atwood to envisage a representation free
from cultural prescriptions, resting on an affinity between women's
bodies and nature (animals) and spirituality. Atwood successfully
avoids the static limits of mythical archetypes. The force of Shamanistic
references in *Surfacing* in particular, emphatically represents a fresh
metaphoric inscription. The novel is structured around rituals which
carry specific connotations in Shamanism.

   Shamanism requires particular potencies. Michele Jamal tells us, 'in
the literal sense there are Shamans who are able outwardly to transform
their physical shape into other forms' (Jamal, 1987, p. 3). In *Surfacing*
the 'shape shifter' protagonist alters her consciousness through similar
rituals of transformation. When she was young she freed frogs and
animals from the masculine sadism of her brother. As an adult she frees
herself from the exchange value of food and drink and moves into a
non-human world. Catherine Clément and Hélène Cixous point to
Atwood's larger intent: 'The Shamans turn themselves into birds ...

and more than any others, women bizarrely embody this group of anomalies showing the cracks in the overall system' (Clément and Cixous, 1986, p. 7). Surfacing endorses the power of a natural order. Water is an organising motif in the novel. Responses to water constitute the plot of Surfacing (for example in the events of her brother's drowning and her father's 'grave') and water is a symmetrical metaphor of revision (for example when the protagonist makes a final dive into the lake and into her Shaman powers). In the spiritually validated frame which is Shamanism, immersion in water represents the moment of body change: 'In vision I have gone into the Pacific Ocean many times where I have eight "dolphin guides" who take me to ... a great vortex of energy' (Jamal, 1987, p. 65).

A water motif intervenes indirectly in The edible woman when Marian moves into a higher degree of consciousness only while being effectively in water in a continually humid city: 'I walked towards the subway station ... it was almost like moving underwater'. Facetiously, Marian becomes the 'washer woman' of her household making frequent trips to the laundromat. Similarly in moments of transformation Atwood's heroines discover liberating changes in their perception. Light, like water, is a key motif of Shamanism. Light represents a 'diamond-heat energy' which Shamans begin to possess when re-envisioning boundaries: 'Feeling my boundaries, and creating a circle of coloured light around me for psychic protection, became crucial' (Jamal, 1987, p. 134).

'Giving Birth', Atwood's strong story of a female artist describes the seer woman in terms of transparency. In the story, light flows through the artist as the sun rises, and buildings and forests appear to resemble water or jelly. In Surfacing, the narrator's anatomical changes and the congruence of water and light forcefully represent a potent body language: 'My bones and the child inside me showing through the green webs of my flesh, the ribs are shadows, the muscles jello, the trees are like this too' (Atwood, 1973, p. 181). In Shamanism such perception has a precise term and function. It is 'dermoptic perception' or skin vision which enables Shamans, for example, to detect colours without seeing. Where historically in the West, visualisation techniques have been used by science to map and to control women's bodies, for example in ultrasound technology, in Atwood's novels transparency emblematises the fluid complexity of female identity. At times transparency represents the psychic withdrawal of heroines as they choose to be invisible within their social worlds. At other moments light and transparency are transformed into metaphors of creative female power.

The symbols of Shamanism, water and light, are the signs, within *Surfacing*, of the efficacy of female power. In addition, Atwood's narrative assertion of Shamanism includes that powerful sign system – totemism. Adopting and respecting totems is the necessary final step to the full grammar of transformation. The paternal totem – the talisman from the protagonist's father, the 'man-animals', is 'complicated, tangled', but the maternal totem, her mother's pictograph – the heroine's own childhood drawings – is 'simple as a hand, it would be final' (Atwood, 1973, p. 149). Pictographs depend on a direct representation of objects and beings. The interpretation of their signs is not easy but it is open ended unlike meanings transmitted by phonetic principles in literate cultures which are fixed and closed.

Atwood's exegesis of Shaman power, represented in the symbolic motifs of water, light and talismanic objects enables the heroine to cross the border of animal and supernatural into a new cosmology. In the novel the boundary between the narrator's human existence and the animal and plant realms is blurred. The narrator's conscious conception of her personal body power is of a hybrid form – one where 'my hair spreads out, moving and fluid in the water. The earth rotates, holding my belly down to it as it holds the moon; the sun pounds in the sky' (Atwood, 1973, p. 149).

Atwood paints a powerful picture of the natural world. The placing of, and interpretation of, women's bodies inside a sign system of Shamanism enables Atwood to escape conservative definitions of women's nature. The symbolic calibration of female potencies abrogates essentialist demarcations – if this is female it must be natural, it's natural to be female – and replaces these demarcations with the mobility of free spirits. Atwood is intensely interested in the signitive possibilities of women's bodies. In *Surfacing*, the narrator's 'divine' dialogue with the environment significantly comes after she refuses human speech. Silence deflects the narrative of patriarchy. The narrator thrills to utopian possibilities. Her baby will have no human language: 'I will never teach it any words' (Atwood, 1973, p. 162). She moves in and out of first person vocalisation to reveal the duplicity of pronouns and names. *Surfacing* is a confessional novel but the speaking voice mixes observations and memories in a temporally disjointed narrative. Similarly *Bodily harm* and *The handmaid's tale* are narratives where women initially describe their bodies in the third person in order to highlight a disjunction between their sensibilities and a dichotomised outer world. The poems most of all, are a measure of how far Atwood allows herself to question syntactical representation. 'This is a photograph of me' bears the impress of 'a transparent' semiotic language where the narrative voice is absolved of body boundaries. It is 'in the lake ... just under the surface' (Atwood, 1968, p. 17). Atwood's multivocal, personal documentary is a dynamic statement about traditional univocal convictions. The poem is a first person narrative which is both repositorial and fragmented because it sometimes exists in photographs and sometimes in water and in invisibility. The autobiographical I is already a deconstructing I.

Surfacing certainly problematises, and erases any meaningful difference between nature and rationality. In other words the novel, through its Shamanistic identification of women with natural cognition and in its propensity to subvert the fundamental difference between cognition and feelings, finally endorses an organic and feminine power. Such textual energy recalls Clément and Cixous' argument that 'the specific power to produce something living of which her flesh is the locus is not only a question of the transformation of the whole perceptive system. How could the woman who has experienced the not-me within me, not have a particular relationship to the written?' (Clément and Cixous, 1986, p. 90). Similarly empowered, the narrator in Surfacing returns to a first person narrative which is now a voice of self-direction and autonomy. The edible woman adopts a similar device. Part II, which describes Marian's immobility, takes the form of a third person narrative while Parts I and III, are in first person and represent Marian's retrieval of her script and her fresh understanding of her body. Atwood often employs the multiple voice. In 'Book of ancestors', 'The double nun' and 'This is a photograph of me' the speaker's voice is split either into separate identities or into different places. The displaced perspectives suggest depth not duplicity.

For decades psychoanalysis has worked to produce the most sustained account of the variability of femininity. The preferred taxonomic label under which psychoanalysis categorises female fluidity is 'hysteria'. In hysteria it is the body which articulates psychic pain. Freud's Studies on hysteria demonstrate very well how patriarchy places woman's multivocal mobility inside the tight 'therapeutic' boundaries of the confession.[9] Freud associates excessive narrativity (which characterises the end of Surfacing) with illness, with hysteria. He permits women to make only mimetic narratives in the form of dreams. Freud sees 'hysteria' in body language – the physical movements a hysteric makes which betray her unconscious sexual desires. By embedding woman's voice in a case history of her body, psychoanalysis controls woman's access to language and to the agency of narration.

Atwood subverts this psychoanalytic boundary with interpellation – her novels directly address a female reader. 'Reading position' describes the assumed relation by an author of the individual reader to a text. Atwood self-consciously addresses a female reader by making access to the plot depend on an identification with the heroine's form of cognition and with her anorexic body.

Atwood does not make a crude positivisation of women's hysteria. The reader shares the narrator's 'hysterical' but slowly consolidated discovery of an alternative consciousness. Her body is not observed from outside or from afar. The body is not specular, it is not distanced in another encompassing discourse. In addition, male characters like Joe certainly have no gift of speech, nor do reader perceptions move in advance of those of the central character. By adopting Shaman/ anorexic motifs Atwood creates descriptions of women unconstrained by the coded norms of narrative femininity. In the same way, as Elaine Showalter observes in The female malady, 'the hunger strikes of militant women prisoners brilliantly put the symptomatology of anorexia nervosa to work in the service of a feminist cause' (Showalter, 1987, p. 162).

Less obvious, however, but equally persuasive is the way in which traditional narrative conventionally privileges male definitions. In narratives, one of the major strategies by which a text nullifies a woman's identity is its use of names. In tandem with her choice of a multivocal woman narrator, Atwood scrutinises the errant appellations of androcentricity. From the first moment of The edible woman, it is clear that the female narrator, Marian, is bounded in every way by androcentric language – both in her work and in her relationships. The first element in this pervasive management is Marian's work on the naming surveys for Seymour Services which catalogue and classify personal (body) products – sanitary napkins and razor blades. Peter's conversations offer Marian no alternative compensation, built as they are on stories of hunting: 'I whipped out my knife, good knife, German steel, and slit the belly and took her by the hind legs and gave her a hell of a crack' (Atwood, 1969, p. 70). The violence and enormity of this masculinity does not bespeak merely Peter's individual appetite for physical pleasure but suggests as well the assaults of heterosexual relations – 'The stream of words was impossible to follow, and my mind withdrew'. Neither can the younger, and potentially more liberal men, Fish and Trevor, provide Marian with any adequate and corrective narrative. Fish's language is, like the condition of his room, a mess of paper generalisations which he employs busily to turn *Alice in wonderland* into a parody Freudian case study. Androcentricity, in Atwood's fiction, is represented by its bulimic nomenclature, a dictionary of irrelevant definitions.

In *Surfacing*, it is men who attempt to capture and fix the meaning of the wilderness with the 'languages' of cameras or guns, or with the formal rules of their scientific discipline. The narrator's father employed a 'Seymour survey' technique of scientific classification to describe the countryside around him. Her brother tried to codify the wilderness beneath the surface of the landscape with his map of mineral rights. David slips into 'yokel dialect' but he can only mimic and does not understand local words. The narrator's husband once wrote his initials on a fence 'leaving his mark' (Atwood, 1973, p. 47). Men's survival magazines contain a collection of absurd maxims: 'avoid unclassified mushrooms' (Atwood, 1973, p. 48). Yet neither the males of her family nor her male peers can stem the tide of the narrator's linguistic skill. In a more literal and figurative vein, she uses appropriate and practical vocabulary. It is not only Anna who finds men to be crazy because they keep 'changing' the rules. The narrator learns how language is tainted with masculine anxieties, in particular with men's fear of women's bodies: 'The worst words in any language were what they were most afraid of and in English it was the body, that was even scarier than God' (Atwood, 1973, p. 45).

In contrast, Shaman names are names of assignation. In Shamanism, names establish differences of function not differences of value. Similarly in *Surfacing*, the heroine from the beginning, insists on the fundamental function of body language and hates predictable behaviour. Atwood orchestrates a choreography of authority expressed in male bodies. Her heroine knows when, or when not, to speak in relation to her lover Joe's arm movements. It is interesting to note the convergence of Atwood's account of gender difference and Shaman techniques. The narrator, like a Shaman, learns to speak her own name by focusing on natural functions, 'on a spider web' (Atwood, 1973, p. 73). Immersed in nature, she comes to know that 'in one of the languages there are no nouns ... the animals have no need for speech, why speak when you are a word' (Atwood, 1973, p. 181).

Epistemologically, Atwood's women characters break with the sign systems of patriarchy. Women learn to turn their bodies into a representational language of feeling, not one of spectacle. Atwood's women are uniquely moral entities acting somewhat in the convention of a thriller where morality depends on the personal morality of its hero. Isolated, and in danger, the thriller hero depends on his professionalism and on the way he thinks about, and articulates, the world around him. Atwood's women adopt a similar stance. The narrator's search for her father, in the convention of a thriller, gives only a meagre theology of 'cold comfort, but comfort, death is logical' where the search for her mother is metaphorical and liberating (Atwood, 1973, p. 170).

The absent father is a central 'lack' in all of Atwood's novels. By coming to create and to control her father's 'history' the narrator comes to terms with patriarchy. The identification of the narrator as her own subject is marked by her return to semiotic language. For example in the final wilderness of the island, the protagonist speaks in fluid sentences without full stops and differentiates objects by their functions, discarding nouns and a referential language system.

Women's discursive mobility is marginal to the ways in which society encapsulates and describes 'woman'. Therefore the representation of translation as we have seen, like the discarding of clothing, is a general metaphor in many women's novels for a defiance of sex-roles. For example in Sylvia Plath's The bell jar, Esther longs to 'crawl into' the body of the Russian translator at the United Nations building. Atwood represents translation as a trajectory of border crossing. In 'Two-headed poems', the English and French try to hold onto their identities by hoarding their languages, their 'stockpiled words'. The interviewing department at Seymour Surveys in The edible woman is a female world dedicated to deciphering interviewers' handwriting and where Marian turns the convoluted and overly subtle prose of the psychologists into simple, useful questions. In Surfacing, translation is very much a female property. The heroine is in control of a series of 'languages'. She interviews Paul, albeit with difficulty, in another language. She talks to a mother deaf in one ear. David can only teach but cannot practice, communication. The narrator, on the other hand, renders experience from one reality (animal language) into another – the human world. It is women who possess linguistic dexterity. The activity of translation becomes a metaphor of the theme of Surfacing: 'a language is everything you do'.

As we have seen, water and light are key metaphors in Atwood's writing and they recall the spiritual status accorded to natural elements by Shamanism. These metaphors, together with the metaphor of translation, confer on the narrator's 'animal' body all the connotations and sacramentality of Shamanism. Similarly, one of the striking aspects of Atwood's poetry is the metaphoric process by which ideas merge into effects so that animals, for example, can be both themselves and stand for mental concepts as they do in 'Landcrab II'. Atwood's use of these metaphors is quite unique. Hence her pronounced affinity with the Gothic, which she uses in Lady oracle to represent women's anxieties about the 'monstrosities' of their bodies and about their gender. As Eve Sedgwick points out in her investigation of the 'paranoid Gothic', which she calls a major genre of gay writing, the Gothic plot above all works to transmute 'the intrapsychic with the intersubjective' (see Sedgwick, 1989).[10]

In Lady oracle the heroine Joan Foster is the author of Lady oracle which she wrote as an experiment in automatic writing while under hypnosis. In Atwood's deployment of the Gothic both heroine and reader share the typical estrangement – the distancing from realism and realistic narratives. Atwood plays with Gothic, with romance, with dramatic dialogue to dislodge the conventional logic of realism by introducing narrative contradictions. These genres above all are those which foreground their own conventions. Atwood clearly disparages the high/low boundary in literary theory between modernism/popular genres. It is in popular imagery that woman's body is a more visible representation of masculine fears. The figures of popular culture are often emblems of ethical and social anxieties. They provide a performative dimension for the prohibitions of contemporary culture. Popular culture is often didactic and informed with moral purpose. Along with the genres of popular culture such as the Gothic, Atwood uses the artifacts of popular culture – its women's magazines, its popular music, its advertising slogans – to address the mismatch between what Jameson calls 'socio-symbolic messages' and women's ethics (see Jameson, 1981). In her criticism, Atwood stresses the emphatic morality of women. In 1961 she praised the novel La belle bête, written by another Canadian woman Marie-Claire Blais, for its handling of characters. Blais, Atwood suggests, tells us 'that a princess is good and a step-mother wicked' (Atwood, 1982, p. 26). It is this ability to promote specific moral characterisations, Atwood feels,

F

which makes Blais's 'world of imagination, somehow more real'.

In The edible woman, Atwood suggests that women's morality needs a new language. Men, like Duncan for example, seem less and less able to handle rhetoric: 'He was writing another term paper, he had told her, called "Monosyllables in Milton"' (Atwood, 1969, p. 188). Marian, on the other hand, gives dextrous attention to the possibilities of metaphor: 'Marian's mind grasped at the word "immature", turning it over like a curious pebble found on a beach. It suggested an unripe ear of corn' (Atwood, 1969, p. 171). Metaphor and simile help Marian to realise the definitive fantasy of a free woman beyond the validated frames of everyday language. In the closing pages of The edible woman, Marian, unconstrained, converts metaphor to metonymy by walking through a ravine with Duncan in a literal evocation of border crossing.

This concern for metonymy, for giving a new 'body' to women's language enters Atwood's writing not only in its overt content, but more drastically in the very syntax itself. For example, Atwood's poems are ideogrammatic. They do not often employ conventional literary tropes. Her poems often refuse sequential development and depend on parallelism, preferring to juxtapose emotional states in synthetic relation to each other. Aural parallels are an important device, too, in Atwood's novels. A key passage in The edible woman evokes the stage routines of Restoration comedy where, in individual scenes, plot dialogue occurs simultaneously with 'to the audience' asides. Trevor prepares a grand meal for Marian and his friends. The scene becomes a metonymic image of Marian's existence as a body on the border between 'hysteria' and 'reality'. Marian eats 'as one would make an offering to a possibly angry God' which Fish can only mimic ludicrously by talking about his theory of a pre-Malthus organic language. When Marian begins to discard her meat, Fish is beginning to argue the case for a new Venus from the sea. The dinner table, as Helena Michie points out with reference to Victorian literature, has long been a testing site of appropriate moral and gendered behaviour. In Victorian novels the table is the place where characters and plots meet to confirm the values of the novel. Conspicuously absent in Victorian literature, are heroines who eat (see Michie, 1987). Atwood however makes plain that parallelism, translation and metaphor are all strategies contemporary women can use to avoid the business-as-usual of masculine monism. The use of paradox is, of course, one of the most expressive symptoms of the anorexic whose body language, like that which Atwood employs, is often a semicomic play with the stereotypical feminine.

In addition to recognising the efficacy of 'hystericized' bodies, Atwood's tactical campaign is to create a specifically gendered morality that depends on a fundamental respect for non-human life. For example, Marian is first aware of the power of her body, and rejects meat, when she talks to Peter 'trying to get a clearer image of what she had meant by "justice". She thought that it ought to mean being fair, but even her notion of that became hazy around the edges' (Atwood, 1969, p. 152). What 'happens' to Marian in this novel and to the protagonist in *Surfacing* becomes fully clear and coherent only, I think, when one takes into account Atwood's explicit attention to women's 'alternative' morality.

Carol Gilligan's notion of female ethics goes some way to explain Marian's 'hazy' opposition to the petrified 'justice'. Gilligan's major studies of gendered morality, *In a different voice* and 'Woman's place in man's life cycle', advance very similar arguments to those of Atwood's *The edible woman* and her other books. Gilligan notes that, from a woman's perspective, morality and the preservation of life are 'contingent on sustaining connection', on seeing the consequences of action 'by keeping the web of relationship intact' (Gilligan, 1987, p. 19). Following Nancy Chodorow, Gilligan takes this gendered difference to stem from the differing object relations which boys and girls experience as infants, when girls affiliate with mothers while boys acquire a masculine identity through opposition to maternal, and hence female, characteristics.[11] Women then have a morality of responsibility in stark contrast to men's concept of 'rights'. The force of Gilligan's argument finds its illustration in *Surfacing*. The narrator's brother has a spurious morality: 'There had to be a good kind and a bad kind of everything'. Atwood deflates his absurd abstractions by highlighting its crazy logic based as it is on good leeches 'with red dots on the back' and 'bad leeches who are mottled' (Atwood, 1973, p. 38). The issue, for women, is to substitute for masculine abstractions 'a mode of thinking that is contextual and narrative rather than formal and abstract' (Gilligan, 1982, p. 19).

Another major gender difference which interests Atwood is men and women's relation to time. Women's bodies are deeply saturated with time. Concepts of periodisation structure women's identities and structure social expectations of what a woman in her 30s or 50s for example, ought to be. In such a Western, linear version of time, woman's social status derives from the appearance of her body which is organised in set decades – the teens, the 40 year old. In everyday habitual memory time is sedimented in the body. Michel de Certeau has exposed the workings of this hermeneutic with respect to race. In an account of the torture of Indian slaves in *Heterologies: discourse on the other*, he describes the Indian body as 'memory'. It carries in 'written' form the law of equality and rebelliousness that not only organises the group's relation to itself, but also its relation to the occupiers (see de Certeau, 1986).[12] Like 'tortured slaves' women's bodies 'carry' the visible, verifiable marks of the social order. Against this background it is inevitable that women try to deny the body its age or its food in order to gain time from patriarchy.

Anorexia is fundamentally about time. This is because, as Kim Chernin explains, food represents memory: 'Food is the archive in which we have stored the record of ourselves' (Chernin, 1986, p. 153). Food carries with it the memory of childhood, and at the heart of an anorexic's 'disordered' relation to food there is a 'disorder' in her memory. Similarly, in *The edible woman*, Marian escapes the androcentric linear countdown to marriage by *progressing*, via the mechanism of food, back into childhood. She 'regresses' from meat to peanut butter and finally to a semiotic world of liquids and sensuality. Food is Marian's metaphoric archive of developing feminism.

Atwood's fiction describes the geography of childhood. She identifies childhood as a positive, not as a finite, state and she identifies it with the female and with creativity. In *Life before man*, the lives of its three protagonists Lesje, Elizabeth and Nate are interwoven by their connection with the Royal Ontario Museum, a symbol of society's lost past. While cataloguing materials in the museum, Lesje re-enters the time of her childhood, remembering her early fossil drawings and this begins to change for her the official history of palaeontology. Similarly, the 'history' of *Surfacing*'s border setting the narrator comes to see, is a mélange of road signs where defaced election posters jostle with religious signs and advertisements – 'an X-ray of it would be the district's entire history' (Atwood, 1973, p. 15). Against this faded androcentric world the narrator poses the time of her body. Time for her is compressed like the fist 'closed on my knee' in which she holds 'the clues and solutions' (Atwood, 1973, p. 76). The assertive, but timeless, closure of *Surfacing* can begin when the heroine at last sees her body: 'I'm crying finally, it's the first time, I watch myself doing it' (Atwood, 1973, p. 172). Men, in Atwood's novels, prefer a mechanical order. Men possess time. David takes with him the only watch held by members of the group. What replaces David's watch is the narrator's creation of her own body time moulded by pictographs. Pictographs represent a prelinear time – one of Native American culture and they also represent the pre-speech time of the narrator's childhood drawings. In Shamanism the ability to draw pictographs or to decode such drawings reveals a calling to power in any individual.

Remembered figures from the narrator's past model these time changing manoeuvres. The narrator's father and mother are not *actual* content within the timed plot of the novel, but belong to the realm of narrator time. They exist, 'mammoths frozen in a glacier', on the border between prehistory and human history. Atwood has the same insight in 'A book of ancestors' which she makes free of linear chronology and in 'After the flood we' where characters metamorphise within evolutionary time as if playing an unclassifiable 'Animal, vegetable, mineral' panel game. Shamanism has a complementary set of manoeuvres. Jamal explains that 'the Shaman draws in the volcanic tides and gravitational pull of the earth, and floods her body with the seismic energy of the cosmos' because the Shaman 'lives in universal time' (Jamal, 1987, p. 176). Similarly, Atwood makes plain that the viable time of *The edible woman* is located in Marian's body changes not in Peter's constricting linear courtship. It is history's function to tirelessly restore the linear. History produces linearity and forces recognition of linearity by arranging time into chronology and periods. Atwood unlocks the handcuffs binding social history with women's psyches by asking women to attend to memories of childhood and to their bodies. The inevitable result is Atwood's contest with narrative form. Narratives present events in a linear sequence called plot. Narratives arbitrarily and quite determinedly, therefore 'naturalize' causal processes and temporal sequences. Atwood's women on the other hand are the subtitles of 'history', which Atwood demystifies as a set of absurdly constricting male priorities.

Atwood breaks with chronology by her frequent attention to the semiotic – a time before the framing of social identity, which is a moment commonly characterised as the 'mirror phase'. In Écrits, Jacques Lacan postulates that the baby gains an individual and unified image when it can look in a mirror and see its mother as another. A transition from the semiotic to the symbolic order therefore depends on separation from the mother. The world of early childhood constitutes, in other words, a fragmented imagistic powerful space whose language can never be entirely recuperated by social history and by the symbolic order.[13]

There are pointed allusions to mirrors in Surfacing, and not only in its title. Mirrors are motifs of androcentricity. It is when standing in front of a mirror that the narrator 'delays' dreaming of her mother: 'She was either ten thousand years behind the rest or fifty years ahead of them' (Atwood, 1973, p. 52). In order that the narrator can celebrate a border crossing, and re-enter her body, she must 'stop being in the mirror ... not to see myself, but to see. I reverse the mirror so it is toward the wall, it no longer traps me' (Atwood, 1973, p. 175). Women best serve their bodies by refusing the social identity which mirrors reflect. Mirrors also play an important role in the symbolism of anorexia. Anorexics learn to deny mirror images in order to enjoy their own non-specular and more spiritual feelings. In A newly born woman Hélène Cixous makes an extensive and positive account of the battle:

To break up, to touch the masculine integrity of the body image, is to return to a stage that is scarcely constituted in human development; it is to return to the disordered imaginary of before the mirror stage, of before the rigid and defensive constitution of subjective armour ... the entire fantastic world made of bits and pieces, opens up beyond the limit, as soon as the line is crossed. (Clément and Cixous, 1986, p. 33)

The link which Cixous makes here between the mirror stage, social boundaries and women's bodies and childhood helps to explain Atwood's use of mirror metaphors. Like the anorexic, Surfacing's narrator must learn to refuse to see her body as a reflected image of the desires of others. If women are to refuse the specular, to refuse to be mirrors of male desires, they must begin Atwood is suggesting, to define themselves in and through the mothering body. The clue to Atwood's fiction lies in her literary criticism. Here not surprisingly, she intensively focuses on the writing of Adrienne Rich. Adrienne Rich has long argued that the mind/body dualism rests at bottom on a concept of gender development as a process of separating from others. However, only men are encouraged to pursue separation. In Of woman born, Rich argues Atwood's case for a clearly confirmed tradition of female power. This power Rich locates in motherhood which, Rich argues, men have mythically and socially misrepresented. Rich carefully distinguishes between motherhood as an institution with its socialised technology, and motherhood as the crucial or potential experience of women and our source of a new creative knowledge.

(see Rich, 1976 and Humm, 1986) When reviewing Rich's book, Atwood is revealingly autobiographical. Atwood claims that Adrienne Rich is 'redeeming herself, creating a new landscape, getting herself born' (Atwood, 1982, p. 162).

The theme that the maternal parent represents both a mythical creativity and a potential and actual social identity for women is repeated throughout Atwood's writing. In such poems as 'A red shirt' and in Lady oracle there is a specific engagement with maternal figures who heroines must 'reparent' in order to gain their own intellectual and moral identities.

The 'experience' and the 'institution' of motherhood, or the personal and political aspects of mothering, are a rich part of the plot of The handmaid's tale. Woman's reproductive capacity always makes her vulnerable to patriarchal institutionalisation. In the future word of Gilgead reproductive control is the centre of social order. Gilgead sets women down into the categories of Marthas, Econowives, Handmaids and Nonwomen. Interspersed with episodes about these 'institutionalised' demarcations there are moments of pleasurable jouissance drawn from Offred's memories or 'experience', of her mother and daughter. Atwood is not simplistically pro-mothering in some essentialist sense. For example, Joan's mother in Lady oracle is a monster who sticks knives into her daughter's arm. Atwood carefully recognises the ambiguities of the mother/daughter dyad in order to emphasise its significance. But, as Kristeva argues, the maternal space breaks with conceptual boundaries because in a maternal body a woman is 'an other' (see Kristeva, 1983).

A profound mother/daughter struggle shapes anorexia. Kim Chernin describes how a woman's guilt at surpassing her mother is directed at her own female flesh: 'Food has taken the place of the mother' (Chernin, 1986, p. 131). Selvini Palazzoli agrees that because the child's original experience of the primary object, the mother, is a 'corporeal-incorporative one' the mother's body is an extension of the child's (Palazzoli, 1974, p. 158). The ideas of Kristeva, Chernin and Palazzoli are very varied but they clarified for me issues involved in my own eating disorder as well as explicating the issues of mother/daughter affiliation which often have fictional equivalents in Atwood's writing. Surfacing resounds with such images. The narrator's mother gives out 'Life savers' sweets, and avoids socially simplistic explanations for birth and death by metonymically giving the narrator 'a piece of dough' (Atwood, 1973, p. 74). The protagonist in her 'anorexic' mode can guiltlessly surpass her mother because she has incorporated her mother's talents. The protagonist gives care and food to her 'children' Anna, David and Joe. She anticipates birthing her baby holistically: 'I'll lick it off and bite the cord, the blood returning to the ground where it belongs' (Atwood, 1973, p. 162). Significantly the protagonist's baby actively works with the mother to birth itself.

Atwood's concern is with the conceptual, cultural glue which patriarchy uses to stick maternity into a limited space. In *Surfacing, The handmaid's tale* and her other writing Atwood exposes the institution-alisation of mothering and, in opposition, explores and validates an anorexic 'corporeal – incorporative' mother/daughter relationship. The strength of Atwood's feminism is clear if, for example, we look at Lévi-Strauss's alternative readings of Shaman rituals performed to facilitate childbirth. Teresa de Lauretis has described how, although Lévi-Strauss's account of the luna incantation prompted him to make similar parallels between Shamanistic practices and psychology, it is notable how in *his* version of the myth the hero is *not* a woman or even a female spirit but a *male* symbolised through phallic attributes. (see de Lauretis, 1984, p. 122)

Women's Shaman and anorexic rituals give voice to the mother's tongue now in the mouth of her daughter. A woman's body need no longer be defined as an *object* of knowledge but can find its affirmation as a set of *procedures* – a way of border crossing. All these motifs are welded and have an exemplary force in the final part of *Surfacing*. Here the event of transition is the moment of the protagonist's dive into the lake and her 'dive' into a new epistemology of the body. It is a tremendous struggle, 'the new effort, my body stumbled. It remembered the motions only imperfectly, like learning to walk after illness' (Atwood, 1973, p. 141). In Shaman ritual the initiation into such psychic power takes the form of a similar homeopathic 'illness': 'I became death ... I let go of my flesh, my bones ... I put myself together again. I had a threshold' (Jamal, 1987, p. 73). The first manifestation of this transition is sickness. In Atwood's poem 'Evening train station before departure' a diseased body which has been 'spineless' is able to regenerate itself through similar metaphors of water and baptism.

In *Surfacing* the heroine crosses over the fence around society's garden and acquires power by experiencing the pre-oedipal materials of her body and its liquid foods. Kim Chernin reminds us that one of the characteristics of the modern world is the disappearance of any meaningful rites of initiation. Intentional ritual, in the context of anorexia she suggests, can 'serve to alleviate the self-destructive excess of the transformational experience by providing forms and measures for the passage from nature into culture' (Chernin, 1986, p. 185). *Surfacing* ends on that note: 'I tense forward, towards the demands and questions, though my feet do not move yet' (Atwood, 1973, p. 192).

In a revealing piece called 'Alphabet', written the year before *Surfacing*, Atwood argues that 'the Canadian habit of mind, for whatever reason – perhaps a history and a social geography which both seem to lack coherent shape – is synthetic' (Atwood, 1982, p. 94). With her 'Canadian habit of mind', the heroine of *Surfacing* moves across the limits of a cabin world into a vision of nature that overwhelms boundaries. She transforms the specularity of patriarchy by, metaphorically, turning her body inside out. Atwood elegantly synthesises that critique of borders which I am arguing is characteristic of much contemporary writing by women. Atwood seems to be constructing alternative and oppositional stories about women beyond the androcentric formulae of time, the family romance and specularity. Like the Shamans in Michele Jamal's account of traditional beliefs, Atwood has consciously chosen 'the ingredients of a new paradigm' (Jamal, 1987, p. 190). Like the anorexics who Kim Chernin describes, Atwood has 'shaped that new woman, dream of the future, out of the transformed obsessions that presently rule our lives' (Chernin, 1986, p. 214).

Occupied territories: Adrienne Rich

In 1983, in 'Blood, bread and poetry' her address to the Institute for Advanced Studies in the Humanities, University of Massachusetts, Adrienne Rich eloquently explored the geography of her own poetics of gender. As usual, Rich spoke about herself as a traveller across the borders of modernism, feminism and the Third World, identifying the now bracketed male writers, Yeats and F. O. Matthieson who had 'heated the blood' before she was able to write 'out of a woman's body' (Rich, 1983, p. 535). As usual she argued emotionally and convincingly that her feminism did not inevitably deny the masculine features of the poetry academy of the 1960s. There is nothing unusual, of course, in poets making symmetrical rhetorical clinches for themselves between radically dissimilar poetry, nor that a woman poet should seek to dismantle 'the master's house' largely through 'a long conversation with the elders' (Rich, 1983, p. 540). One could list scores of love poems to fathers, for example Anne Sexton's 'The death of the fathers', and Diane Wakoski's 'The father of my country'. But the first thing to say about Rich's description of her pivotal position is that she 'locates' herself on the border of a new feminist poetics by admitting to a historicised thematics of masculinity. In two ways: Rich uses the same lexical pointers to describe both the seductive appeal of Yeats and the 'powerful effect' of contemporary Cuban women poets, and Rich consistently promotes the notion of thresholds.

That this is so need not be argued from one keynote address alone. Strong evidence from elsewhere in Rich's career proves it. In Rich's first and major lesbian 'separatist' poetry – 'Twenty-one love poems' – the power of an embodied masculinity has, I would like to argue, a specific energising presence. In conversation with Elly Bulkin, Rich described the 'Twenty-one love poems' as the moment which delineated 'the end and the beginning of a certain part of my life' (Bulkin, 1977, p. 61). Yet Rich steps forward into a lesbian erotics, zig-zagging and curving through the existing poetic tradition. 'Twenty-one love poems' in particular, as Rich herself realised, intermingle and mirror her sources with 'a certain amount of reference back and forth'

(Bulkin, 1977, p. 59). The thematics of masculinity is present as a very particular historicised address to Rich's male peers Robert Lowell and Paul Goodman. 'Twenty-one love poems' is one of the finest feminist poem cycles of its period and yet is one which seems to make a strong claim to a lesbian erotics by being most movingly subject to a masculine voice(s). The second thing to say, sadly, is that it is precisely this articulate polyphony that has been ravenously subsumed in literary criticism about Adrienne Rich, particularly in feminist criticism, into a 'compulsory' feminist model. With few exceptions literary criticism has actively repelled any inquiry into the poetic asymmetries of Rich's feminism. The critical schema follows a familiar line. To judge from most criticism written about Rich, Rich's more 'important' lesbian script emerged from the traditional, male dominated canon when Rich began to describe an autonomous and collective women's culture. Feminist critics, such as Mary DeShazer, read Rich as if Rich herself, in her poetry, positively refuses or evaporates the heterosexual element of her eros (DeShazer, 1986). They suggest that with separatism Rich was able to leave a residue of masculine motifs safely outside the wall of her feminist poetics. Rachel Blau DuPlessis, among others, argues that Rich's sources of inspiration come from her invocation of inspirational women figures – figures who had no place in conventional poetry (DuPlessis, 1985). Joan Fiet Diehl agrees that Rich is clearsightedly replacing male heroes with women adventurers such as the mountain climber and scientist, without any bifocal lens (Diehl, 1980). Feminist critics then, connect Rich's feminist poetry to that sustaining community of women writers and women activists, past and present, with whom Rich intellectually associates only by the late 1970s and 1980s. Susan Stanford Friedman, in particular, feels that it is Rich's transmutation of H.D.'s poetics which enables Rich to create new representations more appropriate for a women-centred world (Friedman, 1984).[1]

Certainly, by the time of The fact of a doorframe (1984), Rich has replaced the valences of a masculine aesthetics with her own feminist vision which incurs a clear distaste for the social order of men. Although this collection is welcome as a feminist arena in which Rich's talents could be more fully displayed, it does not explain when and how Rich became brave enough and separatist enough to be at last erotically inobliterable. To find the evidence of feminism in Rich's poetry, as Diehl does, only in Rich's representation of the everyday world of women elides and subsumes other acute and exciting sexual differences. This repressive blankness ignores, too, how Rich's *male* contemporaries also explore their daily lives in poetry. We feminists are not the first generation of poets to assume that we are closer to the 'common language'.

Rich's poetic topology is complex and it is one not easily read using only a map of female signposts. Certainly, to create a lesbian feminist poetics of experience and identity Rich needed the rhetorical authority of women-identified myths. As critics note, Adrienne Rich makes strong connections between her literary foremothers and her own contemporary practices. Emily Dickinson and Anne Bradstreet are major and continuous sources of inspiration, not only because these writers were brave to write poetry in a deeply patriarchal society but also because they explored, in print, their emotional lives (See Rich, 1986). Virginia Woolf, Sojourner Truth, H.D. and many other emblematic women literary figures appear again and again in Rich's poetry as talismans of women's intellectual powers.

Furthermore, in conversation with the Gelpis, Rich claimed that 'I cannot think of a single male poet, however marvellously he has written about the female principle or intellectual beauty, who hasn't misused and abused actual women' (Gelpi and Gelpi, 1975, p. 116). Rich's essay 'When the dead awaken' appears to reinforce her disengagement from an inherited past. In it Rich describes a woman poet's struggle against a poetic tradition with its alienating iconography of objectified women. But Rich's exploration of the material and collective bases of women's experience is continuous throughout her career. The exploration, in *itself*, is an inadequate explanation for, or indeed proof of, Rich's feminist separatism. Detailing that exploration does not address the *moment* and *place* of Adrienne Rich's break across the boundary of tradition. It does not address the equally full, if equivocal, lexical pointers in her work to men. For example, in Of woman *born*, Rich circulates her poetic identity inexorably among male exemplars claiming that she 'identified more with men than with women; the men I knew seemed less held back by self-doubt and ambivalence, more choices seemed open to them' (Rich, 1976, p. 193). It is worth, then, trying to discriminate that possible plurality of markers to reveal the imaginative quality of Rich's feminist imperative.

The necessary conditions for writing, to follow Harold Bloom, must include the presence of Others. In psychoanalytic terms this is frequently described as the powerful dynamic between parents and offspring of the same gender. In poetry it is represented, as Bloom argues in The anxiety of influence, in the artistic representation of the poetic forerunner in the strongest work of the poetic successor. Until the early 1970s the American poetic space was inhabited in the main by male poets – Robert Duncan, Robert Creely, John Berryman and in particular Robert Lowell. A further examination of Rich's 'strongest' poems – the 'Twenty-one love poems' – reveals a complex poetic reciprocation between that poetic space and Rich's own creativity.

Rich's explicit separatism, and articulation in her poetry of a women-centred world occurs quite abruptly within the period 1970 to 1975 even if it derives, of course, from a premature and conscious identification with women's concerns. To offer a more adequate explanation of that moment, and to resist essentialism, requires an examination of the poetic context of that period and Rich's thematics of response and detachment. The 'Twenty-one love poems' are hugely self referential. They are shaped in such a way as to refer to Rich's external interests at the moment of composition. Not only this but there is an emotional urgency in that composition which produces a sequence of abbreviations and associations which demand to be placed in the context of Rich's other writing and reading in this period.

The transgression of literary boundaries – the moments of discursive parody when the oppressor's own weapons are turned against him – reveal not only the conditions within which any poetry actually exists, but also what new 'networks of meaning' can be created. Rich's poetry is full of voices, not all of them originating from her own tongue. On the contrary, she incorporates a wide variety of signs from other texts. The moment when the structure of the house is shaken – the 'coming out' lesbian poems of the 'Twenty-one love poems' cycle of 1975 – follows and depends on Rich's belief in Necessities of Life: Poems 1962 – 1965 and Leaflets that women's private experiences cannot be separated from their public context which is the discursive and institutional lines of a masculine culture. Shaping that separatism is a heritage, external and internal, which Rich once described as the creative antagonism of 'wandering between two worlds' (Rich, 1980). For example Rich continually fluctuates between private experience and public statement in her writing by obliterating the border between genres – between autobiography and advocacy.

In 1983 in Massachusetts, Rich was describing that difficult relationship a woman poet has with the literary tradition which implicitly modifies the imagery of women's poems as much as it explicitly misrepresents women in the literary canon. Rich's poetics of transgression create an identity for women in her 'Twenty-one love poems'. But the poems draw on male precursors as much as on the detail of the lesbian relationship which the poems describe. If Rich's lesbian relationship offers her a language of subjectivity, of feeling, the authority of the poems comes as much from Rich's clear relation to the masculine poetic ontology. Rich draws on that creative dialectic between subjectivity and ontology when she analyses other women's writing. Women writers, Rich claims, negotiate marginality, they are 'a decorative garnish on the buffet-table of the university curriculum' but women critics are the healers at work in a profoundly fragmented patriarchy (Rich, 1983, p. 521):

In a world in which diverse ancient communities still exist as residues but in which art and social life are deliberately severed, criticism bears an immense responsibility ... the feminist critic ... she is or may be the mediator between the living or the dead, between writers of color and white writers (and their readers), between lesbian writers and heterosexual writers and readers, between writers and readers of the expanding and mixed cultures of a global society. (Rich, 1984, p. 737)

Adrienne Rich demands a hugely expanded programme for feminist criticism but clearly feels that it should dialogue with past and present. The evidence suggests therefore that Adrienne Rich's own poetry should also be read as a continuum of 'residues' and a 'global' feminist culture in which she engages with, and explicitly rewrites, the precursor tradition. There is no foreground or background where a patriarchal past is waiting to be developed into the positive print of feminist poetry. Certainly in her criticism Rich has brilliantly explored the institutions and contexts which inform women's writing, in terms of the various disguises or metaphors with which women poets transform the silencing of women by patriarchy. Yet if Rich's growing commitment to a *separate* world for women coincided with her abandoning the radical humanism which pervades her writing in the 1960s, the resolution which subordinated humanism to lesbian erotics reveals much tension. Rich gradually changes the personae of her poems from anonymous figures with ambiguous genders to more positive women. But when that moment of separatism is investigated the masculine precursors are present in shadowy form. Rich's struggle between a masculine past and the feminist future, between the gendered limits of literary theory and the trajectory of feminist criticism is encapsulated in her most generative feminist term —

re-vision. 'Re-vision — the act of looking back, or seeing with fresh eyes, of entering an old text from a new critical direction — is for women more than a chapter in cultural history: it is an act of survival. Until we can understand the assumptions in which we are drenched we cannot know ourselves' (Rich, 1980, p. 35).

Here 're-vision' becomes the central way in which women's writing is constructed. Yet Adrienne Rich took the term 're-vision' from a male American poet, Robert Duncan. Duncan first used the term in *The artist's view* in 1953. Rich's debt to Duncan is not simply one of terminological appropriation but part of her clear sense that the very category 're-vision' necessarily implies a circumscription from some quarter of poetry or other. The run-on which Rich is making here is instructive. 'Re-vision' is first historical — 'looking back' cataloguing our inequities and rewriting the past. It remains 'cultural' but is always psychic — an analysis of our deepest 'assumptions'. It is worth getting at the precise notions which Rich incorporates into her term since 're-vision' provides her poetry with its sexual politics. Rich passionately believes that critical work is a life-long activity, an almost obsessive noting of patriarchal instances whose notation will eventually help women to cross the boundary of institutionalised misogyny. The task which Rich describes here is akin to Michel Foucault's characterisation of 'archaeology' — a topographical exposure of the forgotten documents traversing social practices and the values embedded in linguistic forms.[2] It is instructive to compare Duncan's original conception with Adrienne Rich's very different understanding. The comparison highlights, I think, that more fundamental difference between the ways in which masculinity and femininity are inscribed in texts.

'ON REVISIONS'. In one way or another to live in the swarm of human speech. This is not to seek perfection but to draw honey or poetry out of all things. After Freud, we are aware that unwittingly we achieve our form. It is, whatever our mastery, the inevitable use we make of the speech that betrays to ourselves and to our hunters (our readers) the spore of what we are becoming.

I study what I write as I study out any mystery. A poem, mine or others, is an occult document, a body awaiting vivisection, analysis, X-rays. My revisions are my new works, each poem a revision of what has gone before. In-sight. 'Re-vision'. (Duncan, 1960, pp. 400-1)

Duncan's organic imagery presages Rich's attraction to categories of the body but Robert Duncan is calling up a very masculine figure. Both poets attend to their perceptions, but Duncan recommends self-perception, a turning inwards, whereas Rich celebrates an open psycho-history of gender. Rich searches for the impress of collective histories to give to her readers. Duncan, on the other hand, is hunted by his readers. Duncan's 're-vision' is the uncovering of his own dead past, a 'body awaiting vivisection' whose new poems are merely 'spores' thrown off his own parent body. Masculinity is present not only in the vocabulary, in a terminology of 'mastery' and 'hunters', but is an implicit part of Duncan's very tropes. Rich refuses this self-exhumation. 'Re-vision', to Rich, is the work of scrutinising language in order to speak freely of women's 'love' which Rich finds also to be a word 'in need of re-vision'. Rich subverts Duncan's masculine usage by including his definition into an intrinsically open and unresolved feminist engagement with literary history. Good writing will recognise and represent the specificities of all women's experience, not merely reconceptualise the poet's own experience. Yet it is deeply significant that Rich's most generative and feminist term should be one she learned from a man. Rich coins a feminist terminology by appropriating the vocabulary of a male poet.

In literary criticism, analyses of sexuality and textuality often reproduce an oedipal model. Harold Bloom's theory of poetic influence, in particular, is one which depends on Freud's theories of gender acquisition and sexuality. Bloom describes the scenario of sexuality within poetry as one which reproduces a confrontation between a son and his powerful poet father. Bloom claims that all strong poets depend for their success on the deliberate absorption of precursor poets into their poetry. In the *Anxiety of influence* he divides poets into 'precursors' and 'ephebes' or revisers, and he defines poetic revision as purposeful misinterpretation. Bloom traces forms of poetic revision in the writing careers of Keats, Wordsworth and other poets. Using Freudian concepts of the Oedipus and sublimation, Bloom explains that a 'strong' poet makes use of his precursor poet in the tropes and imagery of his poem in order to violate or usurp his poetic father. Bloom gives a nomenclature of 'clinamen', 'tessera' and 'apophrades' among other terms to ways in which poets swerve away from, or rewrite, the precursor poet's work inside their own poems in order to 'begat' an individual poetic self (Bloom, 1973).

Bloom's model of literary history is overly masculine. Feminist critics, justifiably, have attacked Bloom's poetic thematics as being intensely patriarchal because he describes only the intra-poetic relationships of male, not of female, poets. Sandra Gilbert and Susan

Gubar, for example, adapt elements of Bloom's oedipal drama in The madwoman in the attic, but apply it very differently to describe the much warmer matriarchal dialectic between the female precursor and contemporary woman poet (Gilbert and Gubar, 1979). This alternative model offers a more adequately feminist way to describe a female poet's relationship to precursor women poets because the female relationship, Gilbert and Gubar claim, depends on affinities rather than on mastery. Yet Adrienne Rich draws as freely upon precursor males as upon precursor female writers. It might be more accurate to explore these cross-gender intra-poetic relations rather than move swiftly past Rich's more traditional symmetries through the open door to a women-identified world. Rich allows the poets Paul Goodman and Robert Lowell their full density of Otherness in her articles in The American poetry review and in the 'Twenty-one love poems'. It is the 'collision' between Rich and Goodman and Lowell which tosses up the moment and manner of Rich's lesbian separatism.

The structure of the poetry which Rich was writing before the 1970s exactly reproduces the energy of this tension. Many of the poems in the volume Poems selected and new 1950-1974 are organised on this very principle. Differences of gender are rendered as contradictory by virtue of their representation as differences between the institutional power of male poets and other discursive possibilities. Summarising the space clearing rhythms and figures of the poems written up to that date we can see the same motifs and themes explored again and again in ways in debt to the literary legacy of earlier male poets. Yeats, in particular, is suggested in symmetrical phrases 'a figure of terrible faith' or in an appropriated nomenclature of 'Erinyes' (Rich, 1974, p. 157). Rich suffers no loss of contact with traditional sources. The poetry written during this period carries the pattern of an embodied masculine aesthetics. 'The Loser' echoes Yeats's 'Sailing to Byzantium' both in its imagery and diction. Rich adopts Yeats's sense of want but directs her desire to the domestic interior. It is not simply that this signals an uncertain notion of a strong female self but that Rich recognises that heroines achieve identity by engagement with, not alienation from, a familiar order. 'Aunt Jennifer's tigers' and 'Orion' can appropriate a masculine formalism but only at the expense of, as Rich reveals in 'When the dead awaken', 'putting the woman in a different generation' or relying on male siblings (Rich, 1980, p. 40). In 'When the dead awaken' Rich describes the poetry which was her undergraduate and graduate culture from the 1940s to the end of the 1950s. Included along with formalism, which Rich in a resonating phrase remembers handling with 'asbestos gloves', are particular male poets and their concomitant baggage of 'universalism'. Even in 'Snapshots of a daughter-in-law', commonly thought to be Rich's major and lengthy description of women's objectification at the hands of men, she refuses a personal pronoun 'I' preferring to juxtapose the oppositional narratives of the cultural tradition with the voices of famous and unknown historical women. 'Planetarium', 'In the woods' and 'Necessities of life' all explore the social implications for women of cultural and physical objectification. The misshapen constellations of 'Planetarium' are a metonymy of women's physical pain which Rich also metaphorically represents in images of the distorted bodies of victims of famine and war. The poems do not declare women's autonomy. Rather they array the strength of masculinity in such figures as doctors and soldiers. Rich understands that women's autonomy will depend on women digesting and absorbing a powerful diet of intellectual authoritarianism, even male brutality, for example in 'After Dark'. As a group, the poems Rich was writing before the early 1970s, begin to arm the narratives of women with the power and strength of masculinity. For example, in 'The Knight', Rich cuts a familiar mythical figure free from his Tennysonian Pre-Raphaelite associations and recasts the Knight as a man imprisoned in his metallic and mechanical armour. In a somewhat mirrored way the Knight is as inhuman as the numbing imagery which Rich is forced to apply to women.

So that until the poems of the later 1970s, Rich's mythical figures, like the three sisters of traditional folk tales in 'Women' from *Leaflets*, remain the Others of male mythology. Such demonic women remain visibly *objects* sitting on 'rocks of black obsidian' – monster paradigms of the Other, tabooed and marginalised female subjects. Women and men are not *equal* oppositional figures in Rich's poems just as the poetic tradition is not a negative, but a persuasive power to which Rich is surprisingly vulnerable. Rich's poems begin to 're-vision' difference in terms of different identities but they never reject a classical story. Deflation and delegitimation are the messages here. Yet such poems are also interrogatives often with a direct address to Rich's reader, to disengage from fixed categories as part of the process of reading. For example Rich chooses different verb tenses for different areas of experience. The present is identified as sensual, empirical and usually organic; the past is identified as a collective patriarchal message; and the future is full of interrogatives with Rich oscillating between feminist transgression and attributed categories. The poems mirror Rich's increasing concern that the border between past and present, like the border between art and life, must be vaulted over. The poems, haunted with images of doors and journeys, stand as Rich's rite of passage.

By 1972 the connectives are made. While the content of the later poems appears similar – houses are still burning down, women are still suffering quietly – in 'For a sister', Rich uses the image of a tow chain to connect herself with the world. 'Essential resources' takes its 'bridge' metaphor from plumbing with Rich, metaphorically, replumbing the house of poetry. By 'Landscape architect' whole new lands are being mapped. Rich begins to describe maternal women, with multi-faceted feelings and a self conscious ability to cross the boundary between inner and outer selves. The vocabulary of the poems grows simpler as Rich's ideas become certain. Rich now uses a direct, less abstract style, which organises a vocabulary of mutuality rather than one of objectification. Speech is freed with 'surgical' cuts, with a direct 'tracheotomy'. In 'Phenomenology of anger' the narrator is an acetylene torch burning away the lies of patriarchy. Rich assumes different temporalities too in her preoccupation with inhabiting a gender. In 'Meditations for a savage child', she time travels centuries to associate with the outcasts of history and to give speech to the silent – to l'enfant sauvage, Vietnam orphans and women in the grip of male doctors.

Rich is beginning to take on the identities of women in a thoroughgoing way. She has a sense of herself as representative of many American women – black slaves, pioneers and miners. 'Diving into the wreck' delineates with rapt attention women's everyday and communal concerns. The moments of collective identity are those of family 'anniversaries' recorded in personal 'diaries'. These studies of 'women's time' are alert to the differing metaphorical weightings of 'woman'. For example, Rich undercuts the solidity of nouns with the transgressive continuous female 'infinitive'. Rich matches her sense of a gendered consolidation with the invocation of a woman reader in abrupt pronoun changes 'we are, I am, you are'.

Rich reinforces her address to that larger community of women by assuming that each woman narrator will have a woman reader, for example, the poem 'For L. G. ∴ unseen for twenty years'. Rich's ongoing dialogue is clearly now with women and less with the male literary tradition. Rich's goal for the 1980s, in other words, is to create a rhetorical firmament of women's differences. And indeed the metaphors of the 1980s speak of separatism, voiced in a language of 'natural history', and specifically of women's lives. Lesbianism is the spoken script of 'Diving into the wreck', *The dream of a common language* and *A wild patience has taken me this far*. The love of women is the emotional source of Rich's 'common' language.

In 'Transcendental Etude', the poem closing *The dream of a common language*, Rich suggests that women need to have contact with each other to remember their history. The material of women's history, here and in Rich's other poems, are the erotic sexualities of women's 'separate' experiences, specifically lesbianism and motherhood. A metaphor of giving birth to oneself was the dominant image of Rich's epic text *Of woman born* as well as it is the dominant theme of poems like 'The mirror in which we two are one'.

Of woman born argues the case for a clearly confirmed history of female power which Rich traces from pre-historical myths of birth and reproduction. This power found in motherhood, Rich argues, has been socially misrepresented as the 'institution' of motherhood. Rich subverts a technological language of reproduction with her historical account of the warm sacramental relationships of mothers and daughters and the replication of these in the lesbian couple. Rich expresses this theme in metaphors from the semiotic, from the psychic as well as from the physiological density of motherhood.

Similarly in her poems the models of women's creativity depend no longer on gloomy references to mechanical knights or great male poets but to a rather different category, – the Great Goddess figures of Demeter and Diana. Rich challenges the traditional image of the female muse which is often portrayed as a static, rotund or virginal woman by creating strong, emblematic women whose survival depends on a metonymy of affiliation, for example the literal roping together of women's bodies needed by the Russian women's climbing team in 'Phantasia for Elvira Shatayev'.

Rich creates a progressive identity of feminism by making a celebratory identification of women in different cultures and by releasing past women poets from the sedimented layers of literary history. The celebration of new women reaches a pitch in Rich's poems of the 1980s. These poems are the tips of an iceberg whose foundation is in the quotidian criticism and reviews which Rich was writing for the *American poetry review* and other journals in the 1970s. Rich claims she experienced a liberating release from the fallacy of universalism with the flowering of the Black and women's movements at the beginning of the 1970s.[3] Rich's major project of the late 1970s – to create a women-centred culture – finds its affirmation in the 'Twenty-one love poems' and in On lies, secrets, and silence. How and where did Rich appropriate that power of naming? Where was the boundary crossed? To understand all the resonances of Rich's 'woman', we need a great elasticity to hold her poetic deployments together with the changing massifications of woman in the cultural climate of the 1970s.

In the early 1970s Rich specifically engages with the stability of 'woman' in the poetry and cultural criticism written by men. Only by demolishing that heterosexual and patriarchal iconography could she place women's relationships at the centre of poetic attention. And it is in Rich's criticism, as much as in her poetry, that the significant break occurs. It is in the pages of the American poetry review that the question of poetic style became Rich's poetics of experience.

Rich was a founding contributor to the journal and wrote a regular column 'Caryatid' and reviews from 1972 to 1974. In her essays Rich assumes an intimate audience, one of known readers, to help her map out that radical relationship between art and politics which she needed for her poetry. Yet, republishing the pieces in On lies, secrets and silence in 1979, Rich prefaces them with a harsh attack on the American poetry review. She claims that the journal had 'white and sexist content, a pervasive lack of purpose – poetic or political', emblematic of the masculine literary arena which worked to flatten and detonate women's words (Rich, 1980, p. 107). Thus, according to Rich, as far back as the early 1970s, the poetic establishment was brutally structured by an aesthetised misogyny which excluded sexual difference as aesthetic fact and as politics. The paths of male entitlement had their margins of literary discourse – the journal the American poetry review.

Rich suggests that she was forced into a feminist, then lesbian separatism with the shock of recognition that even the liberal American poetry review ignored and devalued women's writing. Yet researching carefully in the Review I could not deny that from 1972 onwards, the American poetry review took a consistent feminist line. Its contributors include most of the major feminist, or activist women writers – Marge Piercy, Erica Jong, Denise Levertov and Diane Wakoski. In this decade, these were the poets who pre-eminently were undermining the cultural objectification of women with a writing at once autobiographical and densely certain of female sources of authority – from women's

physiology and family relationships. Whole supplements are given to
the poetry of Ann Sexton and to Rich herself. Photo captions with
Rich's writing connect her poetry specifically with her political role
in the women's movement. Feminism was recognised aloud in the first
issue with a poem by Denise Levertov who uses the imagery of
reproduction to describe the birth of a poet into radical action; and a
piece by Diane Wakoski which argued that a woman's diary is as
important as her poetry because it enables her to translate personal into
textual moments. The *Review* created a space for lesbian writing by
publishing the lesbian journalist Jill Johnston's compelling account of
Janis Joplin's bisexuality. To inscribe static stereotypes, as Rich appears
to do, onto what was arguably a sharp eyed politically liberal journal
seems hardly fair.[4] Yet if we unpack and interpret the substantive
structures shaping the journal's politics a different and less distinctly
liberal agenda is opened up. The *American poetry review* has a very 1960s
tone. Norman O'Brown and Robert Bly wrap autobiographical poetry
with the language of male therapy. Particularly with its publishing of
Russian Samizdat poetry, the journal resembles a group of intellectuals
under seige, with their literature of survival at a moment of crisis in
the master narratives. Although each issue publishes an ethnic voice,
either Chicano, Filipino or American Indian, the *Review* unabashedly
celebrates self expression not the politics of cultural engagement. The
architecture of the *Review* is late modernism. Surrealism re-surfaces with
the *Review*'s endorsement of Paul Eluard, John Berryman is praised for
his 'confessions', John Ashbery is lauded because he is a poet 'in search
of a perfect medium' and Etheridge Knight's poems are about the
'black man's strength'. A professor of religion is chosen to write about
Edward Albee, and Donald Hall argues that the imagery of ritual is
more significant than the imagery of war in Robert Bly's 'Counting the
small boned bodies'. The 1960s struggle on where a new model of
literature should have been created for the 1970s. In one issue a
dialogue between James Baldwin and Nikki Giovanni focuses dramatically the misogyny of liberalism. There is in fact little dialogue in their
discussion. Baldwin expounds his fears about black men's sexuality
and Giovanni describes her mother. Just as the *Review* recuperates Muriel
Rukeyser for modernism so it published only three women in the
trumpeted collection '18 New Poets'. Social and feminist issues are
individualised and hence devalued. The *American poetry review* had no
language in which a lesbian woman could write autobiographically in
an *embodied* poetics. Rich's move from this infusing blank liberalism is

instructive. The topics of her pieces in the *Review* are very revealing both because Rich's contributions are the most overtly political contributions from any writer in the *Review* and because in them, Rich responds directly to issues of sexuality. In her first 'Caryatid' (a punning title referring to the female figures who support Greek temple decorations), Rich chose to write about the American anarchist Paul Goodman. She mourns his recent death particularly because, she claims, it was Goodman's politics which sustained her in the liberal environment of her undergraduate life. Rich also misses she says, in much contemporary writing, Goodman's strong and overt sexuality. The emotional geology of bisexuality, Rich claims, gave a real imaginative and political energy to Goodman's poetry.

Rich's consolidation of a progressive new identity of women very much depends on Goodman's anarchist scaffolding. Paul Goodman was an extraordinary and now unjustly ignored writer. From the 1930s to the 1970s, he was writing philosophy, literary criticism, urban planning, novels, stories, plays, poetry, educational theory, and radical political and psychoanalytic criticism. In *Communitas*, and the *May pamphlet* 'Drawing the line', written during the 1940s, he describes paradigmatic libertarian societies which are tied to precise social groups and institutions in his later writing in the 1960s — *Utopian essays* and *Like a conquered province*. In *Gestalt therapy*, his novel *Empire city* and his poetry and drama Goodman continually meshed together subjective experience with materialist practice, defining culture as the mores and suppressed instincts of society. From the beginning Paul Goodman, very like Adrienne Rich, had a historic sense of an appropriate American culture for the times in which he lived. The reason that *Growing up absurd*, Goodman's book about adolescence, was so immensely popular in 1959, is that it was the first book to show how American society systematically betrays its youth by not providing them with any viable community (see Humm, 1981). Adrienne Rich, twenty years later, argues in very similar terms, that American capitalist patriarchy denies women any serious collectivity. Goodman has clearly taught Rich where to 'draw the line' in an unjust world.

In the fourth issue of the *American poetry review* Rich published her Goodmanesque 'Caryatid: On war, rape and masculine consciousness'. Rich's battle with patriarchal discourse is shaped by Goodman's earlier battle with capitalist aggression in his 'Revolution, sociolatry and war', part of *May pamphlet*. The titles of the essays are similar and the social contexts of their work are akin. Both write in times of war. The context of Goodman's libertarian pamphlet is the pervasive and unremitting pressure of State controls during the Second World War. In 1942 there were up to ten million Office of Civil Defence volunteers, by 1943 a quarter of total broadcast time was on war news or themes. Rich is writing, too, in a time of increasing sexual violence and aggression towards women whose poetry is necessarily a battlefield 'wired with danger'. In her essay, Rich prefers to introduce to the readers of the *Review*, women poets, like Jean Garrique and Natalya Gorbanevskaya who were political activists, rather than judging that the value of contemporary women's poetry comes from its 'confessional' tone.

Both Goodman and Rich emphasise the specifically terroristic workings of masculinity which, for Goodman, was crystallised in a homophobic State and,for Rich, was the continual, but often un-acknowledged, sexual violence of men to women. The argument of Goodman's *May pamphlet* is that individuals are caught coercively by society in a chaotic rather than conspiratorial way. In order to become free, individuals must create a fresh vocabulary and design acts of social worth which will depend on 'natural violence'. Goodman's libertarian argument for establishing communities where people can freely express emotions 'in the interests of rediscovering the primary experiences of birth, infantile sexuality, grief and mourning for death' is repeated by Rich in her essays (Goodman, 1977, p. 23). For example, *Of woman born* is preoccupied by Rich's attention to these psychic experiences. Rich's criticism is a very good example of what Bloom calls 'tessera' where a poet enjoys a reassuring exhilaration of productivity by completing the poem of the precursor in a different sense. Rich and Goodman share an active subjective writing style wide ranging in reference which remains intensely personal in tone and bearing. For both, language is the ramified embodiment of political attack. Both write essays where the vocabulary of personification, indirect hyperbole, attention to value words of 'ought' and 'must' is essentially convictional language. The 'tessera' or fragment of Goodman is antithetically completed by Rich when she retains Goodman's terms but translates them in a 'different' sense into her argument for lesbian separatism.

By the sixth issue of the *American poetry review* Rich has come out. Her 'Caryatid' in that issue praises lesbian-feminist periodicals and she comes out from under the cloak of liberalism in an uncompromising attack on the American poet Robert Lowell. Throughout his early poems – *Poems 1938-1949*, through *Life studies* to *Notebook* and *The dolphin*

- Robert Lowell was soaked in the passionate consciousness of the mythology, history and literature of New England. By the last decade of his life in the 1970s, Lowell's introspective autobiographical poems reveal his uneasy relationship with his Puritan inheritance. Yet Lowell's controlled purchase of poetic form is also continually counterbalanced by often hysterical and violent images. Rich clearly sensed the pain underlying Lowell's overtly tranquil and lyrical celebration of the birth of his first son. Rich chose to review Lowell's Dolphin poems in order to introduce some contemporary women poets and to bravely attack Lowell's descriptions of his wife and mistress. Rich is aggressively feminist. Lowell's need to dominate and objectify the women figures in his poems reveals, Rich states, 'a kind of aggrandized and merciless masculinity at work' (Rich, 1973b, p. 16).

Attacking the high priest of contemporary American poetry was not easy. In the same issue Jerome Mazzaro praises Lowell for his use of 'Ovid, Christianity and international poetry' (Mazzaro, 1973, p. 12). Successive issues appearing after Rich's attack, carried letters rebuking her for resting on 'ideology and sexual prejudice'. Diana Wakoski is upset by Rich's association of Lowell's poetry with his life history, and by Rich's refusal to understand that autobiography is a literary construction: 'Literature is not about the morality of the author' (Wakoski, 1974).

Yet the poems which Adrienne Rich wrote immediately after her attack on Robert Lowell – the 'Twenty-one love poems' – are those which draw most freely on Lowell's imagery and on his topics particularly on the poems in Lowell's Notebook. Rich gives attention to male poets at many points in her writing but nowhere is her debt to Robert Lowell expressed more powerfully than in the 'Twenty-one love poems'. Both the Poems and Lowell's Notebook are constructed in a sequence of short free verse lyrics. Both groups of poems describe lovers addressing their beloveds in intimate tone. It might appear paradoxical that Rich centralises lesbian relations in a poetic tradition for the first time, not directly through calling to H.D. or other women poets but in her rewriting of Robert Lowell. Yet the traces of Lowell are Rich's 'apophrades' or the return of the dead. As Harold Bloom suggests, the strong poet in his final exclusion of the precursor para-doxically accomplishes that separatism by holding his poem fully open 'again to the precursor's work' (Bloom, 1973, p. 15). The 'Twenty-one love poems' are in play with Lowell's Notebook, but although Lowell's image emerges in Rich's topic and metaphors, it does so mirrored, at half its size. In her essays in the *American poetry review* and in the 'Twenty-one love poems', Rich antithetically converts Lowell's misogynist eros into a warm and loving lesbianism and finally escapes the 'anxiety of influence'.

Rich's cycle is haunted by a faded polaroid of Lowell's setting whose lines she observes in order to redraw, redesign and transform its shape. Rich shares Lowell's 'story' – the daily life of a poet balancing sexually private with public moments – but she replaces Lowell's angry tone with a more optimistic poetics. Both 'Twenty-one love poems' and *Notebooks* begin with daily events. Both Lowell and Rich share the same mundane experience of 'waking under the early rising sun' as they equally explore dissatisfaction and alienation in the context of contemporary life (Lowell, 1974, p. 127). Both use the intimate voice of inner conversations to negotiate their sexual experiences. Furthermore Lowell and Rich invoke the same imagery. Both rely heavily on a vocabulary of rivers and borders in a structured ideogram of mental frontiers. The structure for both is a solution of the problems involved in getting a particular thing said, but to move from Lowell to Rich involves exchanging hypostasised bodies for fluid femininity.

In the 'Twenty-one love poems' Rich creates a middle aged heroine whose account of herself and her lover is an erotic history, full of the loved daily moments and objects that draw them together, sharing books, movies and groceries. Lesbian love writes the plot of Rich's daily life where Lowell relies on sexual violence. Rich's poems, however, do focus on the difficulties of language and on the muted fears of the narrator that her resistant syntax might not honestly capture the potential of love. 'Twenty-one love poems' explore the difficulties lesbian lovers experience in sustaining an effortless companionship in historical and political circumstances hostile both to lesbian erotics and to women. Rich depicts the violence of New York city and the violence of military oppression abroad which combine to limit the force and flowering of women's love and politics. What the 'Twenty-one love poems' show is not a refusal of the poetic tradition itself, not a move into some essentialist female iconography; rather the poems represent the daily process of lesbian love as underpinning and sustaining a poet's movement across the boundaries of 'literature and urban life'. Lesbian 'difference' is defined as natural but not as essentialist. The strength of lesbian love making is so powerful, so revolutionary, as to be capable of engendering a new poetry 'close to the Wolverines'.

Not surprisingly, Lowell's *Notebook* accepts the psychosocial position of the male poet. The subject of Notebook is a male having an absolute masculine difference. Woman is of specular interest to the male narrator-lover who fixes her in a gaze as a female Other but never allows her to be a subject with her own articulate sexuality. By contrast, Rich desires to catch the wing of a woman's figure: 'And you, you move toward me with the same tempo. Your eyes are everlasting, the green spark of the blue-eyed grass of early summer' (Rich, 1978, p. 237). The poet's gaze is not specular but marks a moment of mutual female desire. The poems describe a mutual gaze which 'sparks' the two women writers to erotic creativity. Both come to know themselves as women, and as writers, by witnessing each other at work and in love, empathetically, 'and somehow, each of us will help the other live' (Rich, 1978, p. 237). Lowell tells us about himself at fifty with a body where 'overworked central heating bangs the frame' (Lowell, 1974, p. 127). In contrast to Lowell, or perhaps as a feminist complement, Rich imagines a rhapsodic autobiographical figure. Rich is forty five, full of erotic capacity enjoying the 'insatiate dance of your nipples in my mouth' (Rich, 1978, p. 243). Lowell tries to re-enter adolescence remembering life in the sixth grade. Rich, on the other hand, is happily mature: 'Did I ever walk the morning streets at twenty. My limbs streaming with a purer joy?' (Rich, 1978, p. 237).

Lowell's poems represent the processes of repression contained in creative writing. Lowell's concerns are of course with a masculine psyche located in an Oedipal scenario of alienated longing. Lowell's version of the creative process is basically repressive. He finds it necessary to defuse his current erotic longings, to make them safe and controllable by placing them into the objectified setting of adolescence. Lowell's rejection of a contemporary female figure is the burden of his memory of adolescence. The emblematic contemporary figure with 'hair of yellow oak leaves' can be brutally surmounted by returning to adolescence and scratching, 'My four initials, R.T.S.L./like a dirty word across my bare blond desk' (Lowell, 1974, p. 119).

The ellagic acid has transferred from blond oak desk to yellow oak hair. Clearly Lowell is not released from his past but in debt to the misogynist adolescent imagery which it can supply. Lowell is unable to invoke a present woman except in synecdoches of adolescent trauma. Rich continues her dialogue with Lowell in the episode of the pool. Both Lowell and Rich look into water to find their lovers. In Notebooks Lowell's blood is moving solipsistically, however, 'round the single I'. Pools return only 'fungus' carp to him rather than 'our reflection' (Lowell, 1974, p. 128). The same scenario fascinates Rich but it allows her to manoeuvre herself into a position where a dramatic lesbian feminist statement is possible. Raising her lover 'dripping and brought into the sun' Rich discovers the power of lesbian sexuality:

show me what I can do for you, who have
often made the unnameable nameable for others,
even for me. (Rich, 1978, p. 240)

The poolside scene of this encounter is heavy and heady with female-directed desire. There is none of Lowell's retreat into adolescence. Lowell believes women to be 'sadly unfit'. With his lover in bed they become two parallel armies of Greeks engaged in a mental civil war. Like the river they lie beside their passion is policed and patrolled in a 'losing struggle' (Lowell, 1974, p. 126). Rich adopts the same ground and repeats Lowell's elements and verbal particulars. But it is the patriarchal world *outside* the lesbian couple in the 'Twenty-one love poems' which is 'unfit'. Rich's poetic procedure is to break with Lowell's humourless cynicism and displace such hostility onto an outside world which characterises lesbian experience as ugly and perverse.

Rich's project is not so much therefore, as Joan Fiet Diehl and other critics claim, to discover a language *free* from patriarchy. Rather Rich revivifies 'the dead' with her own colour and her own voice. The return of the precursor, as Harold Bloom points out, is, in fact, strongest in those poems that seek to be definitive statements or testaments to a strong poet's most powerful aim. What Rich proposes in the 'Twenty-one love poems', I believe, is Lowell's *Notebooks* revisioned and demisogynised:

Sleeping, turning in turn like planets
rotating in their midnight meadow:
a touch is enough to let us know
we're not alone in the universe, even in sleep:
the dream-ghosts of two worlds
walking their ghost-towns, almost address each other. (Rich, 1978, p. 241)

The narrative scope of the 'Twenty-one love poems' makes isolated quotations difficult. The common language which Rich and Lowell share is shaped by their careful attention to the particular, to the concrete. Yet in her joyful insistence on process, Rich's portrait expands Lowell's vocabulary of 'turning' and 'surviving'. Rich, unlike Lowell with his 'paper-cut finger', is not harmed by her daily life (when safe from 'taut' men in elevators). She overcomes and positively transforms the resistance of ordinary detail – the frequent moments when we touch our bed partner for surety of comfort or to check the passing of the night. Rich bears down hard on just those features of everyday life and language which keep Lowell awake and 'putty-gray'. It is the treachery of near synonyms which give drama to the immediate moment. Rich and her lover, even asleep, stride confidently through their mental towns having to engage in an autonomous creativity because women are 'ghosts' in the daytime world of men. The narrator neither objectifies her lover into a metonymic image from childhood, nor does she want the experience of the text to replace a shared and real erotic sensibility. Rich uses Lowell's scenario, as it were, to reconcile, in figurative terms, feelings whose resonances overrun literal language.

In No man's land, Sandra Gilbert and Susan Gubar pose the issue of Lowell's misogyny among that of other twentieth century men of letters faced with the feminisation of American culture. They describe how Lowell, near the end of his life, attacked Adrienne Rich in a poem as a 'disabled veteran beating time with crutches' (Gilbert and Gubar, 1988, p. 160). Adrienne Rich, as most readers know, is increasingly disabled by arthritis. The savagery of Lowell's unnecessary menace, as Gilbert and Gubar present it, is part of that same psychoanalytical masculine model of loss and anger 'feelings that the mother-muse had abandoned them' (Gilbert and Gubar, 1988, p. 160). Gilbert and Gubar's point, explicated with references to William Carlos Williams, T. S. Eliot and Ezra Pound seems very well taken. Lowell shares the cultural angst of literary men concerned to banish the female from literary history. Nonetheless the decision to put Lowell solely into the context of his masculine peers is an over-determined one. The positioning narrows the possibility of cross-gender dialogues and a purchase on concepts of creativity and inspiration which inform the work of both male and female poets. The implications of categories of gender are not fully explored. What I want to suggest, tentatively, is that a certain appropriation of masculinity from its own limited arena offered Rich a more extensive map of poetry.

To read the 'Twenty-one love poems' alongside stanzas from Notebook is to realise that the poems are deeply indebted to Lowell. The background is Lowell's. The distance between the sexual and the daily life in Lowell is not unlike the gap which Rich describes between her experience of lesbianism and the way society distances lesbianism from any daily agenda. Yet Rich, with great and careful calculation, is not swallowed up in Lowell as he fears being swallowed up alive in 'the huge smile' of his dolphin women.

A form of stylistic osmosis emerges in Rich's poems. How often she observes the lover working alone as if the lover was a co-poet, even muse in a displaced or circular metonymy of Rich's own work place 'at your desk for hours'. Throughout the poems, Rich keeps returning to the dread she reads in the male canon, in its Oedipal power, 'Goethe's dread of the Mothers' (Rich, 1978, p. 238). But she also appears to be attracted to bibliographical metaphors in the production of her own meaning: 'This apartment full of books ... once open the books ... he's been arranging his books ... centuries of books upwritten' (Rich, 1978, p. 238).

When the masculine power remains safely historicised, a displacement most prominently highlighted in Rich's associative litany of 'artists dying in childbirth, wise-women charred at the stake, centuries of books unwritten' (Rich, 1978, p. 239), Rich is safe within feminist deconstruction. But when it comes to *named* male friends' love of literary figures, for example Kenneth looking 'at Blake and Kafka while he types', the subtitled seduction of the fathers emerges.

Uncertain of her place, living in an apartment which 'could crack open to the thick jaws' and placing herself vulnerably on the cusp of past and current misogyny, Rich must turn Lowell's, Goodman's and Duncan's power against themselves, *because* the tradition has an ex-clusively masculine contents and shape. 'Blake and Kafka', 'Swift or Claudel' cannot be undone by substituting a female genealogy 'in woman's form, limping the long path' (Rich, 1978, p. 240). Rich adopts a different strategy for defusing the power of her male peers. The story of lesbian romance draws on the mechanics of intertextuality.

Topologically, the masculine tradition takes on a nominated role easily engorged by feminist culture. As is apparent from her metaphors as well as from her spatial organisation, Rich values her moments on the border, between history and herstory, between cold night and lesbian love making where 'two women together is a work' (Rich, 1978, p. 245). This poetic reversal by which Rich obtains power over Lowell's aesthetic, works so well because Rich herself shares many of the tradition's assumptions about the nature of images and the function of poetry.

Rich uses the imagery of women's bodies, 'every peak a crater' to undermine the topology of her male contemporaries whose sexuality is still an adolescent nightmare. The 'Twenty-one love poems', then are poems about poetry, about constructing sexual identity, about the erotics of work and daily life. Rich brings out the quality of lesbian identity at the borderlines of literature. As the narrator discovers, not all sexual experience is easily expressed. This is the point of Rich's vacillating hint of lesbian S/M:

Such hands might carry out an unavoidable violence
with such restraint, with such a grasp
of the range and limits of violence
that violence ever after would be obsolete. (Rich, 1978, p. 239)

There is a reason for Rich's slippage, for her defensiveness regarding lesbian S/M. Rich knows that to write about lesbian sexuality as if such a totalisable, realisable state simply existed would be to beg a number of questions, for example: what is an appropriate lesbian erotics?

The coming into being of a lesbian erotics seems to involve a dialectic between violence as a connotative, potentially erotic *experience* and violence as a nominative illegitimate form of (possibly masculine) power. Rich ought to be pleased with her sensitivity to the transforming power of women's previously unstated sexuality, this subjection of a masculine power to women's desire. But in Rich's account somehow the pleasures of lesbian desire are partial and provisional when the sexual *activity* of lesbian women is not fully described. Rich remains uncertain what direct and explicit detailing of lesbian S/M 'might' occur although it is 'unavoidable' and, of course, fully 'restrained'. Rich would apparently disavow her lesbian reader a transparent identification with her own lesbian autobiography.

Yet Rich's poetic cycle is not jeopardised by its specifiable links with its historic moment although it remains more than a little influenced by the discursive possibilities of a 1970s poetic production. Rich's resistance to the identity politics of that period was more thoroughgoing in her feminist critiques in the 1980s. If the *materiality* of playful perversity was an unenvisageable moment historically, by engaging in a metaphorics of desire in relation to the poetic canon Rich defies the fixity of an essentialist feminist identity, and the boundary drawn around a feminist icon, around any form of literary canonisation and generalisation.

Rich's dialectical appropriation of the voices of past poets, of Robert Duncan, Paul Goodman, and Robert Lowell, is a means to combat male aggression without diminishing her verbal capacity. Rich has openly transgressed. She has violated poetic expectations. By casting out the masculine standards of Robert Lowell, Rich could place women only relationships at the centre of her critical and poetic attention. Bonnie Zimmerman has drawn attention to the way in which lesbian writers re-vision their own pasts in terms of political theory which, she suggests, 'may be particularly essential to the formation of lesbian identity' (Zimmerman, 1984). Rich's apparently extreme rejection of the *American poetry review* in *On lies, secrets, and silence* might be explained by applying Zimmerman's idea that a lesbian identity can only be embraced by a lesbian writer who distrusts her past. Since one aspect of lesbian oppression is a mutilation of consciousness curable by language it is not surprising that Rich should have been so concerned about the mutilation of women in Lowell's poetic misrepresentation of sexuality. The particular oppression of lesbians is the enforced speechlessness and invisibility of lesbian sexuality.

We can take this deep into the body of Rich's early writing which accounts for many of her euphemisms and obscurities. For example the repeated Greek or Roman names – Corrine and Hadrian – are shorthand for the heroic world pitched beyond the poem and beyond women. Such names stand for the double exclusion of women from the literary tradition: by displacement and by mythical misrepresentation. In Rich's complex matrix, the classical emerges as a problem of tradition. It should encode the images of Sappho and lesbian identity, yet customarily classical poetry circumscribes these images in the patriarchal paradigm of a masculine Greek world.

Similarly misunderstanding the complexity of Rich's *lesbian* poetry impedes the subtlety of her critique of heterosexuality. It is important to recognise that the experience of women bonding which the 'Twenty-one love poems' depicts does not depend only on essentially female metaphors. Debunking the expertise of a poetic hegemony within an expert text, enabled Rich to construct a lesbian ontology. The task of articulating lesbian desire involves Rich in rewriting as well as in writing afresh. In no way must we read Rich's dialogic tolerance as any deconstructive undermining of ostensible feminism but as part of a large subsumption of a masculine poetics within feminism. The reflective mirrors in the 'Twenty-one love poems' signify the strength of Rich's poetic practice which bravely and willingly admits the history of its own unconscious.

Reprinting 'When we dead awaken' in *On lies, secrets and silence*, Rich left out her earlier call in the first version of the essay for women to regenerate culture together with men, by rewriting the final two paragraphs as if to discard any possibility of men's consciousness ever changing. That confidence of separatism is also one of language. In the later edition Rich divests men of the reproductive imagery of 'birth pains' which she first gave them and adds, to her earlier catalogue of women's social victimisation, the subtle victimisation built into 'language, the structures of thought' (Rich, 1980, p. 49).

The two essays which offer definitive statements about a women-identified world are 'Compulsory heterosexuality and lesbian existence' and 'What does separatism mean?'. 'Compulsory hetero-sexuality and lesbian existence' describes two forms of lesbian identity: lesbian 'existence', which is the existence of a lesbian erotics and lesbian 'continuum' which is all women-identified experience. The essay constitutes Rich's thorough formulation of a lesbian culture. She can explicitly separate lesbian affiliation from the imperative of heterosexuality, by having crossed the border into separatism in the early 1970s. By greatly enlarging the categories of 'lesbian' and hence redrawing its system of representation, Rich can set up overlaps and distinctions which overtake the patriarchal tradition. The essay is a clear statement about the meaning(s) of lesbian language, its social and erotic practices and its *range* – 'through each woman's life and throughout history' (Rich, 1983, p. 156).

In 'What does separatism mean?', as in all her work, Rich provides us with a model list of readings about separatism all meticulously documented. Separatism is simultaneously a linguistic and a territorial event – a 'space' where women can 'bear witness' to each other (Rich, 1981, p. 88). All the italicised vocabulary, the most intense statements, are about writing style, voice and meaning. Rich's conclusion is not to conclude. The title of the essay is 'Notes' and the volatility of separatism is coded in the *process* of language 'about how and when and with what kinds of conscious identity it is practised' (Rich, 1981, p. 90). Significantly the particular historical moment which Rich chooses as her own threshold in that essay, her own border crossing, is the 'after-taste' of the 1960s and its 'leftist cult of masculinity and violence and its usage of women' (Rich, 1981, p. 87). In other words the moment of Rich's contribution to the *American poetry review*.

The thematics of anarchist sexuality, male aggression and female misrepresentation which Rich explored in the *American poetry review* go to the very heart of Rich's feminism as it evolves in the 'Twenty-one love poems' and in On *lies, secrets and silence*. Rich confronted the patriarchal poetic canon directly in that journal and, by expressing her own deepest anxieties, could begin to find for her poetry the exuberance of separatism. In *Inspiring women*, Mary DeShazer proposes that the figure of the male master has been a damaging paradigm for women poets (see DeShazer, 1986)[5]. Yet by placing Rich in that larger cultural context of the early 1970s and the 'moment of the break' we can see the extent of her 're-vision' and how Rich is not 'damaged' but appropriates the power of naming.

As a literary space the *American poetry review* did not efface or ignore the effects of writing boundaries but served as best it could the cultural needs, the political needs of gay, and Black men and women poets. The most consistent keynote of the journal's published writing is exactly the sense of a threshold, of a border. The journal was a sort of border camp where the literary outsider could navigate her way through traditional representations on her trajectory to a women-identified culture.

By 1983 in 'Blood, bread and poetry', Adrienne Rich could easily engage in intimate conversation with women of the past and women of the future. That ease depends in part on Rich's active insistence in the *American poetry review*, and in her poetry and other criticism of that period, on placing the chiasmus of feminist difference alongside its masculine poetics. Rich occupied a specific border position in the culture of this period which gives a sure base to her subsequent lesbian separatism. The site of the border – the 'Twenty-one love poems' – has the language of all borders – a vocabulary of mediation, of palimpsest, of mimicry, of bilingualism.

To build a true archway to global feminism in the 1990s, Adrienne Rich needed a firm keystone. She chose hers from the 'fragment or tesserae' of masculine poetics in the 1970s.

Legal aliens: feminist
detective fiction

Tautologically, detective fiction like any other fiction, contains tropes
of gender which represent social and moral values. Yet unlike other
fiction, traditional detective novels often portray men and women as
stereotypical individuals. Traditional detective novels distrust friendships and emphasise the security of stable class and geographic
boundaries. Such novels deny complex sexual and social anxieties in
favour of gender stereotypes which are often depicted in violent and
misogynist vocabulary.

A group of novels by feminist women is now challenging the gender
norms of detective writing. Anglo-American writers, in particular
Gillian Slovo, Barbara Wilson, Mary Wings, Sara Paretsky and Rebecca
O'Rourke, question the limits to women's social progress by questioning the limitations of detective fiction in itself. They explore the
ways in which women overpower male environments by exploiting,
not necessarily having to discount, the feminine. In feminist fiction it
is perhaps the figure of the indecisive detective, for example Barbara
Wilson's printer sleuth Pam Nilson, who personifies the most
deflationary and disruptive contrast to the epistemological graffiti of
traditional detective absolutes. The invention of such strategies which
rupture formulaic conventions joins these texts to their sisters in the
exploration of border crossing. In the celebrated quotation from *A room
of one's own* Virginia Woolf described the role of women in patriarchal
society: 'if one is a woman one is often surprised by a sudden splitting
off of consciousness, say in walking down Whitehall, when from
being the natural inheritor of that civilisation, she becomes, on the
contrary, outside of it, alien and critical' (Woolf, 1929, p. 101). Some
sixty years before Warshowski, Woolf's account foreshadows the way
in which feminist detectives might walk their mean streets. This stance
which Hortense Spillers calls 'neither/nor', suggests that women in
traditional culture are continually working to displace it, and that this
allows the possibility of border crossing. (Spillers, 1987). Such a stance

implies a radical transformation of the character of the detective. One obvious example of change is the way in which feminist detectives prefer self-defence tactics to the violent and phallic gun.

It does not follow of course that women-centred detective fiction need be progressive. Even if there were such a unified category, feminism is not intrinsic to the aims of women-centred writing, nor is it intrinsic to fiction's popularity with women readers (see Coward, 1980).[1] But what marks these writers as feminist is their desire to manipulate both the material base of traditional plots which represent women as a sexualised virus and the bourgeois and violent language of detective writing. The precise specifying of 'detective women' for feminism might replace a traditional masculine antagonism to powerful women.

Although attempts to circumscribe detective fiction with certainty and to make sharp distinctions between mysteries, crime fiction, and thrillers generally fail, critics agree that the genre explores and absorbs the threat of illegality or 'Otherness' in melodramatic tales. Literary detectives are plural in number but they are not multivocal. It is the figure of the detective which focuses reader attention. The classical detective is an isolated man, owning no personal investment in the crime he is to investigate. Even when the detective is permitted subjective reflections, for example in Dashiel Hammett's Sam Spade stories, these reflections are not at all an indication of any emotional involvement in the crime. The detective's ethics may be conservatively personal or they may mirror contemporary social values but they must affirm the continuity of social institutions by holding in opposing values. The victim of the crime has neither psychological nor epistemological complexity. The reader has to come to identify only with the protagonist's sense of value, his sense of time and of place and, most crucially, with his sense of himself. This is because detective fiction gives narrative stress to action which is constant and often violent, described with an emotional charge which avoids psychic or social contradictions.[2] Power is often the basis of personal relationships. All these are characteristics historically signified as masculinist even if they are not characteristics of all men.

Feminist detectives refuse the 'eroticism' of physical violence. They remain continually ambivalent about their responses to aggression. What unites feminist detectives is the potent understanding that moral justice does not depend on forms of personal authority but on collective responsibility. Many feminist detectives share those views of

morality characterised by Carol Gilligan, in In a different voice, as a morality
of 'relationships'. Truncating absurdly Gilligan's subtle analysis, her
book analyses the links between concepts of morality and gender
identity. Gilligan finds that women build their concepts of morality on
affiliation and on a sense of duty to others, whereas men choose moral
absolutes of good or bad.[3] Such opposed characteristics of masculinity
and femininity structure the opposition between traditional detective
novels and feminist writing. Problems arise however, when we try to
distinguish at the level of narrative between the representations chosen
by male authors and those chosen by females. For example a
preoccupation with difference tout court would ignore the sometimes
subtle (and 'feminine') attention to language by Dashiel Hammett and
Raymond Chandler or the subjective poetry of Elmore Leonard. Yet it
is the imagery of gender which precisely and necessarily is chosen
differently by men and by women.

The classic detective is self-critical but he is equally and notoriously,
misogynist. Raymond Chandler's Philip Marlowe is a tough, 'hard-boiled'
emotionally contained individual. The masculinisation of Hammett's
texts occurs both in its violent imagery and in Sam Spade's careful
positioning of women characters. The energy of women's sexuality is
often a cause of plot action but it is contained or qualified out of
existence. Women, in the narratives of Hammett or Chandler, and
particularly in those of Conan Doyle, have no independent movement
or being. Women are conspicuous as erotic triggers of criminality or
as victims of the sexual politics of crime. The closure of female potency
is predicated on women's passive acceptance of the detective's
masculinity or on her 'foreignness' to his Anglo-American ethics, as
for example in Conan Doyle's 'The Greek interpreter' and A scandal in
Bohemia.[4] A romantic or sexual relationship may be desired by the
detective and his female informant/criminal but such a friendship is
often portrayed as hypocritical or threatening to the detective's
independent ethics and masculine ideology.

Yet it is possible to isolate in detective fiction some of the processes
by which a feminist author can make a profoundly different
representation of gender than can a traditional author. For one thing,
feminist authors swerve from classic detective formulae in their
attention to women's roles, to the psychic power of parental authority
and family ties and in the relationship of the work of detection to self
knowledge. It is clear that the breaking of these generic boundaries is
at least partly dictated by the centrality of a heroine and by the textual

urgencies of her desires. Although postmodernism may claim to efface genres in favour of historical collages and a multilevel écriture, the local book store's preference for Teen Romance, Western, Supernatural and Detective and the productive and reproductive spectrum of Western book marketing, relies on tight genre boundaries. Genres are prescriptive, legislative taxonomies of literary representation. Their demons, heroines, monsters and plots depend on a fierce hegemony of exclusionary limits. Within its narrative limits, the masculine detective novel valorises an objective demotic style, for example in the writing of Mickey Spillane, to repress psychic desire. So that the narrative strategies of detective novels written by feminist women have to struggle to express any elements of female psyches. Sometimes this struggle is explicit, for example Sara Paretsky in *Indemnity* only deliberately revises both the title of James M. Cain's *Double indemnity* and his characterisation of women as Other. More often this concern is articulated in an address to issues of sexual politics and to the domestic concerns of women which produces a narrative often in conflict with traditional representations of power, of class and of gender. In sum, feminist authors negotiate new forms of freedom – in the city, in their own histories and in relationships, in order to revise the norms of 'legal' and 'deviant'.

Detective writing by feminist women turns again and again to 're-vision' that embedded confidence in moral, racial, class and gender, superiority which is their cultural 'legacy'. Women detectives may share the marginality of their male peers, perhaps an ambiguous social status, but in feminist writing the marginal is glorified. For example the lesbian couples of Barbara Wilson, turn attention, not only from the conventional boundaries of detective identity, but also from the conventional boundaries of detective fiction itself: '"I could never write a book like that," I said, a little enviously. "Mine would be full of dead ends, tentative conclusions, back pedalling, outright wrong assumptions"'(Wilson, 1989, p. 187). Pam Nilson's epistemological doubts and harrowings both mock and undermine the genre and, at the same time, discredit a solipsistic and selfish detective hero. The stereotypical hard-boiled male detective treats all women as if they are sexually deviant. If this can be excused for those *petit bourgeois* authors keen to escape the tradition of 'literature' and responding to a readership keen to escape the tedium of daily life, it remains true that traditional detective fiction often uses characters specifically to veil and contain sexual ambiguity. The male detective works hard to control his

city and to re-establish the broken chronology of its urban life by
controlling his own and women's sexuality. The aim of traditional
detective fiction is to dispel mystery and the deviant, and subject reality
and mystery to scientific investigation. What so often escapes the
formulae of science and necessitates a turn to narrative formulae is
women's sexuality. The fiction of detective fiction is 'the enigma of
women'.[5]

When a woman chooses detective fiction as her genre, she is faced
then with material that is indifferent to, and often actively hostile to,
women. In addition feminist detectives who want to address ideological
issues such as sexual preference or feminism, lack any categories in the
classic detective text, just as in many other texts. Crossing the border
occurs when writers and their characters discover they need to stand
outside the limits of the genre. Border crossing is most acutely visible
in characters' psychic and material lives, in the time scales in which
they operate, in the language in which they express themselves and in
the environments they inhabit. In common with Atwood, Rhys and
other writers undermining generic boundaries, feminist detectives are
at that felicitous juncture of feminism, literature, and self-identity with
its shifting moods of disruption and transgression. This raises a major
question for feminist writing and critical praxis: how to situate a
female literary subject when the literary canon devalues an articulate
female subjectivity. In feminist detective fiction such positioning
involves an open attachment to other women in friendship, sibling or
lesbian relationships and a reassessment of women's movement
through public spaces and patriarchal time. When writing detective
fiction, feminist writers go to a great deal of trouble and some
awkwardness to show that the forms of knowledge of traditional
detective narratives do not best solve the crime.

In studying the ways in which people pattern their perception of
culture, feminist anthropologists pay special attention to the significance of boundaries, to the categories we use to understand and codify
our interpretations of men's and women's roles. Since, as Margaret
Mead pointed out, the difference between the two sexes is the most
important condition on which we have built the varieties of human
culture, then codes and boundaries must be understood as effects of
sexuality.[6] Taxonomies of gender behaviour, of 'x' opposed to 'non-x',
in any detective fiction will inevitably set the boundaries of detective
work by building it upon sexual difference. As deviancy dramatically
increases, society responds to such boundary threats by ritual

persecution. Scapegoats in detective fiction, as in real life, have frequently been women. Border rituals – the concern with definitions of deviance – emanate in societies trying to hold their members together. Forming views about crime and conspiracy, refusing to compromise with evil and the drawing of symbolic lines and boundaries is a way for cultures and communities to bring order to experience. In detective fiction it is the task of the detective to create a structure of meaning in which individuals are comforted by accepting social classifications coded in literary classifications intrinsic to the genre. Detective formulae are designed to maintain in fictional form a culture's ongoing consensus about the nature of morality. Such formulae enable a reader to explore, but of course only in fantasy, the boundary between the illicit and the legal, watching the spectacle of a criminal irretrievably tarnished by boundary crossing.

Much literary criticism about detective novels forces its readers to replicate the hermeneutic process of traditional detection by encouraging readers to decode and to master the detective fiction. Critic and reader together solve the enigma of a popular genre. If we are to get beyond an analysis of popular writing which depends on simple decoding then we need a theoretical framework like those in anthropology which attends to the cultural expression of gender. More than other anthropologists, as the Introduction showed, Mary Douglas has made a systematic analysis of the cultural boundaries that give symbols their meaning and which are affirmed in rituals and language. The very basis of cultural boundaries, she argues in *Natural symbols*, depends on the presence of symbols that demarcate lines of division (see Douglas, 1970). The ways in which individuals and groups are differentiated one from another are dramatised by the linguistic codes that communities use. People come to internalise and realise boundaries in their social settings expressing themselves in coding procedures in order to make sense of events, particularly if those events are strange or violent. Douglas suggests that the concept of boundary can be understood in diverse ways. It means, often simultaneously, a set of rules which guide behaviour (personal boundaries); the condensation and abbreviation of time (information boundaries), a special language (pollution boundaries) and a structure or pattern behind relationships (social boundaries). All boundaries, Douglas goes on to suggest in *Implicit meanings*, function through an agenda of legality whether this agenda is hidden or explicit. The terms which Douglas throws up adapt well to feminist detective writing. Both Douglas's anthropology and feminist literature stand in a critical relation to a unitary world. The discursive world of anthropology is very analogous to the 'meaning production process' (to use Douglas's term) of feminist detection (see Douglas, 1975).

Why is boundary crossing such a great moment in feminist anthropology and in feminist detective fiction? Because it is then that Otherness has a precisely liminal and not objectified presence. To break out of the interpretative framework of culture or prescriptive loyalties is to identify oneself as/with the Other. The Otherness of other cultures, like the Otherness of the criminal or the Otherness of women are the cracks between the paving stones of capitalism. The contradiction, which an anthropologist often experiences, between Western and Third worlds is like the contradiction between the world of conservative morality and that of the transgressive in plots dealing with the solving of crimes.

One major personification of such a conservative morality is Arthur Conan Doyle's Sherlock Holmes. The Sherlock Holmes stories begin in Holmes's isolated retreat. Like Edgar Allan Poe's Dupin, Holmes has detached himself from society. It is the sudden disruption of Holmes's study which is the metonymic mechanism of social disruption (see Palmer, 1978). Holmes is a key example of the atomised male investigator in a major chord. Leaving his retreat provides the great detective with his, and our, first narrative event and provides the novel with an effective emotional focus in the way Holmes works to displace our panic that the sacramental male space may continue to be violated. The retreat emphasises distance. The door to Holmes's study is his personal boundary, and marks his intellectual, moral and social superiority to the scene of transgression down below which represents the threat of pollution outside the confines of safe capitalism. For example in the cases involving British colonies 'The speckled band' and 'The Boscombe Valley mystery' criminals have illegally bought English land and it is this startling permeation of British life which Holmes must cleanse. The social world outside Holmes's study is there simply to be observed and codified, translated and abstracted through the linear logic of the great detective's keen intelligence. Holmes represents the ideal male scientist detached and far distant from the irrational fears of Irene Adler, and other women characters and certainly detached from a woman reader. Just as the figure of Dr Watson functioned as Holmes's narrator to enable Conan Doyle to represent characters and actions without involving Holmes's emotions or personal opinions so too Watson's simplemindedness forecloses on any *reader* contribution to Holmes's logic.

The androcentric assumptions of Holmes's Baconian investigations debar women readers from significant involvement in each case just as women characters in these texts are anaesthetised despondent observers of the detective's heroic and totalising intellect. Where a male reader at least shares the gender of the male detective, for a woman reader, this masculinity is a major element debarring women from access to self reflexivity and generic embodiment. Not surprisingly, Dr Watson's wife is quickly dispatched from the Holmes series. The failure of any character (except Holmes) to make even a cognitive leap across narrative boundaries enables Holmes to remain in charge of morality, just as he is firmly in control of the aesthetic manoeuvres of his investigations. Each story returns Holmes, with his male reader, to the isolated refuge where he can clear a narrative from complexity and confusion and bind the reader into the small narrative patch they cleared together among the thickets of social dislocation. Popular fiction may potentially be, as Ken Worpole claims, an open-ended text but, as he himself admits, it is the task of detective fiction to role up the murderer's map by leaving the quicksand of civilian emotions.[7] (See Worpole, 1983.) In *A study in scarlet* Holmes applies the investigative techniques of the natural sciences. In this and other stories the values which Holmes endorses include a scientific rationality which distances the material world, a belief in objectification, which distances human reality and its threats, and a belief in a powerful hero. These are all values central to stereotypes of a masculine world. The classic detective novels are for the most part similar and successor inheritors of Conan Doyle's technique at least in one regard – the distancing of the woman reader.

In contrast the issue of enclosure in *She came too late*, by Mary Wings, parallels those of its sister texts: and involves a central character whose occupation and sexual preferences deliberately threaten social boundaries. A lesbian detective is an individual far from traditional power. Wings sets her lesbian detective Emma Victor down in urban Boston to solve the murder of Julie Arbeder by unravelling the strings joining Julie with the rich Allison and Stanley Glassman. Emma negotiates Boston's geographic boundaries, moving between the different feminist groups of the Women's Hotline and Blackstone Women's Clinic and 'illegally' violating the privacy of Glassman's mansion in order to disrupt the economic bounds which Glassman imposes on these marginal groups.

The symbol of a patriarchal boundary is the print by M. C. Escher hanging over Glassman's couch. The print, with its circling and continuous staircase, is a metonymy of the way patriarchy encloses reality in order to hide sexual violence – here the murder of Glassman's wife. Mary Wings's Emma Victor differs in another important regard from Sherlock Holmes. Emma has no 'authority' as conventionally defined. She functions neither to establish a tunnel view of morality nor does she speak to her reader with the cognitive superiority of science or of class.

The city epitomises the economic and the social constraints characteristic of most women's lives. 'The newly-elected female mayor', like other women, has no economic power and 'needed our help in deciding what services would be cut.' (Wings, 1986, p. 3.) The bourgeois budgeting has a double impact: it involves women in 'self mutilating' financial limits and ensures Emma's late response to a message for help from Glassman's second victim. Yet if Emma's room contains the archetypal feminist security blanket – an heirloom patchwork quilt – Emma refuses to hide under its cover in a safe retreat just as she erotically subverts the puritan ethics of detective morality. Emma's ability to talk to women on the 24 hour switchboard is, figuratively as it were, like her ability to cross the boundary of heterosexuality. Mary Wings has constructed a dramatic statement illustrating the threat that women's sexual preferences might pose to the abstractions of city life. The volatility of lesbianism is summed up by Emma's lover Frances who likes 'to see how things on the edge survive. Plants, animals, with little water, rough conditions' (Wings, 1986, p. 65). Emma is freighted with marginality. Glassman thinks of her as 'no more than a gnat buzzing around his head and he was a man who had a cover on the insecticide market' (Wings, 1986, p. 123).

Fundamental to feminist theory is its assumption that the 'public' arena of power is intimately part of the private sphere of sexuality. Feminist writers who challenge the binary opposition between these spheres imposed by society, are also undermining traditional gender boundaries. Wings therefore situates Emma quite concretely on the borders of urban geography, making her work to expose the closed coherence of Glassman's sexual economy. Like other feminist detectives Emma chooses to talk about city streets in terms, not of meanness, but of buildings in use. The domestic vocabulary is historically specific in She came too late. The invocation of tasteless seventies furniture, the over-elaborate caterers' food, the party music and meanings of

Glassman's existence are concretely located in his home. Refusing the area limited to visitors in Glassman's house, Emma slips through a back door into the baroque rooms of Glassman's drugged, gay brother. Glassman encourages his brother Hugo's drug addiction in order to contain Hugo's memory of the murder in physical immobility. Emma is Hugo's conduit through which bits of the story and memories flow together to solve the crime because the very location of their sexuality is outside heterosexuality. The solution to the detective problem that Glassman's violence represents – the joining of the murder to the uncovering of Glassman's motive – is not found in the detailed empiricism of detective science, but rather lies in Emma's ability to identify with other sexual outsiders which deconstructs the architecture of Glassman's patriarchy.

In a complicated and contradictory plot, Allison Glassman is a double signifier. First she is a victim whose murder must be solved, but also, as a lesbian, she is a figure of boundary crossing which patriarchy pays to frame. The place of Allison Glassman's murder is purposefully symbolic. She is pushed from the gang plank which connects her husband's yacht to the shore – pushed, as it were, over the border of capitalist privacy.

Emma's intellectual challenge to one boundary (information boundary) imbricates her challenge to another (sexual boundary). At least since the 1920s, the nature of the way independent women undermine sexual stereotypes has been an exceedingly potent locus of power in detective fiction written by women. For example, Dorothy L. Sayers created women characters who are both intelligent and sexually 'different'. *Gaudy nights* demolishes the familiar female stereotypes of the bitter spinster and dominated mother. The academic spinsters of an Oxford college resist the nexus of heterosexuality and with the help of Harriet Vane resist the violence of a demented and fixated servant wife. Yet if the women of Shrewsbury are vigorous, positive intellectuals, Sayers herself, as Nina Auerbach points out in *Romantic imprisonment*, was contained by the coercive categories of the crude Freudianism available to her in the 1930s.[8]

In *She came too late* Emma happily and confidently transgresses the boundary of heterosexuality and it is this confidence which helps Emma to expose the real limits and dependencies women experience in Boston society. Glassman tries to retrieve his wife for heterosexuality by arranging to have Allison artificially inseminated by Stacy Weldemeer as a payment in kind for his secret financing of Stacy's Women's Clinic.

Thus Wings evokes a causal relation between patriarchy's economic and sexual controls. What Wings arrives at, in fact, is the clear 'solution' that by crossing the boundary of heterosexuality, Emma gains a radical politics.

The same tension between identity and politics, accounts for Wings' portrait of Stacy Weldemeer. Both Weldemeer's work as a medical director and the autonomy it affords her make her an attractive woman: 'She was nearly a media beauty. Fine features, a cultured voice and the posture of a ballerina' (Wings, 1986, p. 5). Stacy allows her deputy Frances, Emma's lover, some independence but manipulates other women and men with a dynamic poise earned from feminism. Stacy is a character, therefore, whom Wings treats with deep ambivalence. None of Stacy's good qualities are allowed to flourish because there has to be something alien about a woman who tries to ignore the effects of patriarchal boundaries.

The pleasure of Frances's body and Emma's economic independence are certainly one axis of feminism in this novel but Emma needs to embrace other goals. Wings insists that Emma's self understanding and solution to the murder can be earned only if Emma listens to the stories told in the informal women's groups – a set of knowledges to be negotiated and achieved but as rewarding for Emma as her work as a telephone therapist. In short, the crime can be solved only through a female facilitation. Stacy Weldemeer, who has no recourse to kinship, is made to suffer the traditional fate of 'independent' women in male detective fiction – suicide. 'I heard the splintering sound of a shot going through Stacy Weldemeer's skull.' (Wings, 1986, p. 176.) In contrast – and the contrasts are finely balanced – Frances's lesbianism enables her to create a truly feminist knowledge by experimenting in biochemistry with 'lesbian frogs' to discover parthenogenesis. It is typical of Wings' sophisticated plotting that Frances's medical breakthrough endorses the political journey which Emma has been taking in order to solve the murder. Lesbian love enables medical breakthroughs, detective breakthroughs are rewarded by the vehement lesbian love of Frances and Emma.

Mary Douglas tells a similar story of how patriarchal cultures work hard to control their boundaries. Camped in the desert, the Israelites refused to regulate any crossing points where useful exchanges could take place; they could accept no theology of mediation. 'When they think of their social organisation in spatial terms they set the holiest place within several concentric boundaries ... inside the boundaries is a small political unit, a people surrounded by powerful rapacious enemies' (Douglas, 1975, p. 304). In the contemporary world the fact that women are constrained in public does not necessarily preclude us from being determinants of, or mediators in, the crossing of spatial limits.[9] If the boundary which frequently marks a hostile city from a woman's family world is gendered, the placing of that boundary may vary widely between cultures and in certain contexts its crossing may be negotiable. Emma crosses into the 'centre' of Glassman's camp, negotiates its 'concentric' Escher world and reveals how violence is innate in patriarchal culture. What formulae, then, empower feminist detectives and arm their investigations if a writer does not depend on physical strength or sexual antagonism? Wings finds one answer in characterisation. She rejects the image of an atomised idiosyncratic detective and displaces the individualistic self-seeker in favour of a mediating detective. One crucial step in this process is the explicit enjoyment of lesbian love which typifies Wings's message for many readers.

'The word "relationship" hanging in the air, admitting to a commitment because we admitted to boundaries. Suddenly we existed as a couple.' (Wings, 1986, p. 78.) The scenes of lesbian love making and feminist collectives have a counterpart in feminist theory. The future for feminism, the poet Adrienne Rich argues in 'Compulsory heterosexuality and lesbian existence', is a similar delineation of 'lesbian existence'. 'Lesbian existence' suggests both the fact of the historical presence of lesbians and our continuing creation of the meaning of that existence. I mean the term *lesbian continuum* to include a range – through each woman's life and throughout history – of woman-identified experience; not simply the fact that a woman has had or consciously desired genital sexual experience with another woman' (Rich, 1983, p. 156).

Like Wings's characters, Rich's definition of lesbian is both political and literary. Rich does not ask us to choose a lesbian existence necessarily for ourselves but rather asks all women to help unveil and describe the cultural 'continuum' of lesbian life. When Rich talks about the construction of lesbianism she means a psychical and literary construction which addresses the absence of a 'natural' language of lesbian sexuality. Similarly feminist detective fiction confronts the absence of an adequate literary construction of 'woman'. In addition, judging from the evidence in Wings, there seems to be a specific sexual drama that has entered and shaped lesbian writing in particular. Such

narratives chart a process of growth and development in uncharted
territory which develops into a literature of social outsiders. For both
Rich and Wings, lesbianism constitutes a position from which to act
and from which to unsettle essentialist stereotypes. In She came too late
lesbian love making is a metaphor of Emma's social transgression and
offers purposeful pleasures rather than the sexual antagonism of most
detective hieroglyphics. The lesbian relationship which Emma enjoys,
like those of her sister detective Pam Nilson, is depicted as a social alternative
to the heterosexual 'norm' matching Rich's case for a 'lesbian
continuum' and 'lesbian existence'.

The image that stays in one's mind at the end of She came too late is
the description of a picture to which Wings dedicates a chapter. Emma
dreams of Glassman sitting in a Calvinistic 'Dutch textile guild'. The
picture is a stern tableau of ill-treated women and children. As 'painter
and patron' Emma deliberately confuses the boundaries of art history
and comically imposes a hugely erotic Rousseauistic nude in the centre
of Dutch capitalism. Similarly in crossing the barrier of sexual privacy
and enjoying lesbian love in the public space, the feminist detective
as 'artist' provides a trope for her detection work as a whole. It is the
feminist detective, not only the murder, which threatens to overturn
property rights and conservative sexuality.

In another work that centres on lesbian women, characters similarly
confront patriarchy in its geographic mode. Jumping the cracks by Rebecca
O'Rourke parallels its sister text She came too late. O'Rourke's narrative
is set in London's Hackney, portrayed as an area of poverty and
dereliction. Startled in this setting by a glimpse of a Rolls Royce
containing a dead man, the detective heroine Rats, explores the links
which might exist between the murder and an exploitative economic
system. O'Rourke begins in an accommodation agency. The opening
setting of the novel is a site primarily concerned with exploitation. It
is a site where capitalism binds people into inferior housing and
impoverished lives. Rats disrupts the geographic stability of East End
blackmail financed by the agency by re-moving information from the
files as she clerks part time.

Where, in the Sherlock Holmes stories the grim London streets
represent an emotive displacement of patriarchal fears, here, Jumping the
cracks gives an obdurate account of people trapped by patriarchy in
squalid rooms and littered streets, and the dangers involved for
heroines when figuratively they surface, rat-like, and jump the fissures
and cracks of patriarchy. In any case Conan Doyle omits much of real

London in his treatment of the city. London appears to Holmes as an emblem of dangers and unpredictable social forces which must be contained. O'Rourke make plain that *Jumping the cracks* concerns desperate physical conditions that create and perpetuate a desperate sexual politics. O'Rourke's detective makes a bold stroke when her investigation simultaneously exposes the social disorder of decaying London as well as its crimes:

Later, Rats couldn't remember exactly when she saw the pattern come clear ... She decided to tell Helen. She wanted to see her anyway, to talk to her about what she had been thinking about them, her willingness to try and change. These last few months had been hard for them both and it seemed to Rats the death kept getting in the way, skewing their sense of each other. As the mystery of the death started to unravel, it cleared a space for herself and Helen. She was excited. (O'Rourke, 1987, p. 139)

To interweave the time and needs of lesbian women with the time of detection is really to speak about the limits of detective fiction and its eternally compromised narratives where 'deaths' 'get in the way' and are more exciting than lives.

Rats, like Emma, breaks with the traditional detective plot which maps and 'owns' a geographic space – a city fiefdom, by seeing the flux of geography as a temporal space where she navigates her way through illegality to a more self-aware lesbian status. Like Wings, O'Rourke rejects a monocular detective by making Rats' exposure of economic practices and sexual oppression as significant as her solution to the crime. For this purpose, O'Rourke's choice of a lesbian detective allows for a serious discussion about designations of 'lesbian' and the distinctiveness of lesbian transgression.

In detective novels, time is one of the main arbiters of moral value. The conventional detective story depends on a comforting certainty about time. Traditionally, the detective manipulates the time of detection with resounding finality by joining 'leads' to infer the precise causes of the crime which then grinds to a close. The generic formula encourages, even privileges, a rigid linear narrative over one of synchronicity. The reader might gain a satisfaction from seeing events from a different perspective but it is always from one which is firmly sequential (see Cawelti, 1976). Where clues and events have been disordered the detective replaces them in their proper order chronologically for the reader. Hence the short detective story is never as satisfactory as the full length novel because part of our involvement

and satisfaction as readers is *durational* because we agree to maintain our
need for solutions during a linear period (see Grossvogel, 1979).

Feminist theory has acutely interrogated those social narratives
which depend most absolutely on evolutionary time. Distinctions in
ways of organising time, as Julia Kristeva argues, are related to
differences of gender. In her essay 'Women's time', Kristeva describes
how patriarchal groups possess a solidity which is rooted in a particular
mode of reproduction represented by linear time. Social identity is
constituted by historical sedimentation and the time of patriarchy can
be said to be the time of linear history. A term which Kristeva uses to
characterise this solidity is 'cursive' time to which she opposes cyclical
or women's time (see Kristeva, 1982). Cursive time in the masculine
detective novel operates in stages to eradicate criminality. By implication criminality represents a primitive aberrant which will be
superseded by a civilised normality.

Feminist detectives are synchronic not diachronic. They prefer to
read clues tangentially from any point to any other point, rather than
in a hierarchic sequence. Barbara Wilson and Gillian Slovo, in
particular, break with the overarching illusion of linear chronology by
seeking to revise the pace of their novels. Both writers contest
conventional narrative linearity by curtailing its two conventional
climaxes: the moments of solution and denouement. Their books are
structured by the progress of character development and character
relationships not by singleminded progress to the solution of the
crime. Barbara Wilson's Pam recharges the work of detection from her
internalised negotiations with her own past 'sometimes I thought it all
had to do with my parents, this odd need to prove the causes of
people's deaths' (Wilson, 1989, p. 125). In Wilson's narratives the
past figures in complex and exhilarating ways rather than containing
the information landmines of traditional detection. To refuse linearity
in detective fiction is to refuse a major aspect of its form. Resisting
chronology gives feminist writers the cognitive bite to chew over and
spit out the sinews of social representation.

Barbara Wilson make plain that *Murder in the collective* concerns the
time of family and of friends. Pam and her twin sister Penny, owners
of a small left-wing press, are faced with the murder of Jeremy one
of their printers. The murder occurs at a time of merger between the
press and B. Violet Typesetting, a lesbian design firm. While
investigating the murder Pam is more concerned to defend her suspect
friends, the black woman June and Zee a Filipino who was married

to Jeremy at his death, than to find the murderer. The plot mutes interest in Jeremy's murder in favour of encouraging 'investigator' Pam to examine her relations with her twin Penny and find a new lesbian sexuality with her lover Hadley. Within this overarching preference we can distinguish two related ways in which Wilson reshapes time. The narration of detection in Murder in the collective takes up less space, less character involvement, has less material purchase, than the narration of relationships. Pam prefers to picnic with Hadley rather than follow her work routine even though the place of her work is the site of the murder: 'I know there's work to do but it kind of gives me the creeps to be there ... I don't know what to think. I feel like I could put it all together if I had some time' (Wilson, 1984, p. 85). Hadley evokes her family background, an outside frame of reference, to explain her feelings about the murder and represses her responses to the daily events of the novel. Perhaps the most suggestive evocation of alternative time is Wilson's references to her own 'autobiographical' time: '"No", we all said in unison, perfect children of the seventies, "No fingerprints"' (Wilson, 1984, p. 40). And it is this 'autobiographical' time which eventually provides the solution to Jeremy's murder. As 'a child of the seventies', Pam's libertarian doubts about government institutions help her discover Jeremy's involvement with the CIA. Unlike the classic masculine detective whose role is to answer doubt with affirmative brutality and restore social order, Pam's arbitrary sense of time and embattled and acutely psychologised attempts to piece clues together create an endemic sense of the importance of self awareness as against legal niceties.

Gillian Slovo has also made a central focus in her writing the split between narrative time and family time, between the linear and the synchronic, that I am taking to be a major feature of border crossing. Death by analysis concerns the murder of a psychoanalyst and figures a detective heroine who is herself experienced in psychoanalytic routines. The whole plot of Death by analysis is informed by the psychoanalytic case study – the model in which patriarchy captures individual time in family memory.[10] Initially conforming to the classic plot, Kate Baeier the detective, begins to investigate the past history of the murder victim Paul Holland. But this involves Kate in discovering the connections between left-wing politics and Holland's ex-patients and ex-lovers Franca and Laura all of whom came to function as a substitute 'family' in Holland's therapy.

Kate Baeier uses her own experience of therapy (her 'family' time) to connect individual characters to the crime through their family pasts rather than through their actions in the present time of the novel: 'It was then that I realised what Arthur was trying to do. He was throwing bait at Sam across the table. It was a well-worn routine between them. They'd met in the early seventies when they'd both served on a Vietnam Solidarity committee. It had been a transition period' (Slovo, 1986, p. 51).

Slovo further shows that it is Kate's interest in her autobiographical time, somewhat in conflict with the trajectory of the time of her detection which enables her to 'recall' solutions from the 'displaced' past, as much as from the conscious present of her investigation. Although Slovo adopts the formulaic apparatus of a meeting between the detective and all her suspects where Kate uncovers the murderer Howard, Kate, like Pam in Murder in the collective, is self reflexive. The time of detection is interspersed with the more significant time of Kate's therapy, and intense relationship, with Franca which is told in detailed flashbacks. It is the abuse of Kate in therapy, the mismatch between psychoanalytic 'family' time and her need for self-identity which is the 'real' plot of the novel.

A companion volume to this 'family' drama is Indemnity only by Sara Paretsky. V. I. Warshawski has strong family memories. The past is knotted, but not cripplingly, into the perspective of the detective. Warshawski is hired simultaneously by a bank's vice-president Thayer to find his son and by McGraw, the head of the International Brotherhood of Knifegrinders, to find his daughter. Son and daughter were lovers, but solving the murder of Peter Thayer and saving Anita McGraw is a less significant family restoration than V. I. Warshawski's memories of her own family history.

'All big men seem old to little girls. I recalled a night more than twenty years ago ... I'd peeped around the door because everyone was making such a commotion and saw him covered in blood' (Paretsky, 1987, p. 35). It is memories of childhood, not the chronology of detection, which enable the crime to be solved. McGraw, Warshawski's patron in the present time of the novel, she discovers to be the 'big man' of her childhood. Classic detective stories often describe an aspect of masculinity which is the fear men possess that daughters may supplant them. (See Knight, 1980.) For example in Conan Doyle's stories fathers are outrageously destructive throwing snakes or imprisonment at their daughters with equanimity. Sara Paretsky, on the other hand, invokes the possibility of the 'daughter's seduction' by the father but can distance it with warm and affectionate memories of her mother, and by supplanting (with her initials V.I.) the paternal surname. By allowing Vic to control her own patronym, Paretsky indicates and displaces, another patriarchal boundary. Not surprisingly, male characters consistently reject Vic's 'open' response to patronymy. Ralph abjures V.I.'s use of initials just as he abjures her professional expertise, characterising Vic's detective work as a 'hobby'. Ralph disparages Vic's explanation of the case and is consequently harmed. More misogynistically, Vic's police force acquaintances coerce her verbally with the feminine and absurd 'Vicki'. Only Lotty Herschel, the feminist doctor with whom V.I. is warmly affectionate has V.I.'s approval to use the name Vic. Lotty is Vic's mothering mirror and Paretsky suggests that it is the bonding of women which might ameliorate the enclosure of patriarchal nomenclature. Each part of Warshawski's memory, then, more than her 'cursive' actions helps her to solve the crime. This concern for memories of childhood, for the time of family and friends, enters the work of feminist thrillers most dramatically, in the place where gender difference is structured, in narrative sequence.

Mary Douglas describes how anomie occurs when people experience the break or border between differently constructed cosmologies, for example the in-between times of dawn and dusk (Douglas, 1975). The resolution subordinating the time of family, friends and autobiography to the time of detection has a similar tension in feminist detective fiction. There is often a disjunction between the introspective self awareness of the heroine and the resolution of illegality. In a distinctive narrative strategy women characters often draw on the resource of childhood memory. For example, in Murder in the collective, Pam pictures Zee as Anne Frank whose Diary was Pam's favourite book as a child. Female characters recuperate the violent events they have to experience with moments of jouissance they can recollect from childhood. Pam often hovers between past and present, retreating into her parents' garden where plants are emblematically 'starting to get out of control among the kale and the lettuce' in order to take 'a time out' from the task of detection.

If the time of feminist detection is incompatible with the genre so too are the subjectivities of feminists' characters. Popular genres such as Westerns and thrillers frequently describe individuals as fixed or archetypal entities. Popular culture relies on character essences which readers can quickly recognise.[11] These often parodic and circumscribed embodiments create intolerable tensions for feminist writers of detective fiction. One passport to discursive freedom, at least for lesbian writers, is a new language of sexuality. Once again anthropology offers a marker, Mary Douglas affirms that in stable societies 'we would expect to find ... that the social body and the *physical* body can focus the identity of individuals in a structured *bounded* [my emphasis] system' (Douglas, 1970, p. 193). The lesbian detective, in particular, is an agent who changes social boundaries by critiquing psychosocial identifications. In *Murder in the collective*, Pam refuses the simplicities of sexual and racial stereotypes. Her own position as a white, middle-class woman is constantly being challenged. As a Black woman who is sexually involved with a white man, June has a more problematic subjectivity than that of a simple suspect. Similarly Zee, a Filipino refugee who has suffered political as well as sexual betrayal, cannot be given the character classification of a stereotypical murderess. Zee is a figure of some political and psychological import to the detective narrator.

The critical problem arises with the definition of marginality, a definition which is the chief concern of all detective work but which is treated very differently by feminist writers. In traditional detective fiction, the detective is himself often a marginal professional surrounded by continual threats to his security and status. Sexual identity is a masculine certitude which, although it is often tested, is inveterately affirmed. His masculinity stems from self-mastery and the ability to define himself as a free agent. One layer of that certitude is built by detective urbanity. The detective controls and polices the public streets. Threats to legality, to ethnic purity or to gender roles perform a jumbled social script. All characters, other than the detective, are at a loss how to read the script of their social lives and it is the detective, reading between the lines, who perceives the solution to social confusion. As we know, there is a narrative theme which assists this perspective. The question of who sees what is at the heart of detective fiction. Traditionally, the detective is able to see as much as the criminal and cognitively much more. This differential of knowledge crystallises that hegemonic set which in her analysis of Hollywood films Laura Mulvey has called the scopic gaze. The detective is traditionally an 'eye' in a fiction about seeing.[12]

The ground of this concept of the eye and its telescoped gaze have been significantly developed by Laura Mulvey in her film theory as I described in chapter 4. Mulvey's theories confirm the 'masculinity' of seeing. She proposes that men look at women in film with two forms of mastery: a sadistic voyeurism which enjoys the way films control women's sexuality by creating dominating male characters *and* a symbolic and masculine fetishisation of women's sexuality in film narrative (see Mulvey, 1975). Mulvey argues that cinema enables this male scopic gaze to exist by creating the illusion, through a complicated system of point-of-view, that the male spectator is producing the gaze. The male character carries the gaze of the male spectator as his assistant. In Hollywood films, women are objectified erotic objects and recipients of the male gaze.

Feminist detectives are, putting things at their most extreme, standing at the impact point of this strong system of interpretation. The feminist detective cannot transfix and immobilise women characters, nor can she herself be totally deprived of a gaze and hence of detective skill. It is the concept of subjectivity which is at issue. It makes sense to reword Anne Kaplan's resonating question 'Is the gaze male?' into 'Is the gaze private?' (see Kaplan, 1983). The feminist detective is not a private eye.

Murder in the collective ends with an epiphanic and ironic comment about the gaze as a primary category of detection. Hadley gives Pam the blue contact lenses which had imaged Hadley's beauty to her lover and which can now give way to Pam's positive vision of lesbian sexuality not the exploitative sexuality of male detectives. Sharing each others' bodies and pleasurable talk, where the 'eyes' can be 'removed' is a paradigmatic counterforce to the scopic gaze. Pam is a facilitator not a female eye. Instead of manipulating her characters Pam mediates between contradictory groups, talking with gay women, with Filipino exiles, with her twin and family, speaking and sharing different languages. The work of detection is also, and at the same time, the scripting of lesbian desire not the script of voyeurism. In *Sisters of the road*, Pam comes to understand the need for multiple points of view and that her feminism can oscillate between the lawyer Janis's arguments against prostitution and the prostitute Dawn's empirical experience. It is the interrelation of the many crimes against women – enforced prostitution, rape and murder – which pushes women to constantly challenge the power of masculine surveillance, and challenges a feminist detective to continually refurbish the category 'woman'. Crime, in feminist detective novels, comes from politics, from injustice, not from individual deviancy.

Pam illustrates Wilson's lucid and optimistic belief that changes in consciousness arise from collective, not from individualistic, action. Pam is an involved narrator who depends on others to work with her in order to restore equilibrium. At the very beginning of *Murder in the collective* she is positioned as someone who 'circumvents useless conflict while encouraging problem resolution' (Wilson 1984, p. 7). In this way Wilson suggests that women's collectives can produce knowledge and power in order to counter the thralldom of masculine individualism, especially since the immediate cause of Jeremy's murder was his sexual violence to women. Jeremy is no innocent victim. He epitomises key aspects of capitalist patriarchy. For example he is both racist and sexist. He betrays Filipinos, reads pornography and gains perverse delight from forcing a lesbian into a heterosexual relationship. Zee, the murderer, is the *real* victim – a scapegoat of American imperialism abroad and its concomitant sexism at home. This revising of victim/ criminal roles is a radical break with the identity boundary of traditional detective fiction. It is male violence which acts as a brake upon detection not the sexual deviance of any woman character. Where the traditional detective plot begins with the murder of a male or female figure but which reasserts masculinity by eradicating women characters, Pam Nilsen understands, correctly, that any genuine ability in detective work depends as an absolute precondition on perceiving the humanity of the victim. At the end of *Murder in the collective* Pam refuses to publicise Zee's crime which she, and we, have come to believe was justifiable homicide. In *The dog collar murders* she admits 'it was the woman I was interested in not the symbol' (Wilson, 1989, p. 100). In *Murder in the collective* Pam knows, 'I also found myself opening up to her and Margaret, feeling community, a desire to share my discovery to see if it was real' (Wilson, 1984, p. 101). The trajectory of each novel is a path to women's affiliation, not a path to the eradication of criminals.

Bonnie Zimmerman in 'What has never been: an overview of lesbian feminist literary criticism' argues that the protagonist of a lesbian novel gains the confidence to come out only through a lesbian community or friendship. Hence in the second Pam Nilsen novel *Sisters on the road*, Pam can live alone because she is secure in her lesbian identity which she gained from the passionate female comradeship of *Murder in the collective*. It is the print collective who decide on the areas to be investigated not the detective, cracking the decades old code by which the entitlement to knowingness always depended on the detective's personal desires. Our relation to knowledge is wrapped in the contiguity of community. Similarly Wilson extends the sexual politics of the text by adding a bibliography of readings about Filipinos and about women in the Third World. Wilson contests the limitations of the genre by using its popularity to open up questions of radical politics, not to foreclose on a social identity. The book both defamiliarises the all too familiar images of detective women, and the sexual politics of a society which created them.

There is a subtly drawn parallel in *Death by analysis*, not about lesbian friendships but in Kate's shared feelings about bourgeois individualism. Kate, and by implication her author and audience, discovers that Paul Holland's murder occurred because of his compulsion to organise the whole course of his life around a selfish and individualised self-seeking, and by his symbolic rejection of the collective, libertarian 1960s. The critical rejection of individualism by Wilson in *Murder in the collective* and by Slovo in *Death By analysis* is elaborated in *She came too late*. Here the persistent everyday rituals of detective life are subjected to equal revisionary scrutiny by Mary Wings, because it is these aspects of character behaviour which embody ideological beliefs about gender. Emma would have a dissolutive place in any traditional detective novel. She has no physical abilities, she is an incompetent pinball player, she is resolutely domestic and she is eloquently delighted to be the vulnerable 'object' of Frances's concern. Emma symbolises Wings's undermining of certain totalising character structures. The social base and physical skills of masculine individualism are displaced from a privileged position in these works. Set in contrast are collectivity, vulnerability and women's friendships. If the function of the feminist detective is to destabilise the fixed boundaries of class and sexual preference then the figure of the detective cannot be reliably constant.

Crime contaminates the world of the traditional detective novel in the unnaturalness of its eruption. For example, in Conan Doyle's 'The speckled band', deviance is dramatised metaphorically as the snakes and Chinese drugs which Holmes repels. As Mary Douglas suggests 'the witch doctor is used as the idiom of control, since it pins blame for misfortune on trouble makers and deviants' (Douglas, 1970, p. 139). Where the traditional detective employs his skills in exorcism, feminist detectives welcome the irrational. Mary Wings challenges with good humour patriarchy's repression of the strange. Emma is reading Daniel Defoe's *A journal of the Plague Year* in a scene resonant of cheap B movies: 'It competed with the sound of a branch scraping against the window. Defoe described one mode of plague prevention by throwing coins in buckets of vinegar. After a while the doorbell rang'. Instead of the traditional male aggressor needing an exorcism of coin or gun, the visitor is Frances who opens her coat 'to show the pale fawn pyjamas. "Gee", was all I could say' (Wings, 1986, p. 161). The heady sexuality which ensues parodies, and refuses, the absurd intensity of conventional detective violence. Wings has used the barren melodrama of the genre to signify its paranoia, the obsessive searching for signs of enemies.

This narrative displacement to the other side of a detective border occurs whenever feminist writers shrug off generic formulae. Barbara Wilson ironically dismisses the incest fantasy, often so fondly a marker of the disordered female personality in conventional fiction: 'Besides, you nasty little Freudian, if you think I'm going to talk about my father with a stubby pink candle in my mouth,' (Wilson, 1984, p. 136). Because traditional detective vocabulary represents the fantasy needs of an anxious male bourgeoisie it has a coloration that Wings and Wilson refuse to print. Emma resists police ciphers, '"Do you have any" – what did they call them – "leads?"' (Wings, 1986, p. 24). An attention to domestic concerns replaces the intimacy of city bars for the engaging mock-heroic heroine (although V. I. Warshawski has a special purchase on that masculine world as well). Any intimation of a new literary space depends extensively on vocabulary. Feminist writers are sensible to the demands of a more feminine epistemology. The physical pleasures of food and cats in these novels incorporate a critical response to the sacramental function and status of violence in traditional novels. Wilson and Wings' obdurate decision to 'make strange' the genre is an ironic move since it is in 'being out of place' that criminal activity first reveals itself in detective fiction.

One of the most sustained examples of a linguistic swerve is the careful calibration of the domestic by feminist writers of detective fiction. The sorority of homely metaphors goes back some way before second wave feminism to Agatha Christie's Hercules Poirot whose precise knowledge of laundry and cooking provides him often with data and with the methods for restoring 'household' order. Domestic chores and the techniques for coping with them are, of course, usually the lot of women. Stephen Knight argues that Christie's popularity derives from her skill in showing that criminals are likely to be family members (see Knight, 1980). As we know, married women are harmed more often by their husbands than by violent strangers. In

contemporary feminist fiction the domestic has additional articulations. In *Murder in the collective* Seattle is a significant and anthropomorphised character: 'Seattle reacted predictably. It called in sick to
work, took off its shoes and sweater and hit the glorious outdoors'
(Wilson, 1984, p. 26). Empathetically, Pam avoids urban anomie and
takes a personalised possession of her time and space by leaving the
place of work. Houses often embody the female emotions of the
detective. In *Indemnity only*, Warshawski's house 'looked to me as it
sometimes looks. A house in transition. The house knew something
was going to happen' (Paretsky, 1987, p. 84). V. I. Warshawski prefers
to anthropomorphise machinery rather than to wield it: 'My chevy felt
embarrassed ... Especially when it saw a small Mercedes' (Paretsky,
1987, p. 84).

The domestic is a strong manoeuvre which feminist writers adopt
to denaturalise and diminish the power of patriarchal law. Pam Nilsen
wittily contests court procedure: 'It sounded like he was asking the
judge to hold the mayo on his BLT. I decided I didn't like him or the
judge either' (Wilson, 1984, p. 142). The same critical view of a
conventional detective agenda is clear in Pam's choice of a new
interpretive grid for her detective work: 'MOTIVES FOR MURDER (I
think I had seen this in a book somewhere; if not it was still a good
start for a person who tended to arrange her shopping lists in
categories: Vegetables; Staples; Sundries). A. Revenge' (Wilson, 1984,
p. 74). If patriarchy categorises knowledge by separating the feminine
trivial from the masculine significant, then women will have to
produce new meanings in mixed modes such as shopping lists, and
other taxonomies.

Sara Paretsky chooses domestic and feminine vocabulary as an
alternative to the violent and restricted language of traditional
detectives.

'He's a department head, and they're like gynecologists – their schedules are
always booked for about twice as many appointments as they can realistically
handle.' Ralph clutched his head. 'You're making me dizzy, Vic, and you're
doing it on purpose. How can a claim department head possibly be like a
gynecologist!' (Paretsky, 1987, p. 73)

Ralph's resistance to the feminine, which symbolises his resistance to
the production of meaning by women, is matched by his inability to
solve the murder.

Any boundary crossing must have implications for sentence and structure. One major example of the representation of Otherness – the investigation of those parts of meaning that are customarily repressed – occurs most often in dreams. Dreams are a common way of introducing a character's irrational or unconscious feelings into a realistic narrative. Many novels depict a character's dreams as a place where fundamental contradictions and personal fears can be exposed but then subsequently *contained* in the succeeding narrative. In detective fiction by feminist women the contradictions in dreams spill over with gusto into the daily world. Dreams are semiporous moments where contradictory versions of female identity and of women's real social needs can intermingle. Warshawski dreams of her mother's Venetian glasses broken by criminals which 'dissolved into a red pool. It was my mother's blood. With a tremendous effort, I pulled myself awake' (Paretsky, 1987, p. 116).[13] Warshawski's task as a detective lies in completing the unfinished and potential work of the mother. Vic's mother invoked the culturally invested power of opera by naming Warshawski, Iphigenia. By entering into and being powerful in a more popular creative form – the detective investigation – Warshawski, the daughter, can make prominent the energy of her mother which resurfaces as Warshawski's desire to break detective formulae. And it is the 'exchange value' of her family history which buys Warshawski's way into the solution of the crime.

Cawelti draws attention to the similarity between dream interpretation and detective work (Cawelti, 1976, p. 92). There is a clear resemblance between the titles of detective stories and the names which Freud gave to dreams and to his cases, for example 'The dream of the botanical monograph'.

Yet in earlier detective writing by women, the psychoanalytic plot is often muffled. Agatha Christie uses the psychoanalytic merely as another contemporary vocabulary. Her detectives are not concerned with the psychological processes of murderers' minds nor do they derive their skill from a psychoanalytically informed general knowledge. Dorothy Sayers makes a more sustained use of psychological theories in her novels, particularly in her innovative introduction of the theme of doubles. For example in the short story 'The image in the mirror' women with opposed moralities mirror each other. Yet although Sayers *does* examine the psychology of women criminals, all too frequently she applies psychoanalysis to the sexually deviant woman and refuses to let psychoanalysis contest socially constructed meanings of sexual difference. For example Sayers' lesbians are all criminally perverted and her male characters have few sexual vulnerabilities.

Gillian Slovo, on the other hand, uses dreams in a positive strategy in order to disrupt the norms of the genre. In *Death by analysis* the detective Kate responds to her dreams of her own past therapy as much as to the past life of the victim Paul – the more traditional source of detective evidence. Dreaming of Franca, her therapist, Kate remembers 'that's what I've learned here. I used to think we could change the world. Now I'm just proud if I survive a hostile encounter' (Slovo, 1986, p. 102).

Kate's therapeutic career models the biographies of those she investigates and the decisions they should have taken to avoid encountering murder. Kate experiences the limits of conventional therapy. '"Come off it, Kate," Franca snapped before catching herself. This time the silence between them was one of surprise ... An unspoken taboo had been broken' (Slovo, 1986, p. 104). The break has come with Franca's insertion of everyday vocabulary into the constrained formulae of psychiatric encounters. The dream also signifies Slovo's critique of the limitations of detective fiction. As the novel progresses Slovo continually interweaves public dialogue with private dreams and feelings. The detective's interior life is no longer a privileged Holmes-like intelligence but is open to investigation. Kate is not a disinterested figure, in control of her own identity, but for example continually questions her ambiguous marital status.

What binds all these feminist writers is their oppositional stance to the constraints of traditional detective fiction and to conventional gender scripts. What marks their fiction as feminist are the strategies they use to unpack and demolish traditional gender representations. By crossing the boundary of linear time and the boundary separating family and domestic concerns from the public space, feminist writers are contesting conventions of containment and displacement. Mary Douglas argues pertinately that 'a people who having nothing to lose by exchange and everything to gain, will be predisposed towards the hybrid being, wearing the conflicting signs' (Douglas, 1975, p. 307). In order to liberate women from the vexed limitations of gender stereotypes it is perhaps not surprising that these writers should focus on synchronicity, on the domestic and on female friendships. But what finally enfranchises feminism in these novels is the recognition by feminist writers that women's investigative, creative capacities come only from other women and not from masculine traditions. It is this passion which finally undermines the border of that traditional country.

In the evolution of the detective novel in the twentieth century what joins all women writers is their desire to scrutinise, and to abandon, the totalising and insidious abstraction of masculinity and femininity signed in the formulae of detective fiction. Agatha Christie undermines masculine individualism by limiting Poirot's omnipotence in her obvious distaste for the powerful male persona. Dorothy Sayers parodies conventional forms of sexual aggression, for example by creating a female murderer in *Gaudy nights* whose pornographic obscenities are so dramatic and so intensely masculine. This trajectory results in Barbara Wilson's radical confounding of the subject/object dichotomy in her appealing metaphor of lesbian S/M in *The Dog Collar Murders*: 'S/M is about the flowing of power back and forth between the top and bottom. It's about exploring limits' (Wilson, 1989, p. 67). Lesbian sexuality represents the collapsing of spectator/consumer practices in a common breaching of limited subjectivities. Since, as V. I. Warshawski realises, 'men can only admire independent women at a distance' it is the project of contemporary feminists to firmly cross the border of detective fiction into a literary landscape of independent feminism.

Notes

Unless otherwise indicated, place of publication is London.

Introduction

1 The field is too vast to list. As well as single author examples such as R. Blau DuPlessis, *Writing beyond the ending* (Indiana University Press, 1985), key and useful grids are provided by:
E. Abel, *Writing and sexual difference* (Harvester, 1982); E. Abel, *The voyage in: fictions of female development* (Pantheon, 1983); M. Eagleton, *Feminist literary theory: a reader* (Basil Blackwell, 1986); G. Green and C. Kahn, *Making a difference: feminist literary criticism* (Methuen, 1985); M. Humm, *Feminist criticism: women as contemporary critics* (Harvester, 1986); C. Moraga and G. Anzaldúa, *This bridge called my back: writings by radical women of color* (Kitchen Table, 1983); J. Newton and D. Rosenfelt, *Feminist criticism and social change: sex, class and race in literature and culture* (Methuen, 1985); S. Roe, *Women reading women's writing* (Harvester, 1987); Showalter, *The new feminist criticism* (Pantheon, 1985); B. Smith, *Home girls: a Black feminist anthology* (Kitchen Table, 1983).
In addition see M. Humm, *An annotated bibliography of feminist criticism* (Harvester, 1987).
2 The feminist criticism most purposefully addressing postmodernism is: L. Hutcheon, *A poetics of postmodernism: history, theory, fiction* (Routledge, 1988); M. Morris, *The pirate's fiancée: feminism, reading, postmodernism* (Verso, 1988); S. Sheridan, *Grafts: feminist cultural criticism* (Verso, 1988); E. Showalter, *Speaking of gender* (Routledge, 1989); P. Waugh, *Feminine fictions: revisiting the postmodern* (Routledge, 1989); E. Weed, *Coming to terms: feminism, theory, politics* (Routledge, 1989).
3 In *Image, music, text* Roland Barthes describes the wide range of languages at work in texts and the polygamous codes which they employ. Barthes's way of opening up the boundary of a text, his concern with the systems by which texts make meaning has been influential in the field of cultural studies.
4 Until recently, women's contribution to literary modernism was downplayed in favour of attention to Pound, Joyce, Yeats and Eliot. Women's distinctive and different articulation is addressed in S. Squier, *Women writers and the city* (University of Tennessee Press, Knoxville, 1984); B. K. Scott, *The gender of modernism* (Indiana University Press, 1990); and S. Gilbert and S. Gubar, *No man's land* (Yale University Press, New Haven, 1988).
5 See Chapter 4, Margaret Atwood, and n.7, p. 219.
6 Embracing deconstruction, Spivak analyses issues of discontinuity and fractures in women's experience with specific reference to race by means of an interdisciplinary perspective. See Gayatri Spivak, 'Scattered speculations on the question of value', in *In other worlds* (Methuen: London, 1987).
7 The concept is discussed by Gloria Anzaldúa in her autobiography in relation to Chicana identity, the history of the south-west and her poetry. See *Borderlands/la frontera: the new mestiza* (Spinsters: San Francisco, 1987).
8 This idea informs Cixous's work on the Brazilian woman writer Clarice Lispector. See 'Extreme fidelity' in *Writing differences*, ed. S. Sellers (Open University Press: Milton Keynes, 1988).

9 Bakhtin describes the ideological horizons of literature in *The formal method in literary scholarship* (Harvard University Press, 1985); and the dualistic universe of permanent dialogue in *Problems of Dostoevsky's poetics* (Manchester University Press, 1984). Allon White sets Bakhtin into the context of deconstruction in 'Bakhtin, sociolinguistics and deconstruction' in *The theory of reading*, ed. F. Gloversmith (Harvester, 1984); and Elaine Rusinko discusses the sources of Bakhtin's ideas in Russian-Soviet literary scholarship in 'Intertextuality: the Soviet approach to subtext', *Dispositio*, IV, 4:11/12, pp. 213-35.

10 An interesting analysis of anthropological representation from the point of view of literary theory is undertaken by Dennis Porter in 'Anthropological tales: unprofessional thoughts on the Mead/Freeman controversy' in *Notebooks in cultural analysis*, ed. N. F. Cantor (Duke University Press; Durham, 1984).

11 Paul Atkinson discusses Bernstein's ideas in relation to structuralism and sociology in *Language, structure and reproduction* (Methuen, 1985). Linda Clarke intriguingly places Bernstein's codes into the generative structure of architecture in 'Explorations into the nature of environmental codes', *JAR*, 3:1, January (1974), pp. 34-38.

12 The question of how gender difference is central to Cixous's feminist mode of research and writing is addressed in S. Sellers (ed.), *Writing differences: readings from the seminars of Hélène Cixous* (Open University Press; Milton Keynes, 1988) which collects examples from Cixous's seminars at the Centre d'Etudes Féminines, Paris. Verena Andermatt describes Cixous's new conceptual art of writing in 'Hélène Cixous and the uncovery of a feminist language', *Women and literature*, 7 (1979), pp. 38-48.

13 See Mary Jacobus, *Reading woman: essays in feminist criticism* (Methuen, 1986).

14 I describe this racist move in British history more fully in Chapter 2: The mother country: Jean Rhys, race, gender and history.

Chapter 1

1 For example feminist historians have successfully analysed women's autobiographies in order to question the problematic categories of women's experience, its historical representation or lack of historical representation. As yet, they have not analysed literary texts as embodied discourses of consciousness, preferring simply to document social and political images. See T. Davis et al. '"The Public Face of Feminism"; early twentieth-century writings on women's suffrage', in *Making Histories*, ed. R. Johnson et al. (Hutchinson, 1982).

2 The Suffrage Movement was more constrained by given definitions of the boundaries between the public and the private because of the containment of suffrage and feminism within the public arena of parliamentary politics. See the Introduction by Ruth First and Ann Scott, in *Olive Schreiner* (André Deutsch, 1980).

3 In her account of women's campaigns about sexuality at the turn of the century, Sheila Jeffreys suggests that the lack of references to their work and activism in histories of the women's movement in Britain ignores how many feminists were arguing that the provision of women's rights to sexual pleasure was a vital component of women's emancipation. See Sheila Jeffreys '"Free From All Uninvited Touch of Man": women's campaigns around sexuality, 1880-1914', *Women's studies international forum*, 5:6 (1982), pp. 629-45.

4 A socialist feminist, Cecily Hamilton argued for the introduction of birth control and a system of voluntary motherhood. See C. Hamilton (1909) *Marriage as a trade* (Rpt 1987, The Women's Press).

5 In her feminist essays Elizabeth Robins speaks feelingfully of women's collective action with other women. See E. Robins, *Way stations* (Dodd, Mead, New York, 1913).

6 Carroll Smith-Rosenberg describes equivalent changing constructions of gender in

America during the pre-war period in *Disorderly conduct: visions of gender in Victorian America* (Alfred Knopf, 1985); and Jane Lewis describes the connections between women's work and roles in the public sphere, the sexual division of labour in the home and concepts of motherhood in *Women in England 1870-1950: sexual divisions and social change* (Harvester, Brighton, 1984).

7   Elaine Showalter makes an extended analysis of the First World War's effect on gender construction in psychotherapy in *The female malady: women, madness and English culture 1830-1980* (Pantheon: New York, 1985).

8   Jane Marcus describes the contradictions, which writers like Rebecca West were facing after the First World War, between a female ethic of heroic self-sacrifice and their newly transformed collective feminist consciousness in 'Writing the Body in/at War', in *Arms and the woman: war, gender and literary representation*, ed. H .M. Cooper, A. Munich and S. M. Squier (University of North Carolina Press: Chapel Hill, 1989).

9   'Welfare feminism' is a phrase coined by Olive Banks in *Faces of feminism* (Martin Robertson: Oxford, 1981).

10 The terms vertical and horizontal segregation were adopted by Catherine Hakim to describe the double discrimination faced by women in work discouraged from promotion and segregated in all-women areas. See *Occupational segregation* (Dept. of Employment 1978). Jane Lewis, *ibid* describes how these forms of segregation mark women's employment in the twentieth century.

11 Wendy Mulford discusses this point in her sensitive biography of Sylvia Townsend Warner and Warner's lover Valentine Ackland. See *This narrow place* (Pandora: London, 1988).

12 Elizabeth Wilson describes how the turn to religion, to the past, to exotic places or to a private morality marks writing by both men and women, in the decade after the Second World War, for example Evelyn Waugh, Elizabeth Bowen and Angela Thirkell. See *Only halfway to paradise: women in postwar Britain 1945-1968* (Tavistock, 1980).

13 Michelene Wandor argues that British theatre has always changed radically during periods of social and political change. For example transvestite theatre flourished at times of changing attitudes to women – the Restoration, the industrial revolution, suffrage agitation and second wave feminism. See M. Wandor, *Understudies* (Methuen, 1981).

14 See Chapter 2, and n. 10, p. 216.

15 See Chapter 4, and n. 6, p. 219.

16 In examining contemporary writing by women, Margaret Homans addresses the question: how is gender inscribed in writing and answers that women are a muted group both socially and in literature. See '"Her Very own howl": the ambiguities of representation in recent women's fiction', *Signs*, IX 1983 pp. 186-205.

17 In terms of feminist theory this concern for a new politics of consciousness and community is expressed in Sheila Rowbotham et al., *Beyond the fragments* (Methuen, 1979).

18 Cixous calls for new definitions of writing which do not depend on a mastery of form but celebrate fluidity, even 'chaos'. Literature is the focus of Cixous's search for a feminine textual economy. In 'Conversations' she argues that biological differences between the sexes create different sources of knowledge. See S. Sellers (ed.), *Writing differences*.

19 The material and cultural impact of immigration to Britain and 'geographical or social and political journeys from the present to the past, from the past to the future' are described in *Charting the journey: writings by Black and Third World women*, ed. S. Grewal et al. (Sheba Press, 1988), p. 2.

Chapter 2

1 Hortense Spillers, although primarily concerned with the mulatto figure in Faulkner's *Absalom, Absalom!* and *Light in August,* similarly argues that the mulatto/mulatta is a metaphor of liminality in literature. See Spillers 'Notes on an alternative model: neither/nor' in *The year left* 2, ed. M. Davis *et al.* (Verso: 1987).

2 To be fair, V. S. Naipaul and other Caribbean writers' adoption of a European perspective may be because, as Incke Plaf points out in 'Women and literature in the Caribbean', there is as yet no broad view of Caribbean literature as a whole, in *Unheard words,* ed. M. Schipper (Allison & Busby, 1985).

3 Mikhail Bakhtin's concepts of dialogy and extopy are discussed in detail in the Introduction.

4 This is, of course, a sweepingly tendentious summary of the literary criticism about deconstruction. For an overview see C. Belsey, *Critical practice* (Methuen, 1980), H. Bloom (ed.), *Deconstruction and criticism* (Routledge & Kegan Paul, 1979), with essays by all the leading deconstructive critics – Harold Bloom, Paul de Man, Jacques Derrida, Geoffrey Hartman and J. Hillis Miller; and Vincent Leitch, *Deconstructive criticism: an advanced introduction* (Columbia: New York, 1983); and C. Norris, *Deconstruction: theory and practice* (Methuen: New York, 1982). For feminist deconstruction see Spivak ibid and B. Johnson, *The critical difference: essays in the contemporary rhetoric of reading* (Johns Hopkins: Baltimore, 1980) and A. Jardine, *Gynesis: configurations of woman and modernity* (Cornell: Ithaca, 1985). J. Culler argues the case that deconstruction has a radical politics in *Deconstruction: theory and criticism after structuralism* (Cornell: Ithaca, 1982). R. Rorty has drawn attention to deconstruction's need to paradoxically 'create' a historically determined practice against which it can react. See 'Deconstruction and circumvention', *Critical inquiry,* 11, 1:pp.1-23.

5 In Britain, it is traditionally the Left which argues, by and large, that romances represent conservative ideologies. Feminist accounts of romance point out that romances are enjoyed by women because in them heroines are at the *centre* of expert care. Romances represent contradictory divisions of the psychic life. See J. Radford (ed.), *The progress of the romance* (Routledge & Kegan Paul, 1986).

6 A marked example of the sequestration of the white woman in a colonial context is the generic cliché of Anglo-Indian romances such as *Ralph Darnell* (1879) or *Pretty Miss Neville* (1884). See B. Moore-Gilbert (ed.), *Literature and imperialism* (Roehampton Institute of Higher Education, 1983). In an alternative, and later, context, Paul Gilroy describes the different responses of whites along gender lines to mixed-race couples in British ballrooms of the early 1950s, arguing that racist ideologies depend on fears of miscenegation. See *'There ain't no black in the Union Jack'* (Hutchinson, 1987).

7 The most direct and forceful feminist critics of Jean Rhys are J. Miller, *Women writing about men* (Virago, 1986); S. James, *The ladies and the mammies: Jane Austin and Jean Rhys* (Falling Wall Press: Bristol, 1983); H. Nebeker, *Jean Rhys: woman in passage* (Women's Publications, 1981); D. Kelly Kloepfer, *Jean Rhys: and the novel as women's text* (University of North Carolina: Chapel Hill, 1988). J. Kegan Gardiner, *Rhys, Stead, Lessing and the Politics of Empathy* (Indiana University Press, Bloomington, 1989).

8 B. Gale Chevigny and G. LaGuardia continue on a more positive note (for decolonialisation) that this imperialist manoeuvre always ends in stasis because colonial romances find solutions to problems either in the colonial past or in Europe itself. The contemporary *reality* of the geography does not provide these writers, as it did Rhys, with comfortable materials. See *Reinventing the Americas* (Cambridge University Press: Cambridge, 1986).

9 Showalter's focus is on the treatment of female insanity by psychiatry and its misrepresentation in social as well as in cultural contexts. Her pertinent and forceful argument is that changes in cultural fashions, psychiatric theory and public policy all

H

combine to keep madness a female malady. See *The female malady* (Virago, 1987). Since psychoanalysis depends conceptually on women's imaginary need for the phallus, Jane Gallop, in *Feminism and psychoanalysis: the daughter's seduction* (Macmillan, 1982), intercuts between Freud and Lacan to challenge the concept of specularity which this essentialism presupposes.

10 Irigaray's insertion into psychoanalysis, and her departure from Lacan, is her creation of a female imaginary which represents woman's desire for the mother. See *Speculum of the other woman* (Cornell: Ithaca, 1985).

11 The Emancipation Act of 1833 followed the abolition of the slave trade in 1807. However Emancipation was to be gradual and former slaves remained the property of their owners after abolition because Emancipation instituted a system of apprenticeship binding former slaves to their owners until 1840. This led to much unrest. See D. McLoughlin 'Notes', to *Wide sargasso sea* (Hodder & Stoughton, 1989).

12 See J. Davy, *The West Indies, before and since the Slave Emancipation* (1854, Rpt 1971 Frank Cass); G. K. Lewis, *Main currents in Caribbean thought: the historical evolution of Caribbean society in its ideological aspects 1492-1900* (Johns Hopkins: Baltimore, 1983); E. Williams, *From Columbus to Castro: the history of the Caribbean 1492-1969* (André Deutsch, 1970).

13 Johannes Fabian points out that anthropology achieved its scientific respectability at a time when the natural histories of evolution reintroduced a history of retroactive salvation. The epistemology of anthropology therefore takes shape from an evolutionary sequential taxonomy based on the episteme of natural history which matches very well with an imperialist discourse employing such terms as 'primitive' and 'underdeveloped'. I use the concept, although not dealing with Fabian specifically, more directly in Chapter 6. See J. Fabian, *Time and the Other: how anthropology makes its object* (Columbia University Press: New York, 1983).

14 Monique Wittig's central focus is on the construction of the feminine subject in psychoanalysis which she believes trivialises experiences of subjectivity in childhood and in lesbianism which are not defined in existing discourses. See Wittig, 'The straight mind', *Feminist issues*, 1,1 (1980), pp. 103-10, and *Les Guérillières* (Viking: New York, 1971).

15 Turner argues that attributes of liminality are necessarily ambiguous because liminal people elude static cultural classifications. However their ambiguous attributes are expressed in a rich variety of symbols in many societies, for example in the instillation rites of the Kumukindyila or Bwiti baptismal ceremonies. See V. W. Turner, *The ritual process: structure and anti-structure* (Routledge & Kegan Paul, 1969).

16 Jean Rhys writes about her family history in *Smile please*: '(my mother) was born in Dominica on what was the Geneva Estate, and Geneva Estate was part of my life'. The estate was founded by James Gibson Lockhart who left Scotland for Dominica in the eighteenth century and it was the freed slaves who burned down the first estate house in the 1830s.

17 Ellis Cashmore traces connections between class, race and gender since the Second World War in terms of structured inequalities in *United Kingdom?* (Unwin Hyman, 1989). Paul Gilroy examines categories of 'race' and anti-racist mobilisation, specifically focusing on the complex and dynamic patterns of Black definitions in post-war Britain in '*There ain't no black in the Union Jack*' (Hutchinson, 1987).

18 A. Mama, 'Black women, the economic crisis and the British State', *Feminist review*, 17, 1984 pp. 21-37 describes the connections between women's immigration and the social services. There is some information about Black women's employment in V. Beechey and E. Whitelegg (eds), *Women in Britain today* (Open University Press, 1986). But a more thoroughgoing account is in *Enterprising women*, ed. S. Westwood and P. Bhachu (Routledge, 1988). Issues of Black women and education are described in *Gender under scrutiny*, ed. G. Weiner and M. Arnot (Open University Press, 1987). Women's autobiographical accounts are in *Charting the journey*, ed. S. Grewal et al. (Sheba Press,

1988) and in E. Dodgson, *Motherland, West Indian women in Britain in the 1950s* (Heinemann Educational Books, 1984).

19 Alice Jardine examines the breakdown in the master narratives of religion, philosophy, history and cultural criticism which, she argues, symbolise the principle of uncertainty, of loss as feminine. See *Gynesis: Configurations of woman and modernity* (Cornell: Ithaca, 1985).

Chapter 3

1 Edward Said's stated preference is for a form of criticism that openly welcomes social and political responsibility. Said, along with other critics such as Gayatri Spivak, aims to give voice to the muted subject of colonial discourse by speaking in criticism with the language, in the case of Said, of the Palestinian nationalist, or in the case of Spivak, of 'Draupadi'. See Spivak, *In other worlds* (Methuen, 1987); Said, *Orientalism* (Pantheon: New York, 1978).

2 By 1930 there were 200,000 Negroes in Harlem. Although not every Black writer lived in Harlem, Langston Hughes, James Weldon Johnston, Claude McKay, Arna Bon Temps, Jean Toomer, Alaine Locke among others felt Harlem to be the source of what Alaine Locke called 'the New Negro' and a Black culture containing dance, jazz, drama and art. See N. Huggins, *Harlem Renaissance* (Oxford University Press: New York, 1971); D. Lewis, *When Harlem was in vogue* (A. Knopf: New York, 1981) and J. Toomer, *The wayward and the seeking: A collection of writings* ed. D. J. Turner (Howard University Press: Washington D.C., 1980).

3 Strategies used by writers to support their verbal message – textual devices incorporated as the memorising mechanisms of Black culture, for example the juxtaposition of codes, is discussed by M. Diaz-Diocaretz, *Black North-American voices: the poetry of G. Brooks, L. Clifton, M. Evans, N. Giovanni, A. Walker and J. Jordan* (Limited Edition, Leeuwarden, the Netherlands; Lesbish Archief). The wresting of language from European culture in post colonial writing is discussed in *The Empire Writes Back*, B. Ashcroft, G. Griffiths and H. Tiffin (Routledge, 1989).

4 While Marxist critics like T. Eagleton argue that the formal experience of literature is always grounded in the social and historical, Linda Hutcheon claims that one of the major concerns of postmodernism is to make the reader aware of the particular nature of the historical referent. See T. Eagleton, *Literary theory: an introduction* (Basil Blackwell, 1983) and L. Hutcheon, *A poetics of postmodernism* (Routledge, 1988). Both Marxist and postmodernist criticism are committed to contesting the totalising master narratives of any culture.

5 The legacy of the political economy of slavery under capitalism and its stimulation of a distinctive Black women's consciousness based on the greater participation rate in the labour force is discussed in D. K. King, 'Multiple jeopardy, multiple consciousness', in *Feminist theory in practice and process*, ed. M. R. Mason et al. (University of Chicago Press: Chicago, 1989); and P. H. Collins, 'The Social Construction of Black Feminist Thought', *Signs*, Special Issue: 'Common Grounds and Crossroads: Race, Ethnicity and Class in Women's Lives', 14: 4 (1989), pp. 745-74.

6 Knowing both the languages of Maya and Nahuatle, La Malincha became the key mechanism by which Cortes was able to gain access to the Mexican interior. The archetypal figure of Malincha provides Rosario Castellanos, in particular, with a rich cluster of metaphors that she uses to explore gender, sexuality and inequality in Mexican culture. Yet in Mexico the Indian woman who was given the name of Doña Marina is a symbol of a cultural traitor, a woman who put foreign concerns before Mexican causes. See M. Ahern (ed.), *A Rosario Castellanos reader* (University of Texas: Austin, 1985).

7   In terms of historical record Bernal Diaz recorded in the sixteenth century that it was
    La Malincha herself who was betrayed when her family sold her into slavery. For first
    hand accounts by participants and commentatory on the Spanish conquest see *Cortés*,
    by Francisco Lopez de Gomara, ed. L.B. Simpson (University of California Press:
    Berkeley, 1966); *The Conquistadors*, ed. P. de Fuento (Orion Press: New York, 1983); Peter
    Martyr D'Anghera, *De Orbe Novo* VII, trans. F. Augustus MacNutt (G. P. Putnam: New
    York, 1912).
8   Hoodoo is often a collective term for traditional Black beliefs in which a healer can
    alter social situations with magical powers. Hurston had a 'holistic' training in Hoodoo
    where she began with simple rituals and advanced to complex ceremonies 'lying nude
    for sixty-nine hours, face downward on a couch at Thompson's house, without food
    or water, with her navel touching a snake skin beneath her' (Hemenway, 1977, p.
    121).
9   Alice Walker's editorship of, and essays about, Hurston did most to restore Hurston's
    work to the AfroAmerican literary canon. In 'Zora Neale Hurston – a cautionary tale
    and a partisan view', in *In search of our mothers' gardens* (Women's Press, 1984), Walker
    identifies with Hurston as a re-visionary writer of Black legend and multifaceted
    language.
10 The Federal Writers Project was an offshoot of the New Deal WPA organised in 1935
    to mitigate the effects of depression. It engaged writers to compile State guide books
    and folklore texts, and employed actors and directors, for example Orson Welles
    directed a now famous Negro *Macbeth* (1936).

Chapter 4

1   The postmodern criticism most concerned with the lingering traces of the economy
    and of politics on the body is: Guy Debord, *Society of the spectacle* (Black and Red Press:
    Detroit, 1985); Jean Baudrillard, *The mirror of production* (Telos Press: St. Louis, 1975)
    and *Simulations* (Semiotext(e): New York, 1983); A. Kroker and D. Cook, *The postmodern
    scene* (Macmillan, 1988); A. Kroker and M. Kroker, *Body invaders* (Macmillan, 1988);
    Teresa de Lauretis, *Technologies of gender* (Macmillan, 1987); S. Sheridan, *Grafts* (Verso,
    1988); S. Rubin Suleiman (ed.), *The female body in Western culture* (Harvard University
    Press: Cambridge, Mass., 1986).
2   In *La jeunne née*, Cixous uses the printed text as a forum, as a laboratory for
    experimentation. Here, and in her later writings, Cixous applies a psychoanalytic
    technique of freeing or rebirthing other authors such as Clarice Lispector.
3   Jean Baker Miller is an American feminist psychoanalyist who devised a 'new
    psychology' for women based on 'affiliation' the sense of a self acquired from the early
    symbiotic bond with the mother. In *Toward a new psychology of women* (Beacon: Boston,
    1976), Miller argues that aspects of women's psychology now regarded as inferior,
    for example our emotions, would become the building blocks of a more humane
    culture.
4   Sherry Ortner argued, following de Beauvoir, that in every culture it is only females
    are 'saturated' with physiological attributes not men. Drawing on the work of Nancy
    Chodorow, Ortner goes on to argue, perhaps with less justification, that these attributes
    are 'real' characteristics of women or attributes we need to display, for example
    'concreteness' rather than 'abstraction'. See 'Is female to male as nature is to culture?'
    in *Woman, culture and society*, M. Z. Rosaldo and L. Lamphere, eds. (Stanford University
    Press: Stanford, 1974, pp. 67-87).
5   For example Native American oral literature expresses truths about experience and
    reality through descriptions of the activities of animals and animal deities who share

typically human emotions and attributes. See K. Kopp and J. Kopp, *Southwest: a contemporary anthology* (Red Earth Press, Albuquerque, 1977). Mary Douglas suggests that Shamanistic cures can manipulate social situations and 'by shuttling back and forth between the arena of the body and the arena of the universe' Shamans create 'harmonious worlds' (Douglas, *Purity and danger* (Ark, 1984, p. 72)).

6   Cixous, drawing a line from the German Romantics Schlegal and Schiller to Nietzsche and to her readings of Heidegger, believes in the creative forces contained in hysteria, and the potential power of unreason over reason.

7   The new network of power in late capitalism, Haraway argues, is a polymorphous information system which has transformed people into cyborgs. Haraway criticises those feminists who oppose the technological with the organic, and adopt anti-science and anti-technology stances. Like Atwood, she is interested in 'cyborg resistance' which lies in boundary transgressions between nature and culture. See 'A manifesto for cyborgs: science, technology and socialist feminism in the 1980s' in *Coming to terms: feminism, theory, politics*, ed. E. Weed (Routledge, 1989).

8   Luise Eichenbaum and Susie Orbach founded the Women's Therapy Centre, London whose premise is that the 'current theory and practice of psychotherapy is imprisoned within conventional patriarchal ideology' (L. Eichenbaum and S. Orbach, *Outside in ... inside out*, Penguin, Harmondsworth, 1982, p. 9). They argue, in opposition, that women's bodies are an integral part of our social and psychic positions.

9   Freud claimed that hysterical symptoms represent the realisation of a fantasy which signifies an arrested sexuality. The case of Dora is a reminder of how the categories of 'hysteria' and 'neurotic woman' were invented by psychoanalysis and given a precise sexual etiology. Mary Jacobus describes the relationship between cultural representations and psychoanalysis in *Reading woman* (Methuen, 1986).

10 Modern critical accounts of the Gothic almost universally agree that the form expresses sexual desires and fears under the mask of monstrosity. Gothic, albeit with different historic conditions, represents the impact of social prohibitions on sexuality as monstrosity and nightmare. See Franco Moretti, *Signs taken for wonders* (Verso, 1983); Eva Kosofsky Sedgwick, *Between men: English literature and male homosocial desire* (Columbia University Press, New York, 1985).

11 See Chapter 6, n. 3 p. 220.

12 Michel de Certeau argues a case very pertinent to feminism. He states that, in the expansionist bourgeois economy, time is considered to be 'other', since the 'past' is an object from which a mode of production, like historiography, needs to distinguish itself, in order to transform the 'past'. Chronology, Certeau believes, is the 'alibi' of time – a way of banishing metaphor from knowledge. See de Certeau, *Heterologies: discourse on the other* (Manchester University Press, 1986). A heterological tradition is one in which a discourse, for example science fiction, operates at the juncture of languages 'in the same place where the past is conjugated in the present' (p. 215).

13 In section II of *Écrits*, Lacan describes the relationship of images to self identity. An awareness of the objective world, and presumably an ability to catalogue in the symbolic, is based, according to Lacan, on alienation – on the moment in the mirror when the child is alienated from his imaginary image. Jacqueline Rose applies Lacan's notion more thoroughly to visual constructions, for example to mainstream cinema, in *Sexuality in the field of vision* (Verso, 1986).

Chapter 5

1   Rich objected to Friedman's essay herself in a reply in *Signs* (1984), pp. 734-8 where she pointed out that 'I am not warning against reading men's books, learning whatever

men have to teach, but against the dangers of identifying with the male mentor to the exclusion of other women' (p. 736).

2 Michel Foucault's *Archaeology of knowledge* sets out to reveal how language changes historically, for example showing how the identification of human with the masculine in discourses like the human sciences, is of recent date. Foucault's fundamental task in all his writing is to connect knowledge to power. It is power which prohibits certain topics (political statements) and certain people (madmen) from participating in social languages. See *Archaeology of knowledge* (Tavistock, 1974).

3 In *Contemporary feminist thought*, Hester Eisenstein claims that the theorists of radical feminism (of whom we could count Rich as the major figure) were influenced by the theorists of the New Left. The re-examination of abstract issues of equality in terms of power relations was a central focus of the New Left, Black Power and Women's Liberation. See Eisenstein, *Contemporary feminist thought* (Unwin Hyman, 1984).

4 The best source in Britain for research into small journals and periodicals of the 1960s and 1970s, including the *American poetry review*, is the Periodicals Library, University of London, Malet Street.

5 DeShazer claims that Adrienne Rich has re-visioned the figure of the Muse which is traditionally defined by men only by mythologising the female self and the 'ordinary' woman. This simplifies the complex relationship between women's poetry, women's gender and the poetic tradition and ignores the full density and power of Rich's sense of otherness. See M. K. DeShazer, *Inspiring women* (Pergamon: New York, 1986).

Chapter 6

1 Ros Coward points out that the representation of women's experience by women writers has no necessary relationship to feminism. Only by paying attention to *practices of writing*, she claims, can we assess fiction's political effect. See Coward, '"This novel changes lives": Are women's novels feminist novels?' *Feminist Review*, 5 (1980) pp. 53–65.

2 Critical accounts of the crime fiction written by male authors are vast in number. Texts which most purposefully address issues of masculinity and popular fiction are: S. Knight, *Form and ideology in crime fiction* (Macmillan, 1980); J. Palmer, *Thrillers* (Edward Arnold, 1978); D. Porter, *The pursuit of crime: art and ideology in detective fiction* (Yale University Press: New Haven, Conn., 1981); D. Longhurst (ed.), *Gender, genre and narrative pleasure* (Unwin Hyman, 1989); C. Bloom (ed.), *Nineteenth century suspense* (Macmillan, 1988) and *Twentieth century suspense* (Macmillan, 1990); B. Docherty (ed.), *American crime fiction* (Macmillan, 1988); K. Worpole, *Dockers and detectives* (Verso, 1983).

3 Carol Gilligan challenged Freud's assumption that men have a well-developed sense of morality whereas women do not. In *A different voice* she describes the decision making of men and women in relation to abortion and finds that no matter their age, class, or ethnic background, women thought that morality comes from relationships with others while men stressed abstract rights. Critics of Gilligan question the lack of variety of Gilligan's respondents and the negative consequences of associating women with caring roles. See C. Gilligan, *In a different voice* (Harvard University Press: Cambridge, Mass., 1982) and R. Tong, *Feminist thought* (Unwin Hyman, 1989).

4 Derek Longhurst in 'Sherlock Holmes: adventures of an English gentleman 1887-1894' carefully details how the preservation of 'Englishness' is fundamental to the class and race boundaries on which Holmes and Watson rest their case. See Longhurst, *Gender, genre and narrative pleasure*.

5 The phrase is from Sarah Kofman's *The enigma of woman* (Cornell: Ithaca, 1985) which argues that although Freud's sign of feminine sexual difference is the sign of hysteria,

the 'slippiness' and complexity of such sexuality positively escapes patriarchal stereotypes.

6 Margaret Mead worked in New Guinea, an area where fear of sexual pollution is a characteristic of cultural boundaries. Mary Douglas points out that, for people in New Guinea, the symbolism of sex occupies a central place in cosmology. See M. Mead, 'The Mountain Arapesh', Anthropological papers 37, American Museum of Natural History (1940) and M. Douglas, Purity and danger (Ark, 1984).

7 From his socialist perspective, Ken Worpole claims that popular literature is highly responsive to popular interests and that it develops in direct relation to popular taste. Therefore, with alternative forms of literary production, crime fiction 'offers the reader some way out at the end'. See K. Worpole, Reading by numbers (Comedia, 1984, p. 55).

8 Agatha Christie's Miss Marple, although not a feminist, often praises feminine qualities and Dorothy L. Sayers's treatment of sexually unconventional women shows that she rejected in part the public morality of her period. See M. T. Reddy, Sisters in crime (Continuum, 1988) and V. B. Morris, 'Arsenic and blue lace: Sayers' criminal women', Modern fiction studies, 29:3, 1983, pp. 485-96.

9 The different and potential roles which women occupy as mediators of space in many cultures is the topic of S. Ardener (ed.), Women and Space (Croom Helm, 1981).

10 In the Psychopathology of everyday life Freud describes 'screen memories' which involve a revision, or re-presentation, of the past when an individual denies sexual difference. See S. Freud, Psychopathology (Penguin, 1938).

11 While it is true that popular culture is difficult to free from stereotypical inscriptions, much of current cultural analysis is sensitive to the complications of popular genres and their expansive creation of pleasure. See T. Modleski (ed.), Studies in mass entertainment (University of Wisconsin: Madison, Wis., 1986) and J. Radford (ed.), The progress of the romance (Routledge, 1986).

12 The creation of photographically exact descriptions is a mark of the writing of Raymond Chandler and Dashiell Hammett in Farewell, my lovely and Red desert.

13 Intriguingly it was Chandler who claimed that Hammett's stylistic development was that he 'took murder out of the Venetian vase and dropped it into the alley'. See R. Layman, Shadow man: the life of Dashiell Hammett (Junction Books, 1981).

References

Unless otherwise indicated, place of publication is London.

Amos, V. and Parmar, P., 'Challenging imperial feminism', Feminist review, 17 (1984) pp. 3-21

D'Anghera, P. M., De orbe novo (New York: G. P. Putnam, 1912)

Angier, C., Jean Rhys (Harmondsworth: Penguin, 1985)

Atwood, M., The animals in that country (Toronto: Oxford University Press, 1968a)

Atwood, M., The circle game (Toronto: Contact Press, 1968b)

Atwood, M., The edible woman (New York: Fawcett, 1969)

Atwood, M., Power politics (Toronto: Anansi, 1971)

Atwood, M., Survival: a thematic guide to Canadian literature (Toronto: Anansi, 1972)

Atwood, M., Surfacing (Wildwood Press, 1973)

Atwood, M., Lady oracle (New York: Simon & Schuster, 1976)

Atwood, M., Dancing girls (Toronto: McClelland & Stewart, 1977)

Atwood, M., Life before man (Toronto: McClelland & Stewart, 1979)

Atwood, M., Bodily harm (Toronto: McClelland & Stewart, 1981a)

Atwood, M., True stories (Toronto: Oxford University Press, 1981b)

Atwood, M., Second words (Toronto: Anansi, 1982)

Atwood, M., The handmaid's tale (Toronto: McClelland & Stewart, 1985)

Atwood, M., Cat's eye (Toronto, McClelland & Stewart, 1988)

Auerbach, N., Romantic imprisonment: women and other glorified outcasts (New York: Columbia, 1985)

Baer, E., 'The sisterhood of Jane Eyre and Antoinette Cosway', in Abel, E. et al., The voyage in (Hanover: University Press of New England, 1983)

Bakhtin, M. M., The dialogic imagination (Austin: University of Texas, 1981)

Bakhtin, M .M., The problems of Dostoevsky's poetics (Manchester: Manchester University Press, 1984)

Banks, O., Faces of feminism (Oxford: Martin Robertson, 1981)

Benjamin, W., Illuminations (New York: Schocken, 1969)

Bernstein, B., Class, codes and control, VI and VII (Routledge & Kegan Paul, 1971-1973)

Bernstein, B., 'On the classification and framing of educational knowledge' in Young, M. F. D. (ed.), New directions for the sociology of education (Collier Macmillan, 1971)

Bhabha, H., 'The other question', Screen, 26:6 (1983) pp. 18-37

Blair, J., 'Private parts in public places: the case of actresses', in S. Ardener (ed.), Women and space (Croom Helm, 1981)

Bloom, H., The anxiety of influence (New York: Oxford University Press, 1973)

Bordo, S., 'Anorexia nervosa: psychopathology as the crystallization of culture', The philosophical forum 17:2 (1985) pp. 33-103

Botkin, B. A., Lay my burden down (Chicago: University of Chicago, 1945)

Brathwaite, E., The development of Creole society in Jamaica (Oxford: Oxford University Press, 1971)

Brittain, V., Testament of youth (1933; Rpt. Virago, 1978)

Brittain, V., Honourable estate (Victor Gollancz, 1936)

Brittain, V. and Holtby, W., Testament of a generation (Virago, 1985)

Brontë, C., Jane Eyre (1847, Rpt. Harmondsworth: Penguin, 1966)

Bruch, H., The Golden Age (Routledge & Kegan Paul, 1976)

Bulkin, E., 'An interview with Adrienne Rich', *Conditions* 2 (1977) pp. 53-66

Burford, B., *The threshing floor* (Sheba, 1986)

Carter, A., *The magic toyshop* (William Heinemann, 1967)

Carter, A., *Heroes and villains* (William Heinemann, 1969)

Carter, A., *The passion of new Eve* (Victor Gollancz, 1977)

Carter, A., *The Sadeian woman* (Virago, 1979)

Carter, A., *The bloody chamber* (Victor Gollancz, 1979)

Carter, A., *Nights at the circus* (Chatto & Windus, 1984)

Cawelti, J., *Mystery, adventure and romance* (Chicago: University of Chicago, 1976)

de Certeau, M., *Heterologies* (Manchester: Manchester University Press, 1986)

Chernin, K. M., *The hungry self* (Virago, 1986)

Chevigny, B. G. and LaGuardia, G., *Reinventing the Americas* (Cambridge: Cambridge University Press, 1986)

Chodorow, N., *The reproduction of mothering* (Berkeley: University of California, 1978)

Chow, R., 'Rereading Mandarin ducks and butterflies: a response to the "Postmodern" condition', *Cultural critique*, 5 (1986/7) pp. 69-93.

Christian, B., *Black women novelists: the development of a tradition 1892-1976* (Westport, Conn.: Greenwood, 1980)

Christian, B., *Black feminist criticism* (New York: Pergamon, 1985)

Christian, B., 'The race for theory', in Kauffman, L. (ed.), *Gender and theory* (Oxford: Basil Blackwell, 1989)

Churchill, C., *Objections to sex and violence*, in Wandor, M. (ed.), *Plays by women: Volume 4* (Methuen, 1975)

Churchill, C., *Light shining in Buckinghamshire* (Pluto Press, 1978a)

Churchill, C., *Traps* (Pluto Press, 1978b)

Churchill, C., *Cloud nine* (Pluto Press, 1978c)

Churchill, C., *Serious money* (Methuen, 1987)

Cixous, H., 'The laugh of the medusa', *Signs*, 1 (1976) pp. 875-93

Clément, C. and Cixous, H., *The newly born woman* (Manchester: Manchester University Press, 1986)

Cobham, R. and Collins, M., (eds.) *Watchers and seekers* (Women's Press, 1987)

Connerton, P., *How societies remember* (Cambridge: Cambridge University Press, 1989)

Cooke, M. G., *Afro-American literature in the twentieth century* (New Haven: Yale University Press, 1984)

Coote, A. and Campbell, B., *Sweet freedom* (Oxford: Basil Blackwell, 1987)

Coward, R., 'Are women's novels feminist novels?', *Feminist review*, 5 (1980) pp. 53-65

Daly, M., *Gyn/ecology* (Boston: Beacon Press, 1978)

Davidson, A. E. and Davidson, C. N., *The art of Margaret Atwood* (Toronto: Anansi, 1981)

Diaz, B., *The Bernal Diaz chronicles* (ed.) Dell, A. (Garden City, NY: Doubleday, 1956)

Diehl, J. F., 'Cartographies of silence: Rich's common language', *Feminist studies*, 6:3 (1980)

Dollimore, J., 'The dominant and the deviant: a violent dialectic', *Critical quarterly*, 28:1/2 (1986)

Donovan, J., 'Animal rights and feminist theory', *Signs*, 15:2 (1990) pp. 350-76

Douglas, M., *Purity and danger: an analysis of concepts of pollution and taboo* (Routledge & Kegan Paul, 1966)

Douglas, M., *Natural symbols* (Barrie and Rockcliffe, 1970)

Douglas, M., *Implicit meanings* (Routledge & Kegan Paul, 1975)

Drabble, M., *The millstone* (Weidenfeld & Nicolson, 1965)

Duncan, R., 'Pages from a notebook', in Allen, D. M., *The new American poetry* (New York: Grove Press, 1960)

Dunn, N., *Poor cow* (McGibbon & Kee, 1967 Rpt. Virago, 1988)

Du Plessis, R., 'The critique of consciousness and myth in Levertov, Rich and Rukeyser', in Gilbert, S. M. and Guber, S., *Shakespeare's sisters* (Bloomington: Indiana University

Press, 1979)

DuPlessis, R., *Writing beyond the ending* (Bloomington: Indiana University Press, 1985)

Eagleton, T., *Literary theory* (Oxford: Basil Blackwell, 1983)

Eichenbaum, L. and Orbach, S., *Outside in ... inside out* (Harmondsworth, Penguin, 1982)

Emecheta, B., *Second-class citizen* (Allison & Busby, 1977)

Emecheta, B., *The joys of motherhood* (Allison & Busby, 1979)

Fabian, J., *Time and the other* (New York: Columbia University Press, 1983)

Fairbairns, Z., *Benefits* (Virago, 1979)

Fekete, J., *Life after postmodernism: essays on value and culture* (Macmillan, 1988)

Forster, H., *Recodings* (Port-Townsend, Washington: Bay Press, 1985)

Freud, S., *Studies on hysteria 1893-1895* (Harmondsworth: Penguin, 1978)

Friedman, S. S., 'Reply to Rich', *Signs* 9:4 (1984)

Frye, N., *The anatomy of criticism* (New York: Atheneum, 1967)

de Fuento, P., *The Conquistadors* (New York: Orion Press, 1963)

Gallop, J., *Feminism and psychoanalysis* (Macmillan, 1982)

Gamarnikow, E., 'Sexual division of labour: the case of nursing', in Kuhn, A. and Wolpe, A. (eds.), *Feminism and materialism* (Routledge & Kegan Paul, 1978)

Gardiner, J. K., 'Good morning midnight; good night modernism', *Boundary 2*, 7:1/2 (1982/ 3) pp. 233-51

Gates, H. L. (ed.), *'Race', writing and difference* (Chicago: University of Chicago Press, 1986)

Gates, H. L., *The signifying monkey* (New York: Oxford University Press, 1988)

Gavron, H., *The captive wife* (Routledge & Kegan Paul, 1966)

Gay Sweatshop, *Care and control*, in Wandor, M. (ed.), *Strike while the iron's hot* (Journeyman Press, 1980)

Gelpi, B. and Gelpi, A. (eds.), *Adrienne Rich's poetry* (New York: W. W. Norton, 1975)

Gems, P., *Queen Christina* (Methuen, 1977)

Gems, P., *Dusa, Fish, Stas and Vi*, in Wandor, M. (ed.), *Plays by women: Volume I* (Methuen, 1982)

Gilbert, S., 'Rider Haggard's heart of darkness', *Partisan review*, 50:3 (1983), pp. 444-53

Gilbert, S. M., and Gubar, S., *The madwoman in the attic* (New Haven: Yale, 1979)

Gilbert, S. M. and Gubar, S., *No man's land V.1: the war of the words* (New Haven: Yale, 1988)

Gilligan, C., *In a different voice* (Cambridge: Harvard University Press, 1982)

Gilligan, C., 'Woman's place in man's life cycle', in Harding, S., *Feminism and methodology* (Bloomington: Indiana University, 1987)

Gilroy, P., *'There ain't no black in the Union Jack'* (Hutchinson, 1987)

Goodman, P., 'Natural violence', in *Drawing the line* (New York: Free Life Editions, 1977)

Goody, J., *The interface between the written and the oral* (Cambridge: Cambridge University Press, 1987)

Greer, G., *The female eunuch* (MacGibbon & Kee, 1970)

Grossvogel, D., *Mystery and its fictions* (Baltimore, Maryland: Johns Hopkins, 1979)

Hakim, C., *Occupational segregation* (Department of Employment, 1978)

Hamilton, C., *How the vote was won* (1909) in Spender, D., and Hayman, C. (eds.), *How the vote was won and other suffragette plays* (Methuen, 1985)

Hamilton, C., *Marriage as a trade* (1909) (Rpt. The Women's Press, 1987)

Haraway, D., 'A manifesto for cyborgs: science, technology and socialist feminism in the 1980s' in Weed, E. (ed.), *Coming to terms* (Routledge, 1989)

Harris, W., *The womb of space* (Connecticut: Greenwood Press, 1983)

Hartsock, N., 'Rethinking modernisms: minority vs. majority theories', *Cultural critique*, 7 (1987), pp. 187-206

Hawking, S., *The large-scale structure of space-time* (Cambridge: Cambridge University Press, 1973)

Hellman, L., *Scoundrel time* (Harmondsworth: Penguin, 1978)

Hemenway, R., *Zora Neale Hurston* (Urbana, Chicago: University of Illinois, 1977)

Heron, L., *Truth, dare or promise* (Virago, 1985)

Hoggart, R., *Uses of literacy* (Harmondsworth: Penguin, 1958)

Holtby, W., *The crowded street* (Bodley Head, 1924)

Holtby, W., *South Riding* (Collins, 1936)

Homans, M., '"Her Very Own Howl": the ambiguities of representation in recent women's fiction', *Signs*, 9:2 (1983) pp. 186-205

Hull, G., 'Afro-American women poets: a bio-critical survey', in Gilbert, S. M., and Gubar, S., *Shakespeare's sisters* (Bloomington: Indiana University Press, 1988)

Hull, G. T., *Color, sex and poetry: three women writers of the Harlem Renaissance* (Bloomington: Indiana University Press, 1987)

Humm, M., 'Paul Goodman and libertarian criticism' (Unpublished Ph.D dissertation, CNAA, 1981)

Humm, M., *Feminist criticism: women as contemporary critics* (Brighton: Harvester Press, 1986)

Hurston, Z. N., *Jonah's gourd vine* (New York: J. B. Lippincott, 1971)

Hurston, Z .N., 'Folklore field notes from Zora Neale Hurston', introduced by R. Hemenway, *The Black scholar*, 7:7 (1976) pp. 41-2

Hurston, Z. N., *Mules and men* (Bloomington: Indiana University Press, 1978)

Hurston, Z. N., *Dust tracks on a road* (Urbana, Chicago: University of Illinois Press, 1984)

Hurston, Z. N., *Their eyes were watching God* (Virago, 1986)

Hurston, Z. N., *The sanctified church* (Berkeley: Turtle Island Foundation, 1986B)

Hurston, Z. N., 'Sweat', in *Spunk* (Camden Press, 1987)

Ibsen, H., *A doll's house* (1879) (Rpt. Harmondsworth: Penguin, 1965)

Irigaray, L., *Speculum of the other woman* (Ithaca: Cornell University Press, 1985)

Jacobus, M., *Reading woman: essays in feminist criticism* (Methuen, 1986)

Jacobus, M. (ed.), *Body/politics* (Routledge, 1990)

Jamal, M., *Shape shifters* (New York: Arkana, 1987)

James, L., *Jean Rhys* (Longman, 1978)

Jameson, F., *The political unconscious: narrative as socially symbolic act* (Methuen, 1981)

Jameson, F., 'Postmodernism and consumer society' in Kaplan, E. A. (ed.), *Postmodernism and its discontents* (Verso, 1988)

Jameson, S., *None turn back* (1936) (Rpt. Virago, 1984)

Jardine, A .A., *Gynesis: configurations of woman and modernity* (Ithaca: Cornell University Press, 1985)

Jeffreys, S., '"Free from all uninvited touch of man": women's campaigns around sexuality 1880-1914', *Women's studies international forum*, 5:6 (1982) pp. 629-45

Jencks, C. A., *The language of post-modern architecture* (Academy Editions, 1977)

Jones, G., *Corregidora* (New York: Random House, 1975)

Kaplan, E. A., *Women and film* (Methuen, 1983)

Kofman, S., *The enigma of woman* (Ithaca: Cornell University Press, 1985)

Kolodny, A., *The lay of the land* (Chapel Hill: University of North Carolina Press, 1975)

Knight, S., *Form and ideology in crime fiction* (Macmillan, 1980)

Kristeva, J., *Desire in language* (Columbia: Columbia University Press, 1980)

Kristeva, J., 'Women's time', in Keohane, N .O. (ed.), *Feminist theory* (Brighton: Harvester Press, 1982)

Kristeva, J., *Powers of horror* (New York: Columbia University Press, 1983)

Kroker, A. and Kroker, M., *Body invaders: sexuality and the postmodern condition* (Macmillan, 1988)

Lacan, J., *Écrits* (Paris: Editions du Seuil, 1966)

de Lauretis, T., *Alice doesn't: feminism, semiotics, cinema* (Bloomington: Indiana University Press, 1984)

Lessing, D., *The golden notebook* (Michael Joseph, 1962)

Lessing, D., *Children of violence* (MacGibbon & Kee, 1964-69)

Lessing, D., *Four gated city* (MacGibbon & Kee, 1969)

Lessing, D., *Memoirs of a survivor* (Octagon Press, 1975)

Lessing, D., *Shikasta* (Jonathan Cape, 1979)

Lewis, G., 'Race relations in Britain: a view from the Caribbean', Race Today, 6:3 (July 1969) p. 80.

Lewis, J., Women in England – 1870-1950: sexual divisions and social change (Brighton: Harvester, 1984)

Llewellyn Davies, M. (ed.), Life as we have known it (Virago, 1977)

Lorde, A., Sister outsider (Trumansberg, NY: Crossing Press, 1984)

Lowell, R., Robert Lowell's poems, ed. Raban, J. (Faber & Faber, 1974)

Lyotard, J-F., 'Answering the question: what is postmodernism?', in The postmodern condition: a report on knowledge, trans. G. Bennington and B. Massumi (Minneapolis: University of Minnesota Press, 1984) pp. 71-82

Macaulay, R., The world my wilderness (1950) (Rpt. Virago, 1983)

McCrindle, J. and Rowbotham, S., Dutiful daughters (Harmondsworth: Penguin, 1979)

MacKinnon, C., Toward a feminist theory of the state (Cambridge, Mass: Harvard University Press, 1989)

Mama, A., 'Black women, the economic crisis and the British State', Feminist review, 17 (1984) pp. 21-36

Mazzaro, J., 'Review', American poetry review, 2:5 (1973)

Michie, H., The flesh made word (New York: Oxford University Press, 1987)

Miller, A., Thou shalt not be aware (New York: Farrar, Strauss & Giroux, 1983)

Miller, J. B., Toward a new psychology of women (Boston: Beacon Press, 1976)

Mitchell, J., 'Women: the longest revolution', New Left review, 40 (1966)

Modleski, T., Loving with a vengeance (New York: Methuen, 1984)

Mulvey, L., 'Visual pleasure and narrative cinema', Screen, 16:3 (1975)

Mulvey, L. 'Afterthoughts', in Visual and other pleasures (Macmillan, 1989)

Nebeker, H., Jean Rhys (Montréal: Eden Press, 1981)

Newton, J. and Rosenfelt, D. (eds.), Feminist criticism and social change (Methuen, 1985)

Ngcobo, L. (ed.), Let it be told (Pluto Press, 1987)

Nunez-Harrell, E., 'The paradoxes of belonging: the white West Indian woman in fiction', Modern fiction studies, 31 (1985) pp. 281-93

O'Rourke, R., Jumping the cracks (Virago, 1987)

Ortner, S., 'Is female to male as nature is to culture?', in Women, culture and society, ed. Rosaldo, M. and Lamphere, L. (Stanford, Cal: Stanford University Press, 1974)

Owen, V. (ed.), Fathers (Virago, 1983)

Page, L., Tissue, in Wandor, M. (ed.) Plays by women: Volume I (Methuen, 1982)

Palazzoli, M. S., Self starvation (Chaucer, 1974)

Palmer, J., Thrillers (Edward Arnold, 1978)

Paretsky, S., Indemnity only (Harmondsworth: Penguin, 1987)

Plante, D., Difficult women (Victor Gollancz, 1983)

Pollock, G. Vision and difference (Routledge, 1988)

Pratt, A., Archetypal patterns in women's fiction (Bloomington: Indiana University Press, 1981)

Pratt, M., 'Fieldwork in common places', in Clifford, J. and Marcus, G. E. (eds.), Writing culture (Berkeley: University of California, 1986)

Pribram, E. D., Female spectators (Virago, 1988)

Pryse, M. and Spillers, H. J., Conjuring (Bloomington: Indiana University Press, 1985)

Radclyffe Hall, The well of loneliness (Jonathan Cape, 1928)

Radford, J. (ed.), The progress of romance (Routledge, 1986)

Radway, J., 'Women read the romance', Feminist studies, 9:1 (1985)

Rhys, J., Wide sargasso sea (André Deutsch, 1966)

Rhys, J., Good morning midnight (Harmondsworth: Penguin, 1969)

Rhys, J., Voyage in the dark (Harmondsworth: Penguin, 1969)

Rhys, J., After leaving Mr MacKenzie (Harmondsworth: Penguin, 1971)

Rhys, J., Quartet (Harmondsworth: Penguin, 1973)

Rhys, J., Smile please (Harmondsworth: Penguin, 1981)

Rhys, J., *Letters* (Harmondsworth: Penguin, 1985)
Rhys, J., *Tales of the wide Caribbean* (William Heinemann, 1987)
Rich, A., 'Caryatid', *American poetry review*, 2:1 (1973a)
Rich, A., 'Review', *American poetry review*, 2:5 (1973b)
Rich, A., *Poems, selected and new, 1950-1974* (New York: W. W. Norton, 1974)
Rich, A., *Of woman born* (New York: W. W. Norton, 1976)
Rich, A., 'Twenty-one love poems' in *The dream of a common language* (New York: W .W. Norton, 1978)
Rich, A., 'Compulsory heterosexuality and lesbian existence', *Signs*, 5:4 (1980) pp. 631-60
Rich, A., *On lies, secrets, silence* (Virago, 1980)
Rich, A., 'Notes for a magazine: what does separatism mean?', *Sinister wisdom*, 18 (1981)
Rich, A., 'Blood, bread and poetry: the location of the poet', *The Massachusetts review*, 24:3 (1983)
Rich, A., 'Comment on Friedman's "I Go Where I Love: An Intertextual Study of H. D and Adrienne Rich"', *Signs*, 9:4 (1984) pp. 734-8
Rich, A., 'Mother-right', in *The fact of a doorframe* (New York: W. W. Norton & Co, 1984)
Richardson, D., *Pilgrimage* (J. M. Dent and Cresset Press, 1938)
Riley, D., *'Am I That Name?'* (Macmillan, 1988)
Riley, J., *The unbelonging* (Women's Press, 1985)
Roberts, D., 'Marxism, modernism, postmodernism', *Thesis Eleven*, 12 (1985)
Robins, E., *The convert* (1901) (Rpt. Women's Press, 1980)
Rowbotham, S., *Woman's consciousness, man's world* (Harmondsworth: Penguin, 1973)
Rowbotham, S., et al., *Beyond the fragments* (Merlin, 1979)
Rubin, G., 'The traffic in women: notes on the "Political Economy" of sex', in Reiter, R.(ed.), *Towards an anthropology of women* (New York: Monthly Review Press, 1975)
Sage, L., *Doris Lessing* (Methuen, 1983)
de Sahagun, B., *The Florentine codex*, eds. Anderson, A., and Dibble C. E. (Sante Fe: The School of American Research and the University of Utah, 1982)
Said, E., *Orientalism* (New York: Vintage, 1979)
Schipper, M., *Unheard words* (Allison & Busby, 1985)
Schreiner, O., *The story of an African farm* (Chapman & Hall, 1883 Rpt. Harmondsworth: Penguin, 1980)
Schreiner, O., *Woman and labour* (1911, Rpt. Virago, 1978)
Schreiner, O., *From man to man* (New York: Harper, 1926)
Sedgwick, E .K., 'The beast in the closet: James and the writing of homosexual panic', in Showalter, E. (ed.), *Speaking of gender* (Routledge, 1989)
Sellers, S. (ed.) *Writing differences: readings from the seminar of Hélène Cixous* (Milton Keynes: Open University Press, 1988)
De Shazer, M. K., *Inspiring women: reimagining the muse* (New York: Pergamon Press, 1986)
Showalter, E., *The Female malady: women, madness and English culture 1830-1980* (Virago, 1987)
Shuttleworth, S., 'Female circulation: medical discourse and popular advertising in the mid-Victorian era', in Jacobus, M., et al. (eds.), *Body politics* (Routledge, 1990)
Sinclair, M., *Mary Olivier: a life* (1919, Rpt. Virago, 1980)
Slovo, G., *Death by analysis* (The Women's Press, 1986)
Spillers, H., 'Notes on an alternative model: neither/nor', in Davis, M. et al. (eds.), *The Year Left 2* (Verso, 1987)
Spillers, H., '"The Permanent Obliquity of an In(pha)llibly Straight": in the time of the daughters and the fathers', in Wall C. A. (ed.), *Changing our own words* (New Brunswick: Rutgers 1989)
Spivak, G., 'Three women's texts and a critique of imperialism', in Gates, H. L., *'Race', writing and difference* (Chicago: University of Chicago Press, 1986)
Spivak, G., *In other worlds* (Methuen, 1987)
Steedman, C., *Landscape for a good woman* (Virago, 1986)

Strachey, R., The cause (Bell & Son, 1928)
Todorov, T., The Conquest of America (New York: Harper Colophon, 1984)
Todorov, T., Mikhail Bakhtin: the dialogic principle (Minneapolis: University of Minnesota, 1984)
Tsing, A. L., 'The vision of a woman Shaman', in Nielsen, J. (ed.), Feminist Research Methods (Boulder, Colorado: Westview Press, 1990)
Turner, D. H., In a minor chord (Carbondale: Southern Illinois Press, 1971)
Turner, V., The ritual process (Routledge & Kegan Paul, 1969)
Valenzuela, L., 'The word, that milk cow', in Meyer, D., and Olmos, M. F. (eds.), Contemporary women authors of Latin America (New York: Brooklyn College Press, 1983)
Volosinov, V. N., Marxism and the philosophy of language (New York: Seminar Press, 1973)
Vreeland, E., 'Jean Rhys', Paris review (1979) pp. 219-37
Wakoski, D., 'Review', American poetry review, 2:5 (1974)
Walker, A., 'Looking for Zora', in I love myself when I am laughing and then again when I am looking mean and impressive: the Zora Neale Hurston reader, ed. Walker, A. (Old Westbury, NY: The Feminist Press, 1979)
Walker, A., In search of our mothers' gardens (The Women's Press, 1984)
Wandor, M., Understudies (Methuen, 1981)
Ward Jouve, N., 'Her legs bestrid the channel: writing in two languages', in Monteith, M., Women's writing: a challenge to theory (Brighton: Harvester Press, 1986)
Warner, Townsend, S., Lolly Willowes (Chatto & Windus, 1926)
Warner, Townsend, S., Summer, will show (1936 Rpt. Virago, 1987)
Warner, Townsend, S., 'Women as writers: the Peter La Neve Foster lecture', Journal of the Royal Society of Arts, 107 (1959) pp. 378-86
Washington, M. H., 'Introduction', in I love myself when I am laughing and then again when I am looking mean and impressive: the Zora Neale Hurston reader, ed. Walker, A. (Old Westbury, NY: The Feminist Press, 1979)
Washington, M. H., Invented lives: narratives of Black women 1860-1960 (New York: Anchor Press, 1987)
Weldon, F., Female friends (William Heinemann, 1975)
Weldon, F., Little sisters (Hodder & Stoughton, 1978)
Weldon, F., Puffball (Hodder & Stoughton, 1980)
West, R., The return of the soldier (1918 Rpt. Virago, 1980)
West, R., Black lamb and grey falcon (New York: Viking Press, 1941)
Wilson, B., Murder in the collective (The Women's Press, 1984)
Wilson, B., Sisters of the road (The Women's Press, 1987)
Wilson, B., The dog collar murders (Virago, 1989)
Wilson, E., Only halfway to paradise (Tavistock, 1980)
Wilson, E., Mirror writing (Virago, 1982)
Wings, M., She came too late (The Women's Press, 1986)
Woolf, V., Mrs Dalloway (Hogarth Press, 1925)
Woolf, V., To the lighthouse (Hogarth Press, 1927)
Woolf, V., Orlando (Hogarth Press, 1928)
Woolf, V., A room of one's own (Hogarth Press, 1929)
Woolf, V., The years (Hogarth Press, 1937)
Woolf, V., Three guineas (Hogarth Press, 1938)
Woolf, V., 'The journal of Mistress Joan Martyn', in Squier, S. (ed.), Twentieth century literature, 25 (1979) pp. 237-69
Woolf, V., The diary of Virginia Woolf, ed. Bell, A. O., and McNeillie A. (Hogarth Press, 1984)
Worpole, K., Dockers and detectives (Verso, 1983)
Wright, R, 'Between laughter and tears: review of For their eyes were watching God by Zora Neale Hurston', New masses, 5 (1937) pp. 25-6
Young, M. and Willmott, P., Family and kinship in East London (Routledge & Kegan Paul, 1957)
Zimmerman, B., 'The politics of transliteration: lesbian personal narratives', Signs, 9:4 (1984)

Index